VERMONT
A STUDY OF INDEPENDENCE

Rowland E. Robinson.

VERMONT

A STUDY OF INDEPENDENCE
by

ROWLAND E. ROBINSON

With An Introduction
To The New Edition By
Professor Paul A. Eschholz

CHARLES E. TUTTLE CO., INC.
RUTLAND, VERMONT

REPRESENTATIVES

For Continental Europe:
BOXERBOOKS, INC., Zurich

For the British Isles:
PRENTICE-HALL INTERNATIONAL, INC., London

For Canada:
HURTIG PUBLISHERS, Edmonton

For Australasia:
PAUL FLESCH & CO., PTY. LTD.
C/O BOOKWISE AUSTRALIA
104 Sussex Street, Sydney

Published by the Charles E. Tuttle Company, Inc.
of Rutland, Vermont

Library of Congress Card No. 75-28714
International Standard Book No. 0-8048-1167-9

First edition published 1892 by Houghton, Mifflin and
Co. Boston
First Tuttle edition published 1975

Printed in USA

ACKNOWLEDGMENTS

IN working on this volume, I have incurred many debts of gratitude. For first introducing me to the work of Rowland Evans Robinson in 1969, thanks go to my colleague Betty Bandel. To the University of Vermont I am grateful for a 1972 Faculty Summer Research Grant which enabled me to undertake research activities at Rokeby. Special thanks go to Leon Dean for his support and encouragement, to the Rowland E. Robinson Memorial Association for making manuscript materials available to me, and to Ted and Janet Williams, Rokeby's curators, for their invaluable assistance. The little-known portrait of the author that appears opposite the title page, Robinson's sketches which illustrate the text, and portions of unpublished letters included in the introduction are printed with the gracious permission of the Board of Directors of the Rowland E. Robinson Memorial Association.

ROWLAND EVANS ROBINSON:
VERMONT HISTORIAN

Rowland Evans Robinson, naturalist, artist, and writer, was born at Rokeby, the Robinson family homestead in Ferrisburg, Vermont, May 14, 1833, the youngest child of Rowland Thomas Robinson and Rachel Gilpin Robinson. Even as a young boy, Robinson was a devoted and omnivorous reader; he was particularly attracted to the historical romances of Sir Walter Scott and the novels of Charles Dickens, as well as the writings of Francis Parkman and the encyclopedic *Documentary History of New York*, a prized holding in the Robinsons' library. With the exception of several years spent in New York City shortly after the Civil War as a draftsman and wood engraver, he lived on the family farm where he raised Merino sheep and wrote for some of the leading periodical journals of the day. Robinson's life, like his stories and sketches, was unpretentious and unsensational, but that is not to say that it was obscure or uninteresting.

Rowland Robinson was a product of the age of regional writing in America, a period which produced such prominent New England local color writers as Rose Terry Cooke, Harriet

Beecher Stowe, Mary Wilkins Freeman, and Sarah Orne Jewett. His writings faithfully depict Vermont's inhabitants as well as her flora and fauna. "As a portrayer of life in Vermont in the middle period of the nineteenth century Rowland Evans Robinson," in the estimate of John Spargo, "has never been equalled." Few disagree. Driven by the strong regional impulse to record and preserve a vanishing past, Robinson, as he relates in the preface to *Danvis Folks*, often wrote

with less purpose of telling any story than of recording the manners, customs, and speech in vogue fifty or sixty years ago in certain parts of New England. Manners have changed, many customs have become obsolete, and though the dialect is yet spoken by some in almost its original quaintness, abounding in odd similes and figures of speech, it is passing away; so that one may look forward to the time when a Yankee may not be known by his speech, unless perhaps he shall speak a little better English than some of his neighbors.

This commitment to capture Vermont's vanishing way of life in his literature is akin to the historian's responsibility to chronicle the events of a people.

Although remembered primarily as a superb writer of local color fiction and as an accomplished journalist, naturalist, and artist-illustrator, Rowland Robinson was foremost an historian of Vermont. It could, and probably should be argued that nearly everything Robinson wrote is history, a meticulous record of the cultural and social conditions of nineteenth century Vermont. His work for Miss Abby Maria Hemenway's *Vermont Gazetteer* in the late 1850's and later his contributions to J. D. Smith's *History of Addison County* helped establish him, within the boundaries of the state at least, as an authority on the history of the area.

In *A Danvis Pioneer* and *A Hero of Ticonderoga*, two historical novels, Robinson narrates the story of the Beeman family: first he recounts the struggles of Seth Beeman's family in settling the Wilderness and later, Seth's son Nathan's heroics in guiding Ethan Allen into Fort Ticonderoga. The author makes use of his many field trips and research to trace the development of the town of Ferrisburg in *Along Three Rivers*. The *Out of Bondage* stories reflect the author's experiences helping his family operate a station on the underground railroad and are valuable for the insights they provide into abolitionist activities in Vermont prior to the war. Other stories and sketches—particularly "A September Election," "The Turkey Shoot at Hamner's," "Raspberrying in Danvis," "Recollections of a Quaker Boy," "In the Sugar Camp," "Bee Hunting," and "The School Meeting in District 13"—are vivid vignettes of rural life; they chronicle Vermonters' occupations, recreations, social life, and folklore. Robinson was a life-long student of human nature; his characterizations are memorable for their fidelity to life. In a catalogue of his characters—Uncle Lisha, Mrs. Purrington, Solon

Briggs, Antoine Bassette, Gran'ther Hill, and Sam Lovel, to name only a few—one finds neither caricature nor exaggeration but instead the whole social spectrum of real Vermont types. Above all, Robinson was an acknowledged master of dialects, a language historian. In his stories he records the curious idioms, unique figures of speech, proverbs, and regional pronunciations of his Vermont neighbors.

At the invitation of Horace E. Scudder, editor of Houghton Mifflin's "American Commonwealths Series," Robinson wrote *Vermont: A Study of Independence.* The appearance of this volume in 1892 marks the culmination of Robinson's efforts as an historian. In his letter of invitation Scudder outlined the intent of each volume within the series:

The volumes of the *Commonwealths* series are not intended to be histories in the sense of being formal annals. The space at the command of writers is not sufficient to permit this, for my purpose is to confine the volumes to about 350pp.—less if possible. But there is room enough for a full account of the development of a state and such presentation of its life as shall give a reader a clear conception of that which characterizes the state and makes it to differ from all other states.

There is a good deal in the early history of Vermont which needs investigation and fresh presentation. I do not think one who was merely generally conversant with the subject could treat it with any satisfaction, unless he availed himself of such documents and obscure sources of information as are open to the historical student; but one who was interested in the subject and had a keen scent would have an opportunity for writing a most attractive book.

By the time Robinson came to write *Vermont: A Study of Independence* his eyesight was failing him. He was forced to compose on a grooved board, a device which enabled him to guide and space his lines. With the determination of a person who has a mission, Robinson continued to write prolifically. He was, however, as he confesses in an autobiographical sketch, "quite dependent on my wife for the revision and copying of my manuscript." Despite the handicap, Robinson produced an attractive and informative book.

Like Dorothy Canfield Fisher after him who drew upon a lifetime of experience and writing to produce *Vermont Tradition: A Biography of An Outlook on Life*, Robinson brought to this work not only his life-long investigations of the history, manners, customs, and occupations of Vermont's people but also his talents as a man of letters. *Vermont: A Study of Independence* immediately achieved distinction in the Houghton Mifflin series and assured its author a prominent place among the historians of Vermont. The subtitle sounds the keynote of the volume, a concise, eminently readable account of what the state has stood for "from the turbulent day of her birth through the period during which she maintained a separate and independent existence, and during the hundred years that she has borne her faithful part as a member of the great republic." Robinson's book, however, is not an historian's history. Robinson did not limit himself to examining important State documents and records and to reading the standard histories written by Vermont's first generation of historians—Ira Allen, Samuel Williams, and Zadock Thompson— because he knew, as folklorist Richard M. Dorson has since stated, that "the historian can find history alive in the field as well as entombed in the library." Robinson's history is, by design, not lifeless and pedantic; instead, it is a story, an accurate biography of a state and her people. "No historian," Edward D. Collins has observed, "was less a slave than he to facts and dates; and no previous author of a single volume on Vermont has revealed such masterly organization of the historical material he chose to use."

Anyone long associated with the state of Vermont is impressed by its marked individuality; Robinson certainly was. He felt that the boundary dispute between New Hampshire and New York constituted "the most unique feature of the history of the commonwealth; and though it retarded its settlement, and afterward for years its admission into the Union, it was the real cause of its becoming an independent State." Robinson's first chapter, "The Highway to War," captures the tenor of early Vermont history. Although familiar to most Vermonters, the battles of Ticonderoga, Hubbardton, Bennington, and the naval operations on Lake Champlain during both the Revolutionary War and the War of 1812 are treated with many a fresh touch. For example, he recognizes the importance of the successful defense of Fort Cassin, a little-known battery on Lake Champlain, to the future of American naval operations.

From out of these trying times—the French and Indian wars, the controversy over the Grants, the Revolutionary War, and the battles on Lake Champlain—state and national heroes emerged. The exuberant Ethan Allen, "Chieftain of the Green Mountain Boys," particularly attracted Robinson's imagination. He recounts Allen's heroics and colorful antics in *A Danvis Pioneer, A Hero of Ticonderoga,* and "The Life of Ethan Allen," an unpublished biography. Robinson never tired of having his characters like Gran-'ther Hill, himself a veteran of the Revolutionary War, reminisce about Allen's conquest of Fort Ti:

'By the Lord Harry! it allers tickled me for tu hear tell what Ethan said when he met the cap'n. He writ a book a-tellin' on't, haow he demanded the fort "In the name o' the Gre't Jehover an' the Continental Congress!" . . . When he came tu the cap'n's quarters he says, says he, "Come aout o' yer hole, you damned ol' skunk, or by the Gre't Jehover I'll let daylight through ye!" '

Despite the legends which even then surrounded the exploits of Ethan Allen and the Green Mountain Boys, Robinson's assessment of Allen as a leader of men is sound and level-headed. Thus he acknowledges that Seth Warner, a modest and practical soldier, was a better choice as leader of the Green Mountain Boys than the impulsive, emotional Allen.

Robinson duly recognizes the state's heroes—the Allens, Warners, Cockrans, Starks, and Chittendens—but he reserves his highest praise for the sturdy yeomen, the hardy and industrious pioneers who bore the distinguishing stamp of "New England character," a trait much prized by Robinson. One of the most attractive and innovative chapters in the history is the one devoted to "Old Time Customs and Industries." In it Robinson examines the activities and interests of Vermonters which gave the state a strong flavor of old-time New England life—husking bees, sugar-making, Merino sheep, Morgan horses, and political elections. He recognizes the importance of the local shoemaker's shop as a gathering place for the exchange of news, ideas, and stories. Later he traces the progress of education, religion, and temperance—of particular historical interest are the strong anti-Canadian sentiments Robinson noted among Vermonters. In "The Vermont People," he examines Vermont's early industries—potash, wool, granite, dairying.

The closing decades of the nineteenth century, the post Civil War years, were bleak and unpromising ones for Vermonters. The Civil War exacted a tremendous toll on Vermont; she paid dearly in human lives for union and the end of slavery. And with new challenges being discovered in the West, other Vermonters drifted into the newer parts of the country and became pioneers in its civilization, builders of new commonwealths. While Robinson was proud of the valor of Vermont's soldiers and the achievements of her emigrant sons, he realized the debilitating effects that the population drain would eventually have on the state. Those who remained stoically weathered the bleak years. The chapters devoted to the people of Vermont give Robinson's history an added dimension; they contribute immeasurably to an understanding of the character of a people of singular intelligence, ingenuity, and patriotism, a people who, as one reviewer of *Vermont* concluded, were "formidable on the field of battle and honest and hospitable neighbors in times of peace."

Finally, Robinson's history is not skeletal, not simply a factual outline of people's lives and events. After the model of Francis Parkman, Robinson paints a detailed scene for the history he presents. These scenes, which are no mere backdrop, evidence his uncommon skill at picturesque description. This skill surfaces in his verbal picture of French soldiers and their Indian cohorts crossing the vast, frozen, unsettled Wilderness:

Marching above the unseen and unheard flow of the river, over whose wintry silence bent the snowladen branches of the graceful birch, the dark hemlock, and the fir, or along the hidden trail, an even whiteness except to the trained instinct of the Indian, seldom a sound came to them out of the forest save the echo of their own footsteps and voices. Sometimes they heard the resonant crack of trees under stress of frost, or the breaking of an overladen bough, the whir of startled grouse, the sudden retreat of a deer or a giant moose tearing through the undergrowth; and sometimes they heard the stealthy tread of their brothers, the wolves, sneaking from some point of observation near their path, but in this remoteness from human haunts, and this deadness of winter, never a sound to alarm men so accustomed to all strange woodland noises.

and again in his description of the state's growth and development at the close of the eighteenth century:

The wild forest had receded and given place to broad fields of tilth, meadow land, and pastures, not now in the uncouth desolation of stumps and log-heads, but dotted with herds and flocks. The jangle of the sheep-bell was as frequent as the note of the thrush in the half-wild upland pastures, for two shillings were deducted from the lists for each pound of wool raised during the year. Orchards were beginning to whiten hillsides with bloom and color them with fruitage, for every acre with forty growing trees was exempted from taxation.

These descriptions are the product of close observation, of a sensitivity to nature in all her various moods. They serve not only to make one's reading pleasureable, but, more importantly, to enrich and give life to the history being recorded.

During his own lifetime, Robinson achieved national prominence both as an illustrator and writer but was not recognized as an historian. His drawings appeared in *Harper's Weekly, Leslie's Magazine, The American Agriculturist* and other leading illustrated periodicals. His essays, nature sketches, and stories, especially those written between 1885 and 1895, Robinson's peak years, were read by subscribers to *Atlantic Monthly, Scribner's, Forest and Stream,* and *Youth's Companion.* Many readers wrote Robinson to tell of their delight with his stories; they noted in particular that his work seemed to "come alive" when read aloud. Robinson died quietly on October 15, 1900 at Rokeby in the same room in which he had been born. His invaluable contribution to the State of Vermont was recorded by joint resolution of the Vermont legislature on October 18, 1900.

Resolved by the Senate and House of Representatives, That in the decease of Rowland E. Robinson, of Ferrisburg, we feel that Vermont hath lost an eminent citizen whose literary work has added to its wealth and renown, and whose general disposition, high character and genuine worth, and whose earnest devotion to his family, his State, his country, to nature, and to the bountiful Creator of every good and perfect gift made his life an illustrious example of Christian patriotism, which will forever preserve his memory in the hearts of the sons and daughters of the Green Mountain State.

Today, as in 1900, Rowland Robinson's merit as a literary artist is unquestioned. The importance of his contribution as an historian of the State of Vermont, however, is only now beginning to be recognized.

Paul A. Eschholz
The University of Vermont
March 23, 1974

CONTENTS.

CONTENTS.

VERMONT.

CHAPTER I.

THE HIGHWAY OF WAR.

CHAMPLAIN, in the account of his voyage made in July, 1609, up the lake to which he gave his name, mentions almost incidentally that, " continuing our route along the west side of the lake, contemplating the country, I saw on the east side very high mountains capped with snow. I asked the Indians if those parts were inhabited. They answered me yes, and that they were Iroquois, and there were in those parts beautiful valleys, and fields fertile in corn as good as any I had ever eaten in the country, with an infinitude of other fruits, and that the lake extended close to the mountains, which were, according to my judgment, fifteen leagues from us."

It was doubtless then that the eyes of white men first beheld the lofty landmarks and western bounds of what is now Vermont. If the wise and brave explorer gave more thought to the region than is indicated in this brief mention of it, perhaps it was to forecast a future wherein those fertile valleys, wrested by his people from the savagery of the wilderness and the heathen, should be made to blossom like the rose, while the church, of which he was so devout a son that he had said "the salvation of one soul was of more value than the conquest of an empire," should here build its altars, and gather to itself a harvest richer by far than any earthly garner. But this was not to be. His people were never to gain more than a brief and unsubstantial foothold in this land of promise. The hereditary enemies of his nation were to sow and reap where France had only struck a furrow, and were to implant a religion as abhorrent to him as paganism, and a form of government that would have seemed to him as evil as impracticable, and he was only a pioneer on the warpath of the nations.

Although the Indians who accompanied Champlain on his inland voyage of discovery told him that the country on the east side of the lake was inhabited by the Iroquois, there is no evidence that it was permanently occupied by them, even then, if it ever had been. There are traces of a more than transient residence of some tribe here at some time, but their identity and the date of their occupancy can only be conjectured. The relics found give no clew by which to determine whether they who fashioned here their rude pottery and implements and weapons of stone were Iroquois or Waubanakee,[1] nor when these beautiful valleys were their home.

[1] The Indians themselves pronounce the word as here given.

A fact affording some proof that the Iroquois abandoned it very long ago is, that not one stream, lake, mountain, or other landmark within the limits of Vermont now bears an Iroquois name. Of all the Indian names that have been preserved, every one is Waubanakee; and though many of them are euphonious, and those least so far better than our commonplace and vulgar nomenclature, none of them have the poetic significance of those so frequently bestowed by the Iroquois on mountain, lake, rock, and river.

It does not seem probable that the warlike nation that conquered all tribes with which it came in contact, having once gained complete possession, should relinquish it. A more reasonable conclusion is, that the country lying east of Lake Champlain was a debatable ground of these aboriginal tribes in the remote past, as it was more recently of civilized nations and states.

Quebec, the town which Champlain had founded in 1608, did not begin to assume much importance till eighteen years afterward, when its wooden fortifications were rebuilt of stone. Nor was the place strong enough three years later to offer any resistance to the English fleet which, under the command of Sir David Kirk, then appeared before the city and presently took possession of it. The conquest was as lightly valued by King Charles I. of

It signifies The White Land. It has been thought better to follow this, than the more common spelling, Abenaki, which has come to us from the French.

England as it had been easily made ; and in 1634, by the treaty of St. Germain, Canada, Acadia, and Cape Breton were restored to France. Thenceforward, for more than a hundred years, these regained possessions of the French were a constant menace and danger to the English colonies in America.

Advances toward the occupation of the country lying between Lake Champlain and the Connecticut River were made slowly by both French and English, though the tide of predatory warfare often ebbed and flowed along the borders of the region and sometimes across it, along the courses of the larger tributary waterways, navigable almost to their narrow and shallow sources by the light birch of the Indian while there was open water, and an easy if crooked path for the snowshoe and toboggan when winter had paved the streams with ice.

One of the earliest of such French incursions into New England was made after the failure of the attempt of De Callieres, the governor of Montreal, to capture New York, and all the English colonies in that province, when less important expeditions were organized against the New York and New England frontiers and the Sieur Hertel went from Trois Rivieres against the English fort at Salmon Falls in New Hampshire. At about the same time, in February, 1690, the expedition under Sieurs Helene and Mantet set forth by the way of Lake Champlain to destroy Schenectady. Both expeditions were organized by Count Frontenac for the purpose of inspiriting the Canadians and their Indian allies, who were sadly disheartened by the recent descent of the Iroquois upon Canada when Montreal had been sacked and destroyed, and most of the frontier settlements broken up.

The wide expanse of pathless woods that lay between the outposts of the hostile colonies gave a false assurance of security to the English settlers, while to their enemies these same solitudes gave almost certain immunity from the chance of a forewarned prey. In the wintry wastes of forest, through which these marauding bands took their way, there ranged no unfriendly scout to spy their stealthy approach, and bear tidings of it to the doomed settlements.

Unburdened by much weight of provision, or more camp equipage than their blankets and axes, these wolfish packs of Canadians and Indians (the whites scarcely less hardy than their wild allies nor much less savage, albeit devout Christians) marched swiftly along frozen lake and ice-bound stream, through mountain pass and pathless woods, subsisting for the most part on the lean-yarded deer which were easily killed by their hunters. At night they bivouacked, with no shelter but the sky and the lofty arches of the forest, beside immense fires, whose glow, though lighting treetops and sky, would not be seen by any foe more dangerous than the wolf and panther. Here each ate his scant ration; the Frenchman smoked his pipe of rank

home-grown tobacco, the Waubanakee his milder
senhalenac, or dried sumac leaves; the Christian
commended his devilish enterprise to God ; the pa-
gan sought by his rites to bring the aid of a superhuman power to their common purpose. The pious
Frenchman may have seen in the starlit sky some
omen of success; the Waubanakee were assured of
it when dread Wohjahose [1] was passed, and each
had tossed toward it his offering of pounded corn
or senhalenac, and the awful guardian of Petowbowk [2] had sent no voice of displeasure, yelling and
groaning after them beneath his icy roof ; and each
lay down to sleep on his bed of evergreen boughs
in an unguarded camp. Not till, like panthers
crouching for the deadly spring, they drew near the
devoted frontier settlement or fort, did they begin
to exercise soldierly vigilance, to send out spies,
and set guards about their camps.

Assured of the defenseless condition of the settlers or the carelessness of the garrison, they swooped
upon their prey. Out of the treacherous stillness
of the woods a brief horror of carnage, rapine, and
fire burst upon the sleeping hamlet. Old men and
helpless infants, stalwart men, taken unawares,

[1] Wohjahose, signifying The Forbidder, is the Waubanakee
name of Rock Dunder, which was supposed to be the guardian
spirit of Petowbowk. Some dire calamity was certain to befall
those who passed his abode without making some propitiatory offering.

[2] Petowbowk, interpreted by some "Alternate Land and Water," by others, "The Water that Lies Between," is the Waubanakee name of Lake Champlain.

fighting bravely with any means at hand, women in whatever condition, though it appealed most to humanity, were slaughtered alike. The booty was hastily gathered, and the torch applied by blood-stained hands, and out of the light of the conflagration of newly built homes the spoilers vanished with their miserable captives in the mysterious depths of the forest as suddenly as they had come forth from them.

So were conducted the expeditions against Salmon Falls and Schenectady. By the first, thirty of the English were killed, and fifty-four, mostly women and children, taken prisoners and carried to Canada. The success of the other expedition spread consternation throughout the province of New York. Sixty persons were killed, and nearly half as many made captive.

In the same year, 1690, the colonies of New York, Massachusetts, and Connecticut organized a formidable expedition by land and sea against Canada, in which they hoped to be aided by the mother country. Having waited till August for the hoped-for arms and ammunition from England which were not sent, the colonies determined to undertake it with such means as they had, Massachusetts to furnish the naval force against Quebec, New York and Connecticut the army to march against Montreal.

The New York and Connecticut troops, commanded by John Winthrop of the last named colony, marched early in August to the head of

Wood Creek, with the expectation of being joined there by a large number of the warriors of the Five Nations, but less than a hundred of them came to the rendezvous. Arrived at the place of embarkation on the lake, not half boats enough had been provided for the transportation of the army, nor sufficient provisions for its sustenance. Encountered by such discouragements, the army returned to Albany.

Captain John Schuyler, however, went forward with twenty-nine Christians and one hundred and twenty savages whom he recruited at Wood Creek as volunteers. In his journal[1] he gives an account of his daily progress and operations; mentions, by names now lost, various points on the lake, such as Tsinondrosie, Canaghsionie and Ogharonde. "The 15th day of August we came one Dutch mile above Crown Point. The 16th ditto we advanced as far as Kanondoro and resolved at that place to travel by night, and have that night, had gone onward to near the spot where Ambrosio Corlear is drowned, and there one of our savages fell in convulsions, charmed and conjured by the devil, and said that a great battle had taken place at Quebeck, and that much heavy cannon must have been fired there." About midnight of the 18th, " saw a light fall down from out the sky to the South, of which we were all perplexed what token this might be." On the 23d, having drawn near to La Prairie, he attacked the people of the fort, who had gone forth

[1] *Doc. Hist. N. Y.* vol. ii. p. 160.

to cut corn. " Christians as well as savages fell on with a war-cry, without orders having been given, but they made nineteen prisoners and six scalps, among which were four womenfolk," and " pierced and shot nearly one hundred and fifty head of oxen and cows, and then we set fire to all their houses and barns which we found in the fields, their hay and everything else which would take fire." Setting out on their return, " the savages killed two French prisoners because they could not travel on account of their wounds," and on the 30th arrived at Albany.

At nearly the same time the fleet sailed from Boston under command of Sir William Phipps, governor of Massachusetts. It consisted of nearly forty vessels, carrying a force of two thousand men. It was not till the 5th of October that it reached Quebec. Precious time was lost in deliberation while the place was defenseless, and then Frontenac, released by the retrograde movement of Winthrop's army from the necessity of defending Montreal, marched to the relief of Quebec with all his forces. After an unsuccessful attack by land and water on the 9th of October, the troops were reëmbarked on the 11th and the storm-scattered fleet straggled back to Boston. Such were the poor results of an enterprise from which so much had been expected.

To remove the unfavorable impression of the English which these failures had made on the Indians of the Five Nations, Major Schuyler of Albany, in the summer of 1691, went through Lake Champlain with a war party of Mohawks, and attacked the French settlements on the Richelieu. De Callieres opposed him with an army of eight hundred men, and, in the numerous encounters which ensued, Schuyler's party killed about three hundred of the enemy, a number exceeding that of their own.

In January, 1695, winter being the chosen time for the French invasions, Frontenac dispatched an army of six hundred or more French and Indians by the way of Lake Champlain into the country of the Mohawks, and inflicted serious injury upon those allies of the English. Retreating with nearly three hundred prisoners, they were pursued by Schuyler with two hundred volunteers and three hundred Indians, and were so harassed by this intrepid partisan leader that most of the prisoners escaped, and they lost more than one hundred of their soldiers in killed and wounded, while Schuyler had but eight killed and fourteen wounded.

Thus, across and along the border of this yet unbroken wilderness, the hostile bands of English and French and their Indian allies carried their murderous warfare to many an exposed settlement, and kept all in constant dread of attack.

Different routes were taken by the predatory bands in their descents upon the frontiers of New England. One was by the St. Francis River and Lake Memphremagog, thence to the Passumpsic, and down that river to the Connecticut, that gave an easy route to the settlements. Another was up the Winooski and down White River to the Connecticut. Another left Lake Champlain at the mouth of Great Otter Creek; then up its slow lower reaches to where it becomes a swift mountain stream, when the trail led to West River, or Wantasticook, emptying into the Connecticut. And still another way to West River and the Connecticut was from the head of the lake up the Pawlet River. Of these routes, that by the Winooski was so frequently taken that the English named the stream the French River; while that of which Otter Creek was a part, being the easiest and the nearest to Crown Point, was perhaps the oftenest used, and was commonly known as the " Indian Road."

All these familiar warpaths to every Waubanakee warrior, with every stream and landmark bearing names his fathers had given them, led through Vermont, then only known to English-speaking men as " The Wilderness."

The treaty of peace between England and France in 1697 gave the colonists a brief respite, till in 1702 war was again declared, and in the summer of the next year five hundred French and Indians assaulted in detachments the settlers on Casco Bay, and that part of the New England coast. In the following winter a force of three hundred French and Indians commanded by Hertel De Rouville, a skilled partisan leader, as had been his father, was dispatched by Vaudreuil, the governor of Canada, against Deerfield, then the northernmost settlement on the Connecticut. It was February, and Champlain was frozen throughout its length. Along it they marched as far as the mouth of the Winooski, and took this their accustomed path through the heart of the wilderness toward the Connecticut. Marching above the unseen and unheard flow of the river, over whose wintry silence bent the snowladen branches of the graceful birch, the dark hemlock, and the fir, or along the hidden trail, an even whiteness except to the trained instinct of the Indian, seldom a sound came to them out of the forest save the echo of their own footsteps and voices. Sometimes they heard the resonant crack of trees under stress of frost, or the breaking of an overladen bough, the whir of startled grouse, the sudden retreat of a deer or a giant moose tearing through the undergrowth; and sometimes they heard the stealthy tread of their brothers, the wolves, sneaking from some point of observation near their path, but in this remoteness from human haunts, and this deadness of winter, never a sound to alarm men so accustomed to all strange woodland noises. Then they came to the broad Connecticut, an open road to lead them to their victims, upon whom they fell in the early morning when the guards were asleep. Winter, the frequent ally of the Canadian bands, aided them now with snowdrifts heaped to the top of the low ramparts about the garrison houses, and upon them the assailants made entrance. All the inhabitants were slain or captured, the village plundered and set on fire, and an hour after sunrise the victorious party was on its way to Canada with its booty and wretched captives.[1]

Such warfare was waged for years, the French and Indians making frequent attacks on the most exposed settlements of the English, and they, at times, retaliating by invasions of the Canadian frontier. In 1709 another grand expedition was planned to operate against Canada in the same manner as that undertaken in 1690. But the troops, which under Nicholson were to advance by the way of Lake Champlain, got no farther than Wood Creek, where Winthrop's advance had ended nineteen years before, for while they were there awaiting the arrival at Boston of the English fleet, with which they were to coöperate, a terrible mortality [2] broke out among them, the fleet never came, and the undertaking was abandoned. In 1711 a still more formidable attempt was made to conquer Canada. But the fleet, commanded by Sir Hovenden Walker, with nine thousand troops on board, met with disaster in the St. Lawrence, and the land force, which again under Nicholson was to invade the French province by Lake Champlain, was not far beyond Albany when news of the fleet's disaster reached it and it was disbanded. Thus, as miserably as had the two preceding ones, this third attempt to conquer

---

[1] White's *Incidents in the Early History of New England.* See *The Redeemed Captive returning to Zion*, by Rev. John Williams, who was one of the Deerfield captives.

[2] In *Summary, Historical and Political*, by William Douglass, M. D., this is said to have been yellow fever.

Canada failed, and a heavier cloud of humiliation and discouragement overcast the English colonies. But after the treaty of Utrecht the eastern Indians made a treaty of peace with the governors of Massachusetts and New Hampshire which gave some assurance of tranquillity to the long-suffering people of those provinces.

Four Scenes in an Important Day of a Farmer Boy's Life   Rowland E. Robinson, 1880

CLEARING UP A FARM.—Drawn by R. E. Robinson.—Engraved for the American Agriculturist. 1850

CHAPTER II.

By the easiest path, in summer and winter, of the larger streams, the English settlements were pushed into the wilderness, and where the alluvial land gave most promise of fertility the sunlight fell upon the virgin soil of new clearings, the log-houses of the pioneers arose, and families were gathered about new hearthstones. They were soon confronted by the old danger, for the Indians, jealous of their encroachments and covertly incited by the governor of Canada, presently began hostilities, and the gun again was as necessary an equipment of the husbandman afield as his axe or hoe or scythe, and his wife and children lived in a besetting fear of death, or a captivity almost as dreadful. Though England and France were at peace during the time for the five years beginning with 1720, a savage war was waged between the eastern Canadian Indians and the provinces of Massachusetts and New Hampshire.

It was in these troublous times that the first permanent occupation was made in the unnamed region which is now Vermont. In 1723 it was voted by the General Court of the Province of Massachusetts Bay, that "it will be of great service to all the western frontiers, both in this and in the neighboring governments of Connecticut, to build a block-house above Northfield, in the most convenient place on the lands called the 'equivalent lands,' [1] and to post in it forty able men, English and western Indians, to be employed in scouting at a good distance up the Connecticut River, West River, Otter Creek, and sometime eastwardly above great Monadnock, for the discovery of the enemy coming toward any of the frontier towns, and so much of the said equivalent lands as shall be necessary for a block-house be taken up with the consent of the owners of the said land, together with five or six acres of their interval land to be broken up or ploughed for the present use of the western Indians, in case any of them shall think fit to bring their families hither."

Accordingly a site was chosen in the southeastern part of the present town of Brattleboro, and in

---

[1] Massachusetts gave 107,793 acres of land to Connecticut as *equivalent* for as many acres she had previously granted that were found to be south of the boundary between the two provinces, and which she wished to retain. One section of these "Equivalent Lands" was on the west bank of Connecticut River, within the present towns of Putney, Dummerston, and Brattleboro'. (*Colonial Boundaries Mass*, vol. iii.) This fell to the share of William Dummer, Anthony Stoddard, William Brattle, and John White. "The Equivalent Lands" were sold at public vendue at Hartford, in 1716, for a little more than a farthing per acre. The proceeds were given to Yale College. (Hall's *History of Eastern Vermont*.)

February, 1724, the work was begun under the superintendence of Colonel John Stoddard of Northampton, by Lieutenant Timothy Dwight, with a force of "four carpenters, twelve soldiers with narrow axes, and two teams." At the beginning of summer the fort was ready for occupancy, and was named Fort Dummer, in honor of the lieutenant-governor of Massachusetts. The fort was built of hewn logs laid horizontally in a square, whose sides were one hundred and eighty feet in length, and outside this was a stockade of square timbers twelve feet in length set upright in the ground. Within the inner inclosure, built against the walls, were the "province houses," the habitation of the garrison and other inmates, and themselves capable of stout defense, should its assailants gain entrance to the interior of the fort. In addition to the small-arms of the garrison, Fort Dummer was furnished with four patereros.[1] There was also a "Great Gun," used only as a signal, when its sudden thunder rolled through leagues of forest to summon aid or announce good tidings. On the 11th of October following its completion, the fort was attacked by seventy hostile Indians, and four or five of its occupants were killed or wounded.

Scouting parties frequently went out to watch for the enemy, sometimes up the Connecticut to the Great Falls, sometimes up West River, and

[1] Light pieces of ordnance mounted on swivels, and sometimes charged with old nails and like missiles, or, upon a pinch, even with stones; hence sometimes called "stone pieces."

thence across the Wilderness to the same point.
Sometimes they were sent to the mountains at
West River and the Great Falls, " to lodge on ye
top," and from these lofty watch-towers the keen
eyes of the rangers scanned the mapped expanse
of forest, when it was green with summer leafage,
or gorgeous as a parterre with innumerable autumnal hues, or veiled in the soft haze of Indian summer, or gray with the snows of winter and the ramage of naked branches, " viewing for smoaks " of
hostile camp-fires. In July, 1725, Captain Wright,
with a volunteer force of sixty men, scouted up the
Connecticut to Wells River, and some distance up
that stream, thence to the Winooski, which they followed till they came within sight of Lake Champlain, when, having penetrated the heart of the
Wilderness farther than any English force had
previously done, the scantiness of their provisions
compelled a return.

By the authority of the General Court of Massachusetts, a " truck house," or trading house, was
established at Fort Dummer in 1728, and the Indians finding that they could make better bargains
here than at the French trading-posts, flocked
hither with their peltry, moose-skins, and tallow.

When, seventeen years after the erection of Fort
Dummer, the boundary line was run between Massachusetts and New Hampshire, the fort fell within
the limits of the latter State, whose government was
appealed to by Massachusetts to maintain it, but declined to do so, on the ground that its own frontier

was better protected by a stronger fort at Number
Four; also that it was more to the interest of Massachusetts than of New Hampshire to continue its
support. Governor Wentworth urged upon a new
assembly the safer and more generous policy, but to
no purpose, and such a maintenance as Fort Dummer
continued to receive was given by Massachusetts.

After pushing their fortified posts up the Richelieu and to Isle la Motte, where they built Fort St.
Anne in 1665, the French made a long stride toward the head of the lake, where in 1730 they built
a small fort and began a settlement on Chimney
Point, called by them Point à la Chevalure, and the
next year began the erection of a more considerable work on the opposite headland of Crown Point,
a position of much greater natural strength. In
the building of this fortress of St. Frederic, which
was for many years to remain a close and constant
menace to the English colonies, they were opposed
only by feeble protest of the government of New
York, though that of Massachusetts urged more
active opposition. The fort was completed, and the
French held the key to the " Gate of the Country,"
as the Iroquois had so fitly named Lake Champlain.
Seigniories were granted on both sides of the lake,
and in that of Sieur Hocquart, which extended
three leagues along the lake and five leagues back
therefrom, was this settlement on Point à la Chevalure. Northward from the fort the habitants
built their cabins of logs in close neighborhood
along the street, and sowed wheat, planted corn and

fruit-trees on their narrow holdings. Flowers new
to the wilderness bloomed beside doorways, and
the fragrance of foreign herbs was mingled with
the balsamic odors of the woods. Where only the
glare of camp-fires had briefly illumined the bivouac
of armed men, the blaze of the hearth was kindled
to shine on happy households; where had been
heard no sound of human voice but the sentinel's
challenge, the stern, sharp call of military command,
or the devilish yell of the savage, now arose the
voice of the mother crooning to her babe, the prattle
of children at play, the gabble of gossiping dames,
and the laughter of the gay habitant; while from
the protecting fort flaunted the lilies of France, an
assurance to these simple people of the permanency
of their newly founded homes. Here the Canadians
tilled their little fields, and shared of the lake's
abundance with the fish - hawks and the otter,
hunted the deer and moose, and trapped the fur-
bearing animals in the broad forest, and at the bidding of their masters went forth with their painted
allies, the Waubanakees, on bloody forays against
the English.

When in 1744 war was again declared between
England and France, the English frontier settlements soon began to suffer from the advantage their
enemies possessed in a stronghold from which they
were so easily reached. During the next year they
were frequently harassed by small parties, and in
August, 1746, Vaudreuil set forth from Fort St.
Frederic with an army of seven hundred French and

Indians to attack Fort Massachusetts, then the most advanced post in the province, whose name had been given it.[1] There were but thirty-three persons in the garrison, including women and children, but Colonel Hawkes bravely defended the place with his insignificant force for twenty-eight hours, when the supply of ammunition was exhausted and he surrendered, with the stipulation that none of his people should be delivered to the Indians. Yet in spite of this, soon after the capitulation, Vaudreuil gave up one half of them to the savages, who thereupon at once killed a prisoner who was unable to travel.

After the capture of Louisburg by the force of New England troops which he had organized, Governor Shirley of Massachusetts proposed a plan for the conquest of Canada, in which a fleet and army promised by the mother country were to attack Quebec, while the colonial troops were to march against Fort St. Frederic.

While active preparations for this enterprise were being made, the colonies were alarmed by news of the arrival at Nova Scotia of a French fleet and army so formidable as to threaten the conquest of all their seaboard, and all their efforts were turned toward defense. When storm and shipwreck had scattered and destroyed the fleet and frustrated its objects, Shirley proposed a winter campaign in which the New Hampshire troops were to go up the Connecticut and destroy the Waubanakee village

---

[1] This fort was situated in what is now Williamstown.

of St. Francis, and the Massachusetts, Connecticut, and New York troops, advancing by the way of Lake George, were to attack Fort St. Frederic ; but Connecticut declining to take part in it, the project was abandoned.

The English had continued to extend their settlements upon the Connecticut, and had built several small forts on the west side of the river. These so-called forts were block-houses, built of hewn logs, with a projecting upper story and pierced with loopholes for muskets. Such was Bridgman's fort in what is now Vernon, and which was twice attacked by Indians, and in the second attack was destroyed. Some years afterward, in July, 1755, a party of Indians, who were lurking near the fort, now rebuilt, waylaid three settlers as they were returning from their work, and killed one Caleb Howe. Another was drowned in attempting to cross the river, and one escaped. The Indians gained entrance to the fort, whose only inmates were the wives and children of the three men, by making the customary signal, which they had learned by observation. After plundering the fort, and taking the helpless inmates captive, they proceeded through the wilderness to Crown Point, and from thence to Canada. Their prisoners suffered there a long captivity, but were at length mostly redeemed.[1]

The most northerly settlement now on the river was at Number Four, on the east side of the Con-

Dr. Dwight's *Travels*, vol. ii. p. 82.

necticut. Three years after its settlement, in 1743, a fort was built under the direction of Colonel Stoddard, the builder of Fort Dummer. It was similar to that fortification in size and construction, but was stockaded only on the north side. It inclosed, as " province houses," the dwellings previously built by five of the settlers, and one built at the same time with the fort. The settlers continued here for three years thereafter, during which they suffered frequent assaults from marauding bands of Indians, in which eight of the soldiers and inhabitants were killed and three taken prisoners. When the Massachusetts troops which for a while had garrisoned the place were withdrawn, the helpless people abandoned their newly made homes, and for months the divested fort remained as silent and desolate as the wintry wastes of forests that surrounded it. In response to representations made to him of the expediency of such a measure, Governor Shirley ordered Captain Phineas Stevens, with thirty men, to march to and occupy the fort at Number Four. Arriving there on the 27th of March, 1747, Captain Stevens found the place in good condition, and was heartily welcomed to it by an old dog and cat which had been left behind in the hurry of the autumnal departure. The garrison had been in possession but a few days when they were attacked by French and Indians commanded by M. Debeline, who opened a musketry fire upon the fort on all sides. Failing to take it in this way, the enemy attempted to burn it by setting fire to the fences and houses near it, by discharging flaming arrows upon the roof, and then by pushing a cart loaded with burning brush [1] against the walls.

Stevens thus describes the ingenious device by which he prevented the firing of the wooden walls by the enemy: "Those who were not employed in firing at the enemy were employed in digging trenches under the bottom of the fort. We dug no less than eleven of them, so deep that a man could go and stand upright on the outside and not endanger himself; so that when these trenches were finished we could wet all the outside of the fort, which we did, and kept it wet all night. We drew some hundreds of barrels of water, and to undergo all this hard service there were but thirty men." [2] All the attempts of the enemy were baffled, fair promises and dire threats alike set at naught by the brave defenders of the fort.

On the third day of the siege Debeline offered to withdraw if Stevens would sell them provisions. Stevens refused, but offered to give them five bushels of corn for every hostage that should be given him to be held till an English captive could be brought from Canada, whereupon, after firing a few more shots, the besiegers withdrew to Fort St. Frederic.[3]

[1] Williams's *History of Vermont.*

[2] Captain Stevens's letter to Colonel Williams.

[3] Stevens's bravery was so much admired by Sir Charles Knowles, an officer of high rank in the British navy, that he presented him a handsome sword, and in honor of the donor the township was named Charlestown. For Captain Stevens's account of this siege see *History of Charlestown*, p. 34.

No other expeditions were afterward undertaken by the French while the war lasted, but the Indians in small parties continued to harry the settlements till after its close in 1748. To guard against these incursions, scouting parties, led by brave and experienced partisans, frequently went out from the frontier forts to watch the motions of the enemy, when oftentimes their perilous adventures and heroic deeds were such that the story of them is more like a tale from an old romance than like a page of history. One memorable incident of this service took place on Vermont soil in the summer of the next year after the gallant defense of Number Four, when Captain Humphrey Hobbs, Stevens's second in command at that post, being on a scout toward Fort Shirley in Massachusetts, with forty men, for four hours held at bay and finally beat off an Indian force more than four times outnumbering his own. It was a brush fight, wherein the scouts had no shelter but such forest cover as their assailants also took advantage of. But three of the scouts were killed; the loss of the Indians, though great, was never known, as when one fell his nearest comrade crept to the body and attached a line to it, by which it was withdrawn to cover. During the fight, the scouts frequently beheld the ghastly sight of a dead Indian gliding away and fading from view in the haze of undergrowth, as if drawn thither by some superhuman power.[1]

[1] This fight took place on Sunday, June 26, 1748, about twelve miles northwest of Fort Dummer, in the present township of Marlboro'.

Until the beginning of another French and English war in 1754, and while the colonies were endeavoring to form a union for their better defense, while elsewhere were occurring such events as Braddock's Defeat and Monckton's and Winslow's Conquest of Acadia, there is little of consequence to record of affairs in this quarter till Colonel William Johnson, with an army of 4,000 or more, began an advance against Fort St. Frederic. The French had occupied Ticonderoga, and begun to fortify the point, which soon became far more important than the older fortress of St. Frederic ; and their army of 2,000 regulars, Canadians and Indians, under Baron Dieskau, taking the offensive, moved against Johnson and attacked his fortified camp at Lake George in September, 1755. The French were defeated with severe loss ; [1] but Johnson did not follow up his success, and the enemy retreated to Ticonderoga unmolested but by the impetuous attack of Captain McGinnis of New Hampshire, with a force of 200 men. Yet in England his barren victory seemed of such importance that he was honored with a baronetcy.

Now, while an army of more than two thousand regulars, under Lord Loudon, was lying at Albany, and Winslow was at Lake George with 7,000 provincial troops, Montcalm besieged Oswego, which presently surrendered with all its garrison, arms, stores, and munitions of war. Montcalm continued

[1] Johnson's " Account of Battle of Lake George, " *Doc. Hist. N. Y.* vol. ii. p. 402.

actively on the offensive, and in August, 1757, undertook the capture of Fort William Henry, which was held by Colonel Monroe with a garrison of 2,500 men. His surrender was at once demanded, but he refused, and defended the fort with great bravery, being confident General Webb would presently send him relief from Fort Edward. But though frequently entreated, no help came from Webb, only a letter protesting his inability to aid him, and advising him to surrender on the best terms obtainable. This fell into the hands of Montcalm, and with renewed demands of surrender was sent by him to Monroe. Thus abandoned, after holding out for more than a week, he signed the articles of capitulation, by the terms of which his paroled army was to be escorted to Fort Edward, his sick and wounded to be cared for by Montcalm, and given up when sufficiently recovered. The story of the perfidious violation of these terms, and the horrors of the carnage when the defenseless prisoners, of whatever age or sex, or sick or wounded, were butchered by the savage allies of the Frenchmen, some of whom stood passive witnesses of the massacre, raising neither hand nor voice to stay it, is a dark and blood-stained page of American history, and an ineffaceable blot on the name of Montcalm. Webb, with increased alarm for his own safety, sent swift messengers to the provinces for reinforcements, which were at once raised and forwarded to him; but Montcalm did not return from Ticonderoga to attack him, and the recruits were not long kept in service.

Loudon at New York was engaged in a controversy with the government of Massachusetts concerning the quartering of British troops, and threatening to send an army to that province if his demands were not speedily complied with, and so the campaign ended without honor or advantage to the English. Its poor results were chiefly due to the inefficiency of the British ministry, and the incapacity of the British commanders to carry on this unaccustomed warfare of the wilderness, and their unwillingness to avail themselves of the experience of the colonial officers, whom they despised, thus leaving to their alert and active enemy all the advantage of familiarity with its methods. So universal was the complaint in England and her American colonies caused by this and the preceding campaigns that the formation of a new ministry became necessary, and William Pitt was appointed secretary of state.

In his plan of the American campaign, which was soon to be vigorously undertaken, one army of 12,000 men was to attempt the conquest of Louisburg; another, still larger, that of the French forts on Lake Champlain; and a third, that of Fort Du Quesne, at the head of the Ohio River. The expedition against Louisburg was commanded by General Amherst, under whom were Generals Wolfe, Whitmore, and Lawrence. The naval force, commanded by Admiral Boscawen, sailed for America early in the spring, and in May, 1758, the whole armament of 157 sail was gathered at Halifax.

Sailing thence on the 28th, a part of the transports arrived near Louisburg, and on the 8th of June the troops, under General Wolfe, disembarked and invested the city. Louisburg was garrisoned by 2,500 regulars, 300 militia, and later by a reinforcement of 350 Canadians and Indians, and the harbor was defended by 11 French ships of war. After a siege of several weeks, during which the French warships were destroyed, the place surrendered to General Amherst on the 26th of July. In the beginning of the same month General Forbes set forth from Philadelphia on his difficult march to Fort Du Quesne. Obstacles which delayed and reverses which checked his progress did not discourage him, although he was so debilitated by a mortal sickness that for much of the distance he was carried on a litter; and in November he took possession of the fort, which had been dismantled and abandoned by the French, and gave it the name of Fort Pitt.

While these undertakings of Amherst and Forbes were progressing, General Abercrombie began his movement upon Ticonderoga with a well-appointed army of more than six thousand regular and nearly ten thousand provincial troops. The army embarked on Lake George in more than a thousand batteaux and whaleboats; and as the flotilla moved down the lake, with glittering arms and gaudy uniforms and flaunting banners shining in the July sunshine, their splendor repeated in innumerable broken reflections on the ruffled waters, this wilderness had never seen such pomp and circumstance

of war ; nor had its solitudes been stirred by such
martial strains as now burst from trumpet, fife,
drum, and Highland pipe, and echoed from shore
and crag in multitudinous reverberations. Having
landed next day without opposition at the lower end
of the lake, the troops began their advance in four
columns. An advanced guard of one battalion of
the enemy, after· firing their tents, retreated from
their fortified camp on the approach of the English,
but afterward engaged in a skirmish with the left
column, when the troops had fallen into some disorder in their march through the dense woods. It
was in this engagement that the English suffered
its first severe loss in the death of Lord Howe, a
gallant young general, who had especially endeared
himself to the provincials by his kindly manners,
by sharing their hardships and perils, and by easily
accommodating himself to the exigencies of this
new service. Israel Putnam, then a major of the
rangers, in which branch of the service he had distinguished himself by his coolness and daring, was
a conspicuous actor in this affair. After the death
of Howe, Putnam and the troops with him attacked
the French with such fury that more than four
hundred of them were killed and taken prisoners.
But the army having fallen into great disorder in
its passage through the woods, it was deemed advis-
·able to withdraw it to the place where it had disembarked. Next day, the sawmill on the outlet of
Lake George was taken possession of by a detachment under Colonel Bradstreet, the bridge there

which the enemy had destroyed was rebuilt, and the army again began its advance on Ticonderoga.

Montcalm had strengthened his position by throwing up a breastwork across the neck of the peninsula on which the fort stood, and by hedging this with an almost impenetrable abatis. Yet the engineer whom Abercrombie had sent to examine the enemy's position was of the opinion that it might be successfully stormed; and as the prisoners taken reported that large reinforcements were likely to arrive soon, it was determined to assault the works at once. The attacking columns were met by a scathing fire of artillery and musketry, but rushed on to the abatis, through which they vainly endeavored to make their way, Murray's regiment of Highlanders hewing at the bristling barrier of pointed branches with their claymores, while a murderous fire from the breastworks thinned the ranks of the brave clansmen. Again and again the assailants were swept back by the pelting storm of bullets, and again they returned to the assault; the few who struggled through the abatis were slain before they reached the intrenchments, or only reached them to be made prisoners, and of the Highland regiment twenty-five of the officers and half the privates fell. With persistent but unavailing valor, the attack was continued for more than four hours, and then a retreat was ordered, and the defeated army sullenly fell back to the camp which it had occupied the night before. Early next morning it was reëmbarked, and the torn and decimated regiments continued their retreat up the lake.

General Abercrombie's defeat did not discourage him from making further efforts against the enemy. He sent General Stanwix to build a fort at Oneida and dispatched Colonel Bradstreet with 3,000 men against Fort Frontenac on the St. Lawrence, and both successfully performed their allotted duties.

General Amherst returned from Louisburg, assumed command, and in the summer of 1757 began a movement for the reduction of Ticonderoga and Crown Point, which was a part of this year's campaign. Moving forward by the same route that Abercrombie had taken, he reached the neighborhood of Ticonderoga without encountering any opposition from the enemy, and made preparations to besiege this fortress; but the French made only a brief defense, in which, however, Colonel Townshend and a few soldiers were killed, and then, leaving the French flag flying and a match burning in the magazine to blow up the fort, evacuated it and retired to Crown Point the night of the 27th of July. An hour after their departure came the thunder of the explosion, which destroyed one bastion and set the barracks on fire. They presently abandoned Crown Point and retired to the Isle aux Noix, while Amherst was repairing and strengthening the fortifications of Ticonderoga.

So at last, with but slight resistance to the tide of conquest that was now overwhelming their northern possessions in America, the French abandoned the strongholds that guarded the "Gate of the Country."

For more than a quarter of a century Fort St. Frederic had been the point from which marauding bands of Indians and their scarcely less ferocious white associates had set forth on errands of rapine and murder, which had made as dangerous and insecure as a crater's brink every frontier settlement of a wide region. Here had been plotted their forays; here they had returned from them with captives, scalps, and plunder; here found safety from pursuit. The two forts had held civilization at bay on the border of this land of "beautiful valleys and fields fertile in corn," and to all the inhabitants of the New England frontier their fall was a deliverance from an ever-threatening danger.

The French held the Isle aux Noix, their last remaining post on Lake Champlain, with a force of 3,500 regular troops and Canadian militia, and had also on the lake four large armed vessels, commanded by experienced officers of the French navy. The presence of this naval force made it necessary for Amherst to build vessels that might successfully oppose it, and while this work was in progress the British general dispatched a body of rangers against the Indians of St. Francis, who for fifty years had been active and relentless foes of the New England colonies.

Early in the century many members of the dif-

ferent tribes of Waubanakees in the eastern part of
New England had been induced by the governor of
Canada to remove to that province, and since then
had lived on the St. Francis River, and were commonly known as the St. Francis tribe, though they
gave themselves the name of "Zooquagese," the
people who withdrew from the others, or literally
"the Little People."[1]

Their intimate knowledge of the region, which
had been the home of many generations of their
people, and their familiarity with every waterway
and mountain pass that gave easiest access to the
English frontiers, made them as valuable instru-
ments, as their hatred of the English made them
willing ones for the hostile purposes of the French.
From none of their enemies had the frontier settlements suffered more, and toward none did they
bear greater enmity.

The wrongs which these tribes had suffered from
the English, since their earliest contact with them,
gave cause for vengeful retaliation, and its atrocities
were such as might be expected of savages accustomed by usage and tradition to inflict on their enemies and receive from them the cruelest tortures
that could be devised, and whose religion taught no
precept of mercy ; but for those Christians, boasting
the highest civilization of the world, the French,
who encouraged the barbarous warfare and seldom
attempted to check its horrors, there can be no excuse.

[1] From John Wadno, an intelligent Indian of St. Francis.

Amherst chose Major Robert Rogers to lead the expedition against St. Francis, and he could not have chosen one better fitted to carry out the scheme of vengeance than this wary, intrepid, and unscrupulous ranger. To him it was a light achievement to creep within the lines of a French camp, and he could slay and scalp an enemy with as little compunction as would an Indian,[1] while the men whom he led had seen or suffered enough of Indian barbarity to make them as unrelenting as he in the infliction of any measure of punishment on these scourges of the border.

Rogers left Crown Point on the night of the 12th of September with a detachment of 200, embarked in batteaux, and went cautiously down the lake. His force was reduced by one fourth on the fifth day out by the explosion of a keg of powder, which wounded several of his men and made it necessary to send them with an escort back to Crown Point.

Arrived at the head of Missisco Bay, the boats and sufficient provisions for the return voyage were concealed, and left in charge of two trusty Indians, when the little army began its march across the country through the wilderness toward the Indian town. Two days later it was overtaken by the boat guard, bringing to Rogers the alarming news of the discovery of the boats by a force of French and Indians, four hundred strong, fifty of whom

---

[1] For some reports of his scouts, see *Doc. Hist. N. Y.* vol. iv. p. 169 *et seq.*

had been sent away with the batteaux, while the others, still doubly outnumbering his force, were following him in hot pursuit. Rogers kept his own counsel, and alone formed the plans that he at once acted upon. He dispatched a lieutenant with eight men to Crown Point to acquaint General Amherst with the turn of affairs, and ask him to send provisions to Coos, on the Connecticut, to which place it now seemed that soon or late he must make his way. The only question was, whether he should do so now, or attempt to strike the contemplated blow before his pursuers could overtake him. It was characteristic of the man to decide upon the bolder course, and he marched his men, as enduring as the enemy and as accustomed to such difficult marching, with such celerity that the pursuing force was left well behind when, on the evening of the 4th of October, the neighborhood of the town was reached.

While his men halted for rest and refreshment, he, disguised as an Indian and accompanied by two of his officers, went forward and entered the village. The Indians, unsuspicious of danger, were celebrating some rite with a grand dance, which quite engrossed their attention while Rogers and his companions thoroughly reconnoitred the place. Returning to his troops some hours before daylight, he marched them within a few hundred yards of the town, and at daybreak, the dance being over and the Indians asleep, the onslaught was made.

Amherst's orders to Rogers, after reminding him of the "barbarities committed by the enemy's Indian scoundrels," and bidding him to "take his revenge," had enjoined that "no women or children shall be killed or hurt;" but if this command was heeded at first, it was presently disregarded. If there was any touch of mercy in the hearts of the rangers when the assault began, the last vestige of it was swept away when daylight revealed hundreds of scalps of their own people displayed on poles, silvered locks of age, tresses of women's hair, golden ringlets of childhood, all ghastly trophies of New England raids.

Old and young, warrior, squaw, and pappoose, alike suffered their vengeance, till of the three hundred inhabitants two thirds were killed and twenty taken prisoners, fifteen of whom were soon "let go their way." The church, adorned with plate and an image of silver, and the well-furnished dwellings, were plundered and burned, and the morning sun shone upon a scene of desolation as complete as these savages themselves had ever wrought.

When the work of destruction was finished, Rogers assembled his men, of whom only one had been killed and six slightly wounded, and after an hour's rest began the return march with the prisoners, five recaptured English captives, and what provisions and booty could be carried.

The route taken was up the St. Francis and to the eastward of Lake Memphremagog, the objective point being the Coos Meadows, where it was expected that the relief party with provisions would be met. They were followed by the enemy, and had lost seven men by their attacks, when Rogers formed an ambuscade upon his own track, into which they fell and suffered so severely that they desisted from further pursuit.

When ten days had elapsed, and Rogers and his men had come some distance within the bounds of what is now Vermont, they began to suffer much from lack of food, and it was thought best to divide the force into small parties, each to make its way as best it could to the expected succor at Coos, or to the English settlements farther down the Connecticut.

While its autumnal glories faded and the primeval forest grew bare and bleak, the little bands struggled bravely on over rugged mountains, through tangled windfalls, and swamps whose miry pools were treacherously hidden beneath the fallen leaves, fighting hour after hour and day after day against fatigue and famine, foes more persistent, insidious, and unrelenting than Awahnock [1] and Waubanakee. Such small game as they could kill, and the few edible roots that they found, were their only subsistence; and they would gladly have bartered the silver image and the golden candlesticks brought from the church, and all their booty, for one day's supply of the coarsest food. They buried the treasure, with scant hope that they might ever unearth it, and cast away unheeded the useless burdens of less valuable plunder.

[1] Awahnock, = Frenchman.

At night they cowered around their camp-fires and shivered out the miserable hours of darkness, then arose unrefreshed, and staggered on the way that each day stretched more wearily and hopelessly before them. Some could go no farther, but fell down and died, and were left unburied by comrades too weak to give them the rudest sepulchre, and some in the delirium of famine wandered away from their companions to become hopelessly lost in the pathless wilderness and die alone.

The officer whom Rogers had dispatched to Crown Point performed the difficult journey in nine days, and General Amherst at once sent a lieutenant with three men to Number Four, to proceed thence up the Connecticut with provisions to the appointed place. The relief party embarked in two canoes laden with provisions, which they safely landed on an island near the mouth of the Passumpsic ; but though ordered to remain there as long as there was any hope of the coming of those whom they were sent to succor, when only two days had passed they became impatient of waiting, or were seized by a panic, and hastily departed with all the supplies.

Rogers and those who remained with him, following the Passumpsic down to the Connecticut, came at last to the place where they hoped to find relief, but only to find it abandoned, and that so recently that the camp-fire of the relief party was still freshly burning. These men were yet so near that they heard the guns which Rogers fired to recall them, but which, supposed by them to be fired by the enemy, only served to hasten their retreat.

Rogers says : " It is hardly possible to describe the grief and consternation of those of us who came to the Cohasse Intervales." [1] Sorely distressed by this shameful desertion but not discouraged, the brave commander left his worn out and starving men at the Passumpsic in charge of a lieutenant, whom he instructed in the method of preparing ground-nuts and lily roots for food, and set forth down the river on a raft with Captain Ogden, one ranger, and a captive Indian boy, in a final endeavor to reach Number Four and obtain relief. At White River Falls the raft was wrecked, and Rogers, too weak to cut trees for another, burned them down and into proper lengths, while Ogden and the ranger hunted red squirrels for food. A second raft was then built, and, after a voyage that would have been perilous to men in the fullness of strength, they at last reached Number Four. Rogers at once dispatched a canoe with supplies to his starving men, which reached them on the tenth day after he had left them, as he had promised. Two days later he himself went up the river with canoes, manned by some of the inhabitants whom he had hired, and laden with provisions for those who might come in by the same route, and he sent expresses to towns on the Merrimac that relief parties might be sent up that river.

On the 1st of December he returned to Crown

[1] Rogers's Journal.

Point with what remained of his force, having lost, since beginning the retreat from St. Francis, three lieutenants and forty-six non-commissioned officers and privates. Notwithstanding its losses and dire hardships, the expedition was successful in the infliction of a chastisement that the Indians of St. Francis never recovered from and never forgot, and which relieved the New England frontier from the continual dread of the bloody incursions that it had so long suffered. Throughout the whole of it, in leading it to victory and in retreat, in sharing their hardships and in heroic efforts to succor and save his men, Rogers's conduct was such as should make his name honorably remembered in spite of the suspicions which tarnished it in after years.

While Rogers's expedition was in progress, a sloop of sixteen guns and a raft carrying six guns were built at Ticonderoga. With these and a brigantine, Captain Loring sailed down the lake and engaged the French vessels, sinking two of them and capturing a third, which was repaired and brought away after being run aground and deserted by its crew, leaving to the enemy but one schooner on these waters.

Amherst at the same time embarked his whole army in batteaux, and began his advance against Isle aux Noix, but, being delayed by storms and adverse winds, deemed it best to abandon for this season the attempt, and returned to Crown Point, arriving there on the 27th of October. He now began the erection of a new and larger fortress and three new outworks there; completed the road between Crown Point and Ticonderoga, and began another from the latter fort to Number Four.

Meanwhile events of great moment had occurred elsewhere. In July, after the death of General Prideaux, who commanded the army besieging Niagara, Sir William Johnson had defeated the French army sent to its relief, and the fort had surrendered to him. On the 13th of September Wolfe, on the Heights of Abraham, had given his life for imperishable renown; and six days later Quebec, the most impregnable stronghold of the French in America, was surrendered to the enemy, whose attempts to reduce it had for seventy years been unsuccessful.

All the English colonies in America rejoiced in its fall, for the conquest of Canada was now assured, and the day of their deliverance from French and Indian invasion had dawned.

Levis's attempt to recapture Quebec had failed, though sickness and death had sorely weakened Murray's garrison, and now at Montreal the French were to make the last stand against English conquest. Amherst was to advance upon it down the St. Lawrence, Murray from Quebec, and Haviland from the south, to break the last bar of the "Gate of the Country," held by Bougainville at Isle aux Noix.

On the 15th of July Murray embarked with nearly 2,500 men. He met no great opposition from the superior forces of Bourlamaque and Dumas, which on either shore of the river withdrew slowly toward Montreal as the fleet advanced. He issued a proclamation promising safety of person and property to all the inhabitants who remained peaceably at home, and threatening to burn the houses of all who were in arms. He kept his word to the letter in the protection and in the punishment, and the result was the rapid dwindling away of Bourlamaque's army.

Toward the end of August he encamped below the town on the island of Ste. Therese, and awaited the arrival of the other English armies. A regiment of New Hampshire men commanded by Colonel Goffe opened the road which Amherst had ordered to be made from Number Four to Crown Point, and performed the labor in such good time that on the 31st of July they arrived, and, turned drovers as well as pioneers, brought with them a herd of cattle for the supply of the army there.[1] This road ran from Wentworth's Ferry, near Charlestown, up the right bank of Black River to the present township of Ludlow, thence across the mountains to Otter Creek, and down that stream to a station opposite Crown Point, to which it ran across the country. That part of the road across and on the west side of the mountains was begun and nearly completed in the previous year, under the supervision of Colonel Zadok Hawks and Captain John Stark; Stark and 200 rangers being employed on the western portion.[2]

---

[1] Belknap's *History of New Hampshire.*
[2] Sanderson's *History of Charlestown*, p. 87.

Haviland embarked at Crown Point on the 12th of August with 3,400 regulars, provincials, and Indians in whaleboats and batteaux, which, under sunny skies and on quiet waters, came in four days to Isle aux Noix. Cannon were planted in front and rear of Bougainville's position. The largest vessel of his naval force was cut adrift by a cannon-shot and drifted into the hands of the English; and the others, endeavoring to escape to St. John's, ran aground and were taken by the rangers, who swam out and boarded one, tomahawk in hand, when the others presently surrendered.[2]

Bougainville, abandoning the island, made a difficult night retreat to St. John's, and from thence fell back with Roquemaure to the St. Lawrence. Haviland was soon opposite Montreal, and in communication with Murray, and both awaited the coming of Amherst's army. This force had assembled at Oswego in July, and numbered something more than 10,000 men, exclusive of about 700 Indians under Sir William Johnson, and had embarked on Lake Ontario on the 10th of August, and within five days reached Oswigatchee. After the capture by five gunboats of a French armed brig that threatened the destruction of the batteaux and whaleboats, the army continued its advance to Fort Levis, near the head of the rapids. Amherst invested the fort, and opened fire upon it from land and water; and when for three days rocky islet and wooded shore had been shaken by

[1] Parkman's *Montcalm and Wolfe.*

```
        THE DARTMOUTH BOOKSTORE, INC.
             33 SOUTH MAIN STREET
        HANOVER, NEW HAMPSHIRE 03755

QTY        PRODUCT          DEPT    PRICE

  1    18-91-07781-X        8400    1.98
  1    15-76-02315-X        8400    3.98
  2    15-98-36242-9        8400    5.98
  1    18-99-00477-7        8400    5.98
  2    15-96-01213-9        8400    5.96
  1    15-98-01516-8        8400   14.98
  1    018111511728         5717    4.99
       20 ZZ DISCOUNT               1.00-
  1    018111511728         5717    4.99
       20 ZZ DISCOUNT               1.00-
  1    028942102828         5703    7.99
       20 ZZ DISCOUNT               1.60-
  1    018111580229         5717    5.99
       20 ZZ DISCOUNT               1.20-
  1    047163004520         5703    4.99
       20 ZZ DISCOUNT               1.00-

         SUB-TOTAL            $67.81
           *DISCOUNT           $5.80-
113245   TOTAL SALE          $62.01

         MASTERCARD          $62.01

STORE-00001 01-WLM  10/27/90  11:32 AM
      THANK YOU FOR YOUR PATRONAGE
```

the thunder of the cannon that splintered the wooden walls, the French commandant, Pouchot, was compelled to surrender the ruined works and his garrison. Johnson's Indians were so enraged at not being allowed to kill the prisoners that three fourths of them went home.[1] There was no further resistance from the French, but there was yet a terrible enemy to be encountered in the long and dangerous rapids that must be descended. Several were passed with but slight loss; but in the most perilous passage of the last three, forty-seven boats were wrecked, several damaged, some artillery, ammunition, and stores lost, and eighty-four men drowned in the angry turmoil of wild waters. When these perils were past, an uneventful and unopposed voyage ensued, till on the 6th of September the army landed at Lachine, and, marching to the city, encamped before its walls.

The defenses of Montreal were too weak to resist a siege; the troops, abandoned by the militia, too few to give battle to the three armies that hemmed them in; and there was nothing left for Vaudreuil but surrender. Some of the terms of capitulation proposed by him were rejected by Amherst, who demanded that "the whole garrison of Montreal and all the French troops in Canada must lay down their arms, and shall not serve again during the war." In answer to the remonstrances of Vaudreuil and his generals he said: "I am fully resolved, for the infamous part the troops of France

[1] Parkman's *Montcalm and Wolfe*, vol. ii. p. 370.

have acted in exciting the savages to perpetrate the most horrid and unheard-of barbarities in the whole progress of the war, and for other open treacheries and flagrant breaches of faith, to manifest to all the world, by this capitulation, my detestation of such practices." [1]

Vaudreuil yielded, as perforce he must, and on the 8th of September signed the capitulation by which Canada passed into the possession of England. The French officers, civil and military, the troops and sailors, were to be sent to France, and the inhabitants were to be protected in their property and religion.

The Indian allies of the English, and those who had lately been the allies of the French but were now as ready to turn against them as they had been to serve, were held in such firm restraint that not a person suffered any injury from them more than from the soldiers of the victorious armies.

The long struggle was over, the conquest of Canada was accomplished, and great was the rejoicing of the people of all the English colonies, especially those of New England. The toilsome march through the savage forest, the cheerless bivouac on remote and lonely shores, were no longer to be endured; nor the deadly ambuscade dreaded by the home-loving husbandman, who for love of home had turned soldier; nor was his family to live in the constant fear of the horrors of nightly attack, massacre, or captivity that had made anxious every hour of day and night.

[1] Parkman.

CHAPTER III.

OCCUPATION AND SETTLEMENT.

Now that Canada was conquered and the French armies withdrawn from Ticonderoga and Crown Point, all the country lying between Lake Champlain and the Connecticut, commonly called the Wilderness, was open to settlement.

In 1696, long before the granting of French seigniories on Lake Champlain, Godfrey Dellius, a Dutch clergyman of Albany, had purchased of the Mohawks, who claimed all this territory, an immense tract, extending from Saratoga along both sides of the Hudson River and Wood Creek, and on the east side of Lake Champlain, twenty miles north of Crown Point. The purchase was confirmed by New York, but three years later was repealed, " as an extravagant favor to one subject."

In 1732 Colonel John Henry Lydius purchased of the Mohawks a large tract of land situated on " the Otter Creek, which emptieth itself into Lake Champlain in North America, easterly from and near Crown Point." The deed was confirmed by Governor Shirley of Massachusetts in 1744. This tract embraced nearly the whole of the present counties of Addison and Rutland. It was divided into townships, and most of it sold by Lydius to a great number of purchasers,[1] some of whom settled upon it. The township of Durham was originally settled under this grant, but the settlers, finding the title imperfect, applied for and obtained letters-patent under New York.[2]

The French colony at Point à Chevalure vanished with the shadow of the banner of France. The young forest soon repossessed the fields where almost the only trace of husbandry was the rank growth of foreign weeds. House walls were crumbling about cold hearthstones and smokeless chimneys, and thresholds untrodden but by the nightly prowling beast or the foot of the curious hunter. There was no remembrance of the housewife's hand but the self-sown lilies and marigolds that mingled their strange bloom with native asters and goldenrods above the graves of forsaken homes. From where the sluggish waters of the narrow channel are first stirred by Wood Creek, to where the waves of Champlain break on Canadian shores, there was not one settlement on its eastern border, nor any inhabitant save where some trapper had built his cabin in the solitude of the woods, and

[1] In an indenture made 30th December, 1761, Colonel Lydius grants to Thomas Robinson, merchant, of Newport, in the Colony of Rhode Island, one sixtieth of the township No. 24, called Danvis, for the "sum of one Shilling money one peppercorn each year for seventy years (if demanded) and after twenty years five Shillings sterling annually, forever, on the Feast Day of St. Michael the Archangel, for each hundred acres of arable Land."

[2] Petition of Colonel Spencer and others. *Doc. Hist. N. Y.* vol. iv. p. 575.

dwelt hermit-like for a time while he plied his lonely craft.

The Wilderness had not long rested in the silence of peace when it was invaded by a throng of pioneers, who came to wrest its soil from the ancient domination of the forest, and upon it to build their homes. Farmers and sons of farmers, while serving in the colonial armies, had noted during their painful marches through it what goodly soil slept in the shadow of this wilderness; keen-eyed rangers, chosen from hunters and trappers for their skill in woodcraft, when on their perilous errands had penetrated its depths wherever led an Indian trail or wound a stream to float a canoe, and knew what it held for men of their craft, and each had planned, when peace should come, to return to the land that gave such promise of fruitful fields or the easier garner of peltry. Lumbermen, too, knew its wealth of great pines; and speculators were casting greedy eyes upon the region, and plotting for its acquisition.

As the soldiers who guarded its posts, or crossed and recrossed the savage wilderness, were of New England origin, it naturally followed that most of the actual settlers came from the same provinces. Thus, from the very first, each little community of hardy and industrious pioneers was clearly stamped with the New England character. Such inspiration, such love of home, as glows in the hearts of all mountaineers, they drew from the grand companionship of the stern and steadfast mountains, the Crouching Lion, Mansfield, Ascutney, whose heavenward-reaching peaks shone white with snow when winter reigned, or summer came or lingered in the valleys, — landmarks enduring as the world, that stand while nations are born and flourish and pass away.

Sometimes the pioneer left his family in the older settlements while he, with a neighbor or two, or often alone, went into the wilderness to make the beginning of a new home. A pitch was located, and the herculean task of making a clearing begun, the apparently hopeless warfare of one puny hand against a countless army of giants that towered above him. Yet one by one the great trees toppled and fell before his valiant strokes. The trunks of some were built into a log-house, with a puncheon floor and roof of bark ; more were rolled into heaps and burned, and the first patch of cleared soil was planted with corn or sown with wheat. After weeks and months of this toil and hardship and loneliness, perhaps not once broken by the sight of a fellow - being, when the tasseled corn and the nodding wheat hid the blackened stumps of the scant clearing, the giants still hemmed him in, their lofty heads the horizon of his little world, the bounds of his briefly sunlit sky. When his crops were housed, and the woods were gaudy with a thousand autumnal tints to where the glory of the deciduous trees was bounded by the dark wall of "black growth" on the mountains whose peaks were white with snow, he shouldered axe and gun and went southward, following the army of crows that raised a clamor of amazement at this intrusion on their immemorial domain. While the little clearing slept under the snow, and the silent cabin made the wintry loneliness of the forest more lonely, he spent a winter of content among old friends and neighbors, and in the spring set forth on horseback, or with an ox-team, with wife and children or newly wedded bride, and scant outfit of household stuff, to take permanent possession of the new home, where, if the burden of loneliness was lightened, the weariness of toil, privation, and anxiety was not lessened. Nature was the only neighbor of the new-comers, kind or unkind, according to her impartial mood to all her children, now a friend and consoler, with sunshine and timely shower, flowers and birdsong and hymns of wind-swept pines, now relentless, assailing with storm and bitter stress of cold. Miles of weary forest path marked only by blazed trees, or miles of toilsome waterway, lay between them and their kind, or help or sympathy in whatever trouble might befall them. Such consolation as religion might give must be sought at the fountain-head of all religion, since church and gospel ministrations were left behind.

The old warpaths became the ways of peace, and on lake and river, that before had borne none but warlike craft, now fared the settler's boat, laden with his family and household goods, skirting the quiet shore or up the slow current of a stream, through intervales whose fat soil as yet nourished only a luxuriant verdure of the forest. From afar the eternal roar of a cataract boomed in swelling thunder along the green walls of the lane of waters, foretelling the approaching toil of a portage. But no foeman lurked behind the green thicket, and the voyagers were startled by no sound more alarming than the sudden uprising of innumerable water-fowl, the plunge of an otter disturbed in his sport, or the mellow cadence of the great owl's solemn note.

The granting of lands, which had been inter-rupted by the war, was again begun by the gov-ernor of New Hampshire, Benning Wentworth, and in different parts of the region surveyors were busy running the lines of townships and lots. There was a flavor of discovery and adventure in their weary toil that gave it zest, as, with no guide but the com-pass, they were led through sombre depths of the primeval forest, where the footsteps of civilized man had never before fallen, and set the bounds of own-ership where had never been sign of possession but the mark of the patient beaver's tooth, bark frayed by the claw of the bear, the antler of the moose, and the brands of the brief camp-fire of the savage. At night they bivouacked where with the fading of daylight their labors ended, prepared their rude supper by the fire that summoned a host of weird and grotesque shadows to surround them, and slept to the grewsome serenade of the wolf's long howl and the panther's scream.

The conditions of the grants or charters were, that every grantee should plant and cultivate five acres within five years for every fifty acres granted ; that all white and other pine trees fit for masting the royal navy should be reserved for that use, and none felled without royal license ; that after ten years a yearly rent of one shilling for each hundred acres, also for a town lot of one acre, which was set to each proprietor, a yearly tribute of one ear of Indian corn, both to be paid on Christmas Day.   In each township that he granted, the thrifty governor had five hundred acres set apart to himself, still known as the governor's lot, and marked on the old township maps, drawn on the backs of the charters, with the initials " B. W."   In each township one share of two hundred acres was set apart for the Society for the Propagation of the Gospel in Foreign Parts, one for a glebe for the Church of England, one for the first settled minister, and one for a school in said town.

The isolated townships constituted little commonwealths, with governments of their own, every inhabitant and freeholder having liberty to vote in the town-meetings, and the three or five selectmen being invested with the chief authority.

Naturally the proprietors to whom the township was granted were the most potent factors in its welfare and government, and, if actual settlers, took the most prominent part in its affairs.

Frequently they offered bounties for the building of gristmills and sawmills, and the forty dollars bounty offered induced the building of such mills, that in their turn failed not to attract settlers; for it was not unusual for pioneers to go twenty miles on foot with a grist to the nearest mill, or to make as tedious journeys for a load of boards, the more tedious that all the environing forest was full of unattainable lumber.

Many of the towns now most populous and important were then uninhabited and unnamed. Bennington, the first township granted by New Hampshire, had its hamlet, its principal building, the Green Mountain Tavern, conspicuous for its sign, a stuffed catamount. Here the fathers of the unborn State often sat in council, moistening their dry deliberations with copious mugs of flip served by their confrère, landlord Stephen Fay. Brattleboro, within whose limits Fort Dummer was built and the first permanent settlement made, although it boasted the only store in the State, was of less importance; while Westminster, with its court-house and jail, assumed more. But at Vergennes, then known as the First Falls of Otter Creek, where the beavers had scarcely quit building their lodges on the driftwood that choked the head of the fall, there lived only Donald McIntosh, the stout old soldier of the Pretender's futile array and of Wolfe's victorious army, and half a dozen other settlers, whose cabins clustered about the frequently harried mills. Where now is the beautiful city of Burlington, the unbroken forest sloped to the placid shores of Petowbowk; and the Winooski, from its torrential source to where its slow current crawls through the broad intervales to the lake, turned no mills, and, but for its one block-house and the infrequent cabins of adventurous pioneers, was as wild as when its devious course was but the warpath of the Waubanakee. Thence to Canada stretched the Wilderness, its solitude as supreme as when, a century and a half before, the French explorer first beheld its snow-clad mountain peaks.

Oftener than human voice, the sonorous call of the moose, the wolf's long howl, the panther's cry, awoke its echoes, and the thud of the axe was a stranger sound than the rarest voice of nature. The eagle, swinging in majestic survey of the region, beheld far beneath him to the southward, here and there, a clustering hamlet and settlements creeping slowly upon his domain ; here and there a mill, where a stream had been stayed in its idle straying ; and here and there on the green bosom of the forest the unhealed wound of a new clearing, the bark roof of a settler's cabin, and the hazy upward drift of its chimney smoke; then to the northward, as far as his telescopic vision ranged, no break in the variegated verdure but the silver gleam of lake and stream, or the rugged barrenness of mountain tops.

Although the settlement of the newly opened region did not progress with anything like the marvelous rapidity that has marked the occupation of new Territories and States in later times, yet it was remarkable, in consideration of the tedious journeys that must be made to the new pitch, with slow ox-cart or sled, or on horseback, where, if there were roads at all, they were of the worst, or they were made by weary oar or waft of unstable wind. Furthermore, there was but comparatively slight overflow of population from the older provinces, or influx of immigration to American shores.

The settlers in the Wilderness soon found their peaceable possession obstructed by an obstacle which they had scarcely foreseen, — not by the harassments of a foreign or savage foe, which now seemed hardly possible, nor by the inert and active forces of nature that had always to be taken into account, but by the jealous rivalry and greed of two provincial governments, both claiming the same territory, and both deriving their authority from the same royal source.

This controversy between New Hampshire and New York, concerning their respective boundaries, began with the first English settlement of the region, and continued till after the close of the Revolution. It constitutes the most unique feature of the history of the commonwealth; and though it retarded its settlement, and afterward for years its admission into the Union, it was the real cause of its becoming an independent State. For undoubtedly, if the claims of either province had been undisputed by the other, the region would have quietly taken its place as part of that, and have had no individual existence. But the aggressions which the people were compelled to resist schooled them to a spirit of independence that most naturally led them to establish a separate government.

CHAPTER IV.

THE NEW HAMPSHIRE GRANTS.

As early as 1749, a dispute concerning the boundaries of their provinces had arisen between the governments of New Hampshire and New York, when Governor Benning Wentworth of New Hampshire had communicated to Governor Clinton of New York his intention of granting unimproved lands within his government under instructions received from his Majesty King George Second, and inclosed his Majesty's description of the province of New Hampshire.[1] In 1740 the king had determined "that the northern boundary of Massachusetts be a similar curve line pursuing the course of the Merrimack River at three miles distance on the north side thereof, beginning at the Atlantic Ocean and ending at a point due north of a place called Pautucket Falls, and by a straight line drawn from thence due west till it meets with his Majesty's other governments."

By this decision, reaffirmed in Governor Wentworth's commission, the government of New Hampshire held that its jurisdiction extended as far west as that of Massachusetts, which was to a line twenty

[1] *Doc. Hist. N. Y.* vol. iv. pp. 331, 332.

miles east of Hudson River. Furthermore, the king had repeatedly recommended to New Hampshire the support of Fort Dummer, as having now fallen within its limits, and which was well known to be west of the Connecticut.[1]

But it was ordered by the governor's council of New York " that his Excellency do acquaint Governor Wentworth that this Province is bounded eastward by Connecticut River, the letters Patent from King Charles the Second to the Duke of York expressly granting all the Lands from the West side of Connecticut River to the East side of Delaware Bay." [2]

Governor Wentworth had already, in January, 1749, granted one township west of the Connecticut, which in his honor was named Bennington, but he now promised for the present to make no further grants on the western frontier of his government that might have the least probability of interfering with that of New York. Later he agreed, by the advice of his council, to lay the matter before the king and await his decision, which his government would " esteem it their duty to acquiesce in without further dispute," and furthermore agreed to exchange with the government of New York copies of the representation made to the king.[3]

This the council of New York reported in November, 1753, that he had failed to do.

This wrangling of governors and councils con-

<hr/>

[1] Williams's *Hist. of Vt.* vol. ii. pp. 12, 13.
[2] *Doc. Hist. N. Y.* vol. iv. p. 332.　　　　*Ibid.* p. 333.

tinued till the beginning of the war in 1754 stopped for the time applications for grants, when the mutterings of the inter-provincial quarrel were drowned by the thunder of the more momentous contest of nations.

With the subjugation of Canada, the granting of lands in the debatable ground was resumed. Governor Wentworth had a survey made sixty miles up the Connecticut, and three lines of townships were laid out on each side of the river. During the next year sixty townships were granted on the west side of the river, and within two years 108 grants were made, extending to a line twenty miles east of the Hudson, and north of that to the eastern shore of Lake Champlain.

It was reported in New York that a party of New Hampshire surveyors, who were laying out lands on the east side of the lake in September, 1762, asserted that Crown Point was in the limits of their government. In December, 1763, Lieutenant-Governor Colden issued a proclamation reiterating the claim of New York to the Connecticut as her eastern boundary, still basing it on the grant to the Duke of York, and also on the description of the eastern boundary of New Hampshire as given in the letters-patent of his Majesty dated July 3, 1741. He commands the civil officers of his government to exercise jurisdiction as far as the banks of the Connecticut River, and the high sheriff of the county of Albany to return the names of all persons who, under the grants of New

Hampshire, shall hold possession of any lands westward of Connecticut River, that they may be proceeded against according to law. This was followed by a proclamation of Governor Wentworth on March 13, 1764, in which he reviews and denies the claim of New York. He says: " At present the boundaries of New York to the Northward are unknown, and as soon as it shall be His Majesty's pleasure to determine them, New Hampshire will pay a ready and cheerful obedience thereunto, not doubting but that all Grants made by New Hampshire that are fulfilled by the Grantees will be confirmed to them if it should be His Majesty's pleasure to alter the jurisdiction." He encouraged the grantees under his government to be industrious in clearing and cultivating their lands, and commanded all civil officers within his province to be diligent in exercising jurisdiction as far westward as grants had been made by his government, and deal with all persons who " may presume to interrupt the settlers on said lands as to law and justice doth appertain." [1]

Though the claims of New York had thus far been founded on the grant to the Duke of York, she now sought to establish it on a less doubtful tenure, and made application to the crown for a confirmation of the same grant. This was supported by a petition representing that it would be greatly for the advantage of the settlers on the New Hampshire Grants to be annexed to New York. To

[1] *Doc. Hist. N. Y.* vol. iv. p. 353.

this were appended the names of many such inhabitants, who afterwards asserted that it was done without their knowledge.[1]

In response came a royal order declaring "the Western bank of the Connecticut, from where it enters the province of Massachusetts Bay as far north as the 45th degree of northern latitude, to be the boundary line between the said two provinces of New Hampshire and New York."

Though this decision was not in accordance with the wishes of many of the inhabitants of the Grants, it gave them no uneasiness concerning the validity of their titles. They had obtained their lands under grants from the crown, and had no fear that under the same authority they would or could be compelled to relinquish or repurchase them. Governor Wentworth remonstrated against the change of jurisdiction, but finally by proclamation, "recommended to the proprietors and settlers due obedience to the authorities and laws of the colony of New York."[2]

But the government of New York chose to construe his Majesty's order as annulling the grants made by Governor Wentworth west of the Connecticut. It divided its newly confirmed territory into four counties, annexing the southwestern part to the county of Albany, which was termed by the New Hampshire grantees the "unlimited county of Albany." North of this was the county of

---

[1] Slade's *State Papers*, p. 62.
[2] *State Papers*, p. 20.

Charlotte, east of it the county of Cumberland, and north of this the county of Gloucester.

The New Hampshire grantees were required to surrender their charters, and repurchase their lands under New York grants. Some complied, and paid the excessive fees demanded by the New York officials, which were twenty fold greater than those exacted by the government of New Hampshire ; [1] but for the most part the settlers were not men of the metal to submit to what seemed to them rank injustice, and they refused to comply with the demand. Thereupon New York regranted their lands to others, and actions of ejectment were brought against them. It was an easy matter to obtain judgments in the county of Albany against the settlers, but the execution of them was met by stubborn resistance, in which the people soon associated for mutual protection.

A convention of representatives from the towns on the west side of the mountains was called, and by it Samuel Robinson of Bennington was appointed as agent to present the grievances of the settlers to the British government, and obtain, if possible, a confirmation of New Hampshire grants.

The mission of Robinson [2] was so far successful that the governor of New York was commanded by

[1] The fees to the governor of New Hampshire for granting a township were about $100. Under the government of New York, they generally amounted to $2,000, or $2,600. Williams's *Hist. Vt.* vol. ii. p. 9.

[2] Governor Moore sneers at him as " a driver of an ox-cart for the sutlers." *Doc. Hist. N. Y.*

his Majesty " to make no grant whatever of any part of the lands in dispute until his Majesty's pleasure should be further known " (July 24, 1767).

But the governor's council of New York decided that this order did not restrain the granting of any land formerly claimed by New Hampshire, but not already granted by that government; and the governor continued to make grants, and writs of ejectment were issued as before, returnable to the Supreme Court at Albany. It was decided in this court that authenticated copies of the royal orders to the governor of New Hampshire, and the grants made in pursuance thereof, should not be used in evidence.

Ethan Allen, soon to become one of the most prominent actors in this controvery, was attending suits at Albany when this decision was made. Being urged by some of the officials there to use his influence with the settlers to induce them to make the best terms they could with their New York landlords, and reminded that "might often prevails against right," Allen replied, in the Scriptural language which he was so fond of employing, that " the gods of the valleys were not the gods of the hills; " and when asked by the attorney-general to explain his meaning, answered that, " if he would accompany him to Bennington Hill, it would be made plain to him." [1]

Thus debarred from obtaining justice in the courts, the people, assembled in convention at Ben-

[1] Thompson's *Vermont*, part ii. p. 21.

nington, " resolved to support their rights and property in the New Hampshire Grants against the usurpations and unjust claims of the Governor and Council of New York by force, as law and justice were denied them." [1]

A more thoroughly organized resistance was now opposed to all attempts of the New York officers to make arrests or serve writs of ejectment. Surveyors who undertook to run the lines of New York grants across lands already granted by New Hampshire were compelled to desist. A sheriff could not come so secretly that vigilant eyes did not discover his approach, nor with so strong a posse that, when he attempted to execute his duties, he did not find a formidable force gathered to resist him. If he persisted, he was, in Allen's quaint phrase, " severely chastised with twigs of the wilderness," though the " blue beech " rod, whose efficacy in reducing a refractory ox to submission had been so often proved by the rough yeomen of the Grants, and which they now applied to the backs of their oppressors, could hardly be termed a twig. This mode of punishment, with grim humor, they termed the " beech seal."

A proclamation was issued by the governor of New York for apprehending some of the principal actors, and in the January (1770) term of the court at Albany several of the inhabitants of Bennington were indicted as rioters, but none of them were arrested.

[1] Slade's *State Papers*, p. 21.

Each party in the quarrel accused the other of being incited by the greed of the land-jobber and speculator, and no doubt there was some foundation for the charge, even on the part of the New Hampshire grantees. But with them, as against an aristocracy of monopolists, were the sympathies of the yeomen of New York, who, when called upon to enforce the authority of their own officers against their brethren of the Grants, held aloof, or feebly rendered their perfunctory aid.

Sheriff Ten Eyck, being required to serve a writ of ejectment on James Breckenridge of Bennington, called to his aid, by order of the governor, a posse of 750 armed militia. About 300 of the settlers, being apprised of his coming, assembled to oppose him. Nineteen of them were posted in the house; the others, divided in two forces of about equal number, were concealed along the road by which the sheriff and his men were advancing, and behind a ridge within gunshot of the house. Unsuspicious of their presence, the sheriff and his men marched to the house and were within the ambuscade. On threatening to make forcible entry, the sheriff was answered by those within, "Attempt it and you are a dead man." The ambuscading forces now made their presence known, and, displaying their hats upon the muzzles of their guns, made a show of twice their actual strength. The sheriff and his posse became aware of their dangerous position, and as one of the first historians of Vermont, Ira Allen, quaintly remarks, "not being interested in the dispute," and Mr. Ten Eyck remembering that important business required his immediate presence in Albany,[1] they discreetly withdrew without a shot being fired on either side.[2]

The New York officers were not always so easily vanquished, nor so unsuccessful in their attempts. The doughty esquire John Munro, who held lands in the Grants under a New York title, and lived upon them among his tenants in Shaftsbury, was a justice of the peace for the county of Albany. He was a man of other metal than Sheriff Ten Eyck, whom he assisted to arrest Silas Robinson, of Bennington, at his own door; and though the house wherein they lodged with their prisoner the night thereafter was surrounded by forty armed men who demanded his release, they carried him to Albany. Robinson was there indicted as a rioter in January, 1771, and held in jail till the next October, when he was released on bail. Upon another occasion, Munro, accompanied by the deputy sheriff and twelve men whom he called to his aid, demanded entrance to the house of Isaiah Carpenter, to serve a writ of ejectment upon him. Carpenter threatened to blow out the brains of any one who should attempt to enter, whereupon the deputy and his men forced the door, and Munro, entering alone, seized Carpenter with his gun in his hand. Two other men were found in the house, and two guns in a corner, "one loaded with powder and

[1] *Doc. Hist. N. Y.* vol iv. p. 422.
[2] Thompson's *Vermont*, part ii. p. 22.

Bullets and the other with Powder and kidney Beans."

The New York claimants now sought to draw some of the prominent persons of the Grants to their interest by offers of New York titles on favorable terms, and by the bestowal of offices upon them, and they induced people of their own province to settle upon unoccupied New Hampshire Grants. By such means they hoped to smother the unmanageable element which had so far thwarted their attempts to gain control of the coveted region, and insidiously overcome the turbulent faction termed by them the " Bennington Mob."

Committees of Safety were organized in several towns of the Grants, and a convention of the settlers decreed that no New York officer should be allowed to take any person out of the district without permission of the Committee of Safety, and that no surveys should be made there, nor lines run, nor settlements made, under the authority of New York. The punishment for violation of this decree was to be discretionary with a court formed by the Committee of Safety. Civil officers, however, were permitted to perform their proper functions in the collection of debts, and in other matters not connected with the controversy.[1] Thus the inhabitants of the Grants established a crude but efficient civil government of their own.

[1] Thompson's *Vermont*, p. 22.

CHAPTER V.

THE GREEN MOUNTAIN BOYS.

A MILITARY force was organized, of which Ethan Allen was colonel commandant, and his active coadjutors, Warner, Baker, Cockran, Sunderland, and others, were captains. Of the name which they assumed, and which Vermonters are always proud to bear, Ira Allen says: " The governor of New York had threatened to drive the military (his opponents) into the Green Mountains, from which circumstance they took the name of Green Mountain Boys."[1]

The necessities of backwoods life accustomed every man of this force to the use of the musket, the long smooth-bore, or the rifle, and most were expert marksmen with any of these weapons, while many, from ranger service in the late war, were accomplished bush-fighters. Inured to hardship and toil, they could not but be enduring, and, to face the dangers that ever beset the pioneer, they must be brave. Rough but kindly and honest backwoods yeomen, they were of the same spirit, as they were of the same race and generation, as the men who fought at Lexington and Bunker Hill.

[1] *Hist. Vt.* p. 345.

They were occasionally mustered for practice and drill. Esquire Munro informed Governor Tryon in 1772 that the company in Bennington, commanded by John Warner,[1] was on New Year's Day " received and continued all day fireing at marks," and again that " the Rioters had brought to Bennington two pieces of Cannon and a Morter piece from the small Fort at East Hoseck with powder and Ball."

Ethan Allen was the chosen as well as the self-appointed leader of the people in their resistance to the claims of New York and its attempts to enforce them. Early in the controversy, he, with four of his brothers, came from Connecticut, and taking up lands under grants from New Hampshire in the southern part of the territory, west of the Green Mountains, very naturally espoused the cause of the New Hampshire grantees. His rude eloquence was of the sort to fire the hearts of the uncultivated backwoodsmen, whether he harangued them from the stump of a clearing, or, addressing a larger audience in the gray pages of his ill-printed pamphlets, he recited their wrongs and exhorted them to defend their rights. His interests and sympathy, his hearty good-fellowship and rough manners, though upon occasion he could assume the deportment of the fine gentleman, brought him into the most intimate relations with them ; while his undoubted bravery, his commanding figure, and herculean strength set this rough-cast hero apart to

[1] Meaning *Seth* Warner.

the chieftaincy which his self-asserting spirit was
not slow to assume.

His brother Ira afterwards became a man of
great note and influence in the young commonwealth, but was more distinguished for civil than
military service, though he was a lieutenant in
Warner's regiment, and afterward captain, colonel,
and major-general of militia.

Seth Warner was of a commanding presence,
" rising six feet in height, erect and well-propor-
tioned, his countenance, attitude, and movements
indicative of great strength and vigor of body and
mind," says Daniel Chipman, who in his boyhood
had often seen him.[1]   But he was cast in a finer
mould than was his more renowned compatriot,
Ethan Allen.   Modest and unassuming, he was no
less brave, and with no lack of firmness, energy,
and promptness to act, his bravery was tempered
with a coolness, deliberation, and good judgment
which made him a safe and trusted leader.   He
was no pamphleteer.   In the public documents to
which his name is appended with those of his associates, Allen's peculiar style is most apparent, yet his
letters show that he could express himself with ease,
clearness, and force.   He too was of Connecticut
birth, and removed with his father to Bennington in
1763, when he was twenty years of age.   The abundant game of the region gave a first direction to his
adventurous spirit, and he became a skillful hunter,
expert in marksmanship and woodcraft.   The same

---

[1] Chipman's *Memoirs of Seth Warner.*

spirit presently led him to take an active part in the controversy respecting the Grants, and he soon took his place among the leaders of the opponents of New York. Remember Baker, the kinsman of both, was a native of Connecticut. He was killed early in the War of the Revolution while with the army invading Canada he was reconnoitring the enemy's position at St. John's. Ira Allen says: "He was a curious marksman, and always kept his musket in the best possible order," which was the cause of his death, for he had so over-nicely sharpened his flint that it caught, and prevented his firing so quickly as did the Indian who killed him. Robert Cockran was another of the border captains, and made himself particularly obnoxious to the government of New York by his active resistance to its encroachments. He served during the Revolution first in a Connecticut, then in a New York regiment, and rose to the rank of lieutenant-colonel.[1] Peleg Sunderland, who in peaceful times was a wood-ranger, hunting moose in the loneliest depths of the Wilderness and setting his beaver-traps on streams that were strange to the eyes of white men, was another leader of the Green Mountain Boys, prominent enough to suffer outlawry.

When, under the encouragement of the New York claimants, settlements were made on the western border of the Grants, though armed to defend themselves, the new-comers were driven away,

[1] He died among his former enemies, the Yorkers, at Sandy Hill, N. Y., in 1812.

their log-houses torn down and burned by Allen, Baker, Cockran, and six others. For their apprehension as rioters, warrants were thereupon issued. But the justice who issued them gave it as his opinion that no officer could arrest them, and recommended that a reward be offered to induce " some person of their own sort " to "artfully betray them." Accordingly Governor Tryon offered a reward of twenty pounds each for their apprehension.[1] Thereupon Allen, Baker, and Cockran issued a proclamation offering a reward of fifteen pounds and ten pounds respectively for the apprehension and delivery at the Catamount Tavern in Bennington of James Duane and John Kemp, two New York officials who were conspicuously active in pushing their claims to lands in the disputed territory. And one proclamation was as effective as the other.

However, some months later Esquire Munro was impelled to undertake the capture of Remember Baker at his home in Arlington, and in the early morning of March 22, 1772, with a dozen of his friends and dependents at his back, forcibly entered Baker's house. In the fray that ensued, Baker and his wife and boy were all severely wounded by sword-cuts, and he being overcome and bound was thrown into a sleigh and driven with all speed toward Albany. But the triumph of his captors was brief, for before reaching the Hudson they were overtaken by a rescue party that followed on horseback in swift pursuit upon the first alarm, and aban-

[1] 1771.

doning their bleeding and exhausted prisoner, they fled into the woods, and Baker, after being cared for by his friends, was triumphantly carried to his home. Munro also attempted the arrest of Seth Warner, who while riding with a friend was met by the squire and several adherents. Seizing the bridle of Warner's horse, Munro called on the others to aid him. When, in spite of all entreaty, he would not desist, Warner struck him to the ground with a blow from a dull cutlass delivered on his head, and went his way. The pugnacious squire had now had enough of the barren honors of his magistracy. "What can a justice do," he asks, "when the whole country combines against him?" and begs Governor Tryon to excuse his acting any longer. He gave his neighbors of the Green Mountains no further trouble, and in 1777 fled to the army of Burgoyne. His property was confiscated, and he was one of those who were forever proscribed by the Vermont act of February 26, 1779.[1]

The Green Mountain Boys were ready to resist more formidable attempts to bring them to submission. When news came to Bennington that Governor Tryon was ascending the Hudson with a considerable force to invade their territory, the Committee of Safety and the officers convened and resolved that it was "their duty to oppose Governor Tryon and his troops to the utmost of their power." Accordingly the fighting men of Bennington and the neighboring towns were assembled.

[1] *Governor and Council,* p. 149.

The cannon, mortar, and ammunition were brought out. Sharpshooters were to ambuscade the narrow passes of the road by which Tryon's force must approach, and cripple the invaders by picking off his officer.

While this warlike preparation was in progress a messenger, who had been sent to Albany to gain information of the strength and intended march of the enemy, returned with the news that the troops, which were wind-bound somewhere below that town, were not coming to invade the Grants, but to garrison the lake forts. In fact, during this season of alarm, Governor Tryon was contemplating a milder policy than had so far been pursued, and presently dispatched a letter " to Rev. Mr. Dewy and the inhabitants of Bennington and the adjacent country on the east side of Hudson's River."

Though he censured their acts of violence, and warned them that a continuance of such acts would bring the " exertions of the Powers of Government " against them, and reasserted the claim of New York to the Connecticut as its eastern boundary, his tone was conciliatory, and he invited them to lay before his government the causes of their illegal proceedings, which should be examined with " deliberation and candor," and such relief given as the circumstances would justify. To accomplish this, such persons as they might choose to send to New York were promised safe conduct and protection, excepting Ethan Allen, Warner, Baker, Cockran, and Sevil. This was briefly replied to by those to whom it was addressed, and at more length by Allen, Warner, Baker, and Cockran.[1] In both replies the validity of the titles given by New Hampshire was maintained, and Allen and his associates declared their resistance had not been to the government of New York, but to land-jobbers and speculators who were endeavoring to deprive them of their property.

These were delivered by the settlers' appointed agents, Captain Stephen Fay and his son, and were laid before his council by Governor Tryon. Upon due consideration, the council recommended that all prosecutions in behalf of the crown, for crimes with which the settlers were charged, should be suspended till his Majesty's pleasure should be known, and that owners of contested lands under grants from New York should stop all civil suits concerning the same during the like period, and agree with the settlers for the purchase thereof on moderate terms, on condition that the inhabitants concerned in the late disorders should conform to the law of New York that settlers on both sides in the controversy should continue undisturbed, and such as had been dispossessed, or forced by threats or other means, to desert their farms, should in future enjoy their possessions unmolested.

This report was approved by the governor. When the agents, returning with it, laid it before the Committee of Safety and the people assembled in the meeting-house at Bennington, there was

[1] *State Papers*, p. 22.

great rejoicing over it. There was a universal expression of a desire for peace. The "whole artillery of Bennington, and the small arms," thundered and rattled salutes in honor of the governor and council of New York, and healths to the king, to Governor Tryon, and to the council were drunk " by sundry respectable Gentlemen."

Unfortunately for the continuance of this promising condition of affairs, news had come before the return of the agents that a surveyor employed by the New York claimants was surveying lands for them in some of the townships to the northward. Thereupon Ethan Allen, with a small party, went in pursuit of him, took him prisoner, and returned with him to Castleton, where he was tried and sentenced to banishment, under pain of death if again found within the limits of the Grants. Upon learning the favorable progress of the negotiations with New York, his judges revoked the rigorous decree and set him at liberty. Making the most of their time while in pursuit of the surveyor, Allen and his men halted at the First Falls of Otter Creek, in the present city of Vergennes, to dispossess the tenants of Colonel Reid; who had himself previously dispossessed persons who, under a New Hampshire grant issued in 1761, had settled there and built a sawmill. Allen's party drove the intruders away, burned their log-houses, and broke the stones of the gristmill Reid had built, and reëstablished the New Hampshire grantee in his sawmill.

Governor Tryon was soon informed of the summary proceedings of the mountaineers, and in a letter dated August 11, 1772, he sharply reprimanded the people of the Grants for " so manifest a breach of public confidence," and, to " insure a continuance of his friendly intentions," required their assistance to reinstate in their possessions the persons who had been ejected." To this an answer was returned by the Committees of Safety of Bennington and ten other towns, in which they denied that any breach of faith had been committed in the seizure of the surveyor, or the dispossession of Reid's tenants, as at that time the proposals of Governor Tryon had not been accepted or even received, and asserted that not they but Reid and the surveyor who was acting for the land-jobbers were the aggressors, and they declined giving any aid in reinstating Reid's tenants in possession so unjustly obtained.[1] They respectfully asked a reply, but it does not appear that any was vouchsafed them, or that further advances were made by the government of New York.

Colonel John Reid, who had been lieutenant-colonel of the Forty-Second or Royal Highland Regiment, held to the purpose of maintaining his settlement on Otter Creek, and in the summer following he repaired thither with a company of his countrymen lately arrived in America. The New Hampshire settlers were again ousted, the gristmill was made serviceable by hooping the stones, and the Scotchmen were installed in their wilderness home,

[1] *State Papers*, pp. 29, 30.

with orders to hold possession against all claimants. Ira Allen chanced soon after to come that way, at nightfall of a stormy day, on his return from an exploration of lands on the Winooski with a view to settlement there. The wet and weary traveler sought admittance at a log-house, whose cheerful firelight promised such welcome as had before been given him there. He was met instead by the savage thrust of a Highlander's skene dhu, delivered through the scarcely opened door, and was questioned, not in the familiar drawl of his compatriots, but in such broad Scotch dialect as unaccustomed ears could scarcely comprehend. He was grudgingly permitted to enter, and then discovered who his unwilling hosts were. He was given shelter for the night, and then went his way to Bennington with the news of this latest intrusion of the " Yorkers."

Ethan Allen and Seth Warner then mustered a force of sixty Green Mountain Boys, and set forth for Otter Creek. Arriving there after a march of four days, they at once set about dispossessing the Scotchmen and their families, burned their houses after their effects had been removed, and destroyed their corn by turning their horses loose in the fields. Allen's party was joined next morning by Remember Baker, with a force nearly as large, when they completed the work of destruction by tearing down the mill, breaking the millstones past all mending, and throwing the pieces into the river. With his sword Baker cut the bolt-cloth into pieces, which

he distributed among his men to wear in their hats
as cockades. When the sturdy miller, John Cameron, demanded by what authority or law he and
his men committed such acts, Baker answered,
" We live out of the bounds of the law," and,
holding up his gun, said, " This is my law." [1]
Cameron told him that with twenty good men he
would have undertaken to defend his house and mill,
though there were a hundred and ten of them, and
was answered that he and his countrymen were all
for the broadsword, but they were for bush fighting ! Perhaps it was in admiration of his brave
Scotch spirit that they offered him a gift of land if
he would jöin them, an offer which he rejected,
while it may be that Donald McIntosh, who had
fought at Culloden and under Wolfe at Quebec,
at least took the proposal into canny consideration,
for his house was not molested, nor he forced to
leave it.

Cameron deposed that he was informed some
three weeks later by one Irwin, who lived on the
east shore of the lake not far from Crown Point,
that Baker and eight others had lain in wait a
whole day near the mouth of Otter Creek, with the
intention of murdering Colonel Reid and his boat's
company on their way to Crown Point, and would
have done so, had not Reid departed a day sooner
than expected. The story seems unlikely, as the

---

[1] Baker showed James Henderson the stump of a lost thumb,
as his commission (possibly given by Esquire Munro), for per-
forming this " very disagreeable work."

Green Mountain Boys, who had come so far to enforce their laws of the green wood, could have had no means of gaining information of Colonel Reid's intended movements, even had they desired to take his life. They retaliated with hard and unrelenting hand the oppressive acts and the encroachments of New York, but never, though the opportunities were frequent and the chances of retribution few, did they, in all the course of this bitter feud, take the life of one of their opponents,[1] even when their leaders were outlawed and a price set upon their heads. Having destroyed six houses, the mill, and most of the growing and harvested crops, the "Bennington Mob" departed from the desolated settlement, Thompson says to build a block-house at the lower falls of the Winooski, to prevent the intrusion of New York claimants there, but it was not reported to the New York government that such fortifications had been built at that place and at Otter Creek till September of the next year.

The controversy engaged the attention of the British government in a direction favorable to the New Hampshire grantees, the Board of Trade, in a report to his Majesty's Privy Council, proposing measures [2] which, if carried out, would have confirmed the rights of settlers under the grants of New Hampshire.

It is worthy of notice that in this report the

---

[1] *Doc. Hist.* vol. iv. pp. 512-516.

[2] *Ibid.* p. 488.

board spoke with considerable severity of the conduct of the governor of New York in passing pa-
tents of confirmation of townships before granted
by New Hampshire, and in granting other lands
within the district, and in like manner called attention to the exorbitant fees exacted for grants by the
governor, secretary, and surveyor of New York,
which were more than double those established by
an ordinance of 1710. Added to these were unauthorized fees taken by other officers, making "the
whole amount of these fees upon a Grant of one
thousand acres of Land in many instances not far
short of the real value of the Fee Simple." It was
in consideration of these emoluments, the board
supposed, " that His Majesty's governors of New
York have of late years taken upon themselves the
most unwarrantable pretenses to elude the restrictions contained in His Majesty's Instructions with
regard to the quantity of Land to be granted to
any one person," by the insertion in one grant of
numbers of fictitious or borrowed names, for the
purpose of conveying to one person a grant of from
twenty thousand to forty thousand acres. They
recommended that his Majesty be advised to give
the most positive instructions to the governor of
New York that the granting of lands should be attended by no fees to the attorney-general, the re-
ceiver-general, or the auditor ; and that neither the
governor, the secretary, nor the surveyor-general
should take any fees but those prescribed by the
ordinance of 1710, which were greater than those

taken by the same officers for similar service in any other colony.[1]

That portion of the report proposing a method of settling the dispute was transmitted by Lord Dartmouth to Governor Tryon, who in a lengthy reply set forth the impossibility of an adjustment upon the plan proposed.

No further conciliatory measures were proposed or entertained by either party in the quarrel, which after this brief respite grew more bitter. New York attempted to make herself friends in the grants by appointing some of the prominent settlers to office. To prevent the success of this policy, the Committees of Safety assembled in convention decreed that no inhabitant of the Grants should hold or accept any office of honor or profit under the government of New York, and all civil and military officers who had acted under the authority of that government were required to "suspend their functions on pain of being viewed." It was further decreed that no person should take grants or the confirmation of them under the government of New York. The punishment for violation of these decrees was to be discretionary with the court, except that for the first offense it must not be capital.[2] Banishment from the Grants was a frequent punishment, and as frequent was the application of the "beech seal." As may be imagined, when the spirit of the times and the rough

[1] *Doc. Hist. N. Y.* vol. iv. p. 493.

[2] Thompson's *Vermont*, part ii. p. 25.

character of a backwoods community are considered, this was often inflicted with cruel severity. Yet it must be remembered in extenuation that the whipping-post was then a common adjunct of justice, and that, by the sentence of properly constituted courts, the scourge was mercilessly applied for the correction of very venial crimes.

The chastisement of offenders was sometimes more ridiculous than severe. A Dr. Adams of Arlington, who made himself obnoxious to the Green Mountain Boys by his persistent sympathy with their enemies, suffered at Bennington, according to his sentence, only the indignity of being suspended in an armchair for two hours beneath the famous Green Mountain Tavern sign, whereon stood the stuffed hide of a great panther, a tawny monster that grinned a menace to all intruders from the country of the hated " Yorkers."

Not long after Allen's raid on the Lower Falls of Otter Creek, he and his men appeared in Durham and Socialborough, whose inhabitants were for the most part friendly to New York, some of them having accepted office under that government. The officials sought safety within its established bounds at Crown Point and Albany, flooding courts and council with depositions, complaints, and petitions. Those who remained were obliged to recognize the validity of the New Hampshire titles.

By the advice of his council, Governor Tryon requested General Haldimand, the commander-in-chief of his Majesty's forces, to order a sufficient

number of regular troops to Ticonderoga and Crown
Point to aid the civil authorities in enforcing the
laws, but the general declined on the ground that,
in the present state of American affairs, the employment of regular troops to suppress "a few
lawless vagabonds" would have a bad tendency as
an acknowledgment of the weakness of the civil
government; also that "Crown Point, being entirely destroyed, and unprovided for the quartering
of troops, and Ticonderoga being in a most ruinous
state, such troops as might be sent thither would
not be able to stay a sufficient time to render them
of much utility." If the request was persisted in,
however, he wished to know what force would be
deemed sufficient. The council thought that 200
men at Ticonderoga might be enough, — a very
modest demand upon the commander-in-chief, but
not on the individuals of a force so insignificant
that it might as well have undertaken to level the
Green Mountains as to attempt to subdue in their
fastnesses these accomplished bush-fighters of the
Grants. The requisition was not approved by the
king, and the troops were not sent.

In consideration of the representations and petitions laid before it, a committee of the General
Assembly of New York resolved that the governor
be requested to issue a proclamation offering a reward of fifty pounds each for the apprehension, and
securing in his Majesty's gaol at Albany, of Ethan
Allen, Warner, Baker, and five others, and that a
bill be brought in more effectually to suppress the

riotous proceedings and bring the offenders to condign punishment. These resolutions having come to the Grants in the columns of the "New York Mercury," the committees of the towns on the west side of the mountains met at Manchester and made answer thereto. They said that in consequence of the report of the British Board of Trade, so favorable to them, they were in daily expectation of a royal confirmation of the New Hampshire grants, and declared themselves loyal and devoted subjects of his Majesty; that the government of New York was more rebellious than they, in that it had acted in direct opposition to the orders of the king; that they had purchased their lands of one of his Majesty's governors on the good faith of the crown of Great Britain, and would maintain those grants against all opposition, till his Majesty's pleasure should be known, and recommended to the governor of New York to await the same before proceeding to the harsh measures proposed, "to prevent the unhappy consequences that may result from such an attempt." They resolved to defend with their lives and fortunes their neighbors and friends who should be indicted as rioters, and that the inhabitants would hold themselves "in readiness to aid and defend such friends of ours who, for their merit to the great and general cause, are falsely denominated rioters," but they would act only on the defensive, and would "encourage execution of the law in civil cases, and in criminal prosecutions that were so indeed." [1]

[1] *State Papers*, p. 42.

But before this answer was approved by the general committee, the New York Assembly had enacted a law (March 9, 1774) as stringent as its committee could have urged, or its report had foreshadowed, and with it or following close upon its passage was issued Governor Tryon's proclamation of a reward of one hundred pounds each for the arrest of Ethan Allen and Remember Baker, and fifty pounds for the apprehension of Seth Warner and five others. Some of the provisions of this extraordinary law were, that if three or more persons, " being unlawfully, riotously, and tumultuously assembled within the counties of Charlotte and Albany," did not disperse when commanded to do so by proclamation made by a justice, sheriff, or coroner, they should upon conviction suffer twelve months' imprisonment without bail; and any person opposing, letting, hindering, or hurting the person making or going to make such proclamation, should be adjudged a felon, and suffer death without benefit of clergy. It should also be adjudged felony without benefit of clergy for an unauthorized person to assume judicial powers, or for any person to assist them, or to execute their sentences, or to seize, detain, or assault and beat any magistrate or civil officer, to compel him to resign his office, or to prevent his discharging its duties; or to burn or destroy the grain or hay of any other person; or to demolish or pull down any dwelling-house, barn, stable, or gristmill, sawmill, or outhouse within either of the said counties. When the persons named in the governor's proclamation, or any other persons, were indicted for any offense committed after the passage of this act, and made capital by it or any other law, did not, within seventy days after the publication of the governor's command to do so, surrender themselves to one of his Majesty's justices of the peace for either of the said counties, they were to be adjudged guilty of the offense for which they had been indicted; and if for a capital offense thereafter to be perpetrated, they should be convicted and attainted of felony, and should suffer death, as in the case of persons so convicted by verdict and judgment, without benefit of clergy; and it should be lawful for the supreme court of New York, or the courts of oyer and terminer or general gaol delivery, to award execution against such offenders as if they had been convicted in such courts. It was provided that, as it was impracticable to bring offenders to justice within the county of Charlotte, all persons committed within its limits should be proceeded against by any grand jury of the county of Albany, and tried in that county by a jury thereof, as if the crime or offense had been perpetrated therein.[1]

Here was indeed an " exertion of the powers of government," but it was barren of any result but to strengthen the spirit of opposition in those against whom it was directed, and, instead of terrorizing them into abject submission, as its authors had confidently expected, it served rather to unite them in more stubborn resistance.

[1] *State Papers.*

In response, Allen and his proscribed associates put forth a manifesto and an address " to the people of the counties of Albany and Charlotte which inhabit to the westward, and are situated contiguous to the New Hampshire Grants," wherein, for the most part, the case is forcibly stated in Allen's peculiar style, and closes with the declaration that " We are under the necessity of resisting even unto blood every person who may attempt to take us as felons or rioters as aforesaid, for in this case it is not resisting law, but only opposing force by force ; therefore, inasmuch as, by the oppressions aforesaid, the New Hampshire settlers are reduced to the disagreeable state of anarchy and confusion ; in which state we hope for wisdom, patience, and fortitude till the happy hour his Majesty shall graciously be pleased to restore us to the privileges of Englishmen."

Not many times, if ever, thereafter, was the authority of the king invoked by those who set their names to this paper : but little more than a year had elapsed when most of them were engaged in wresting from the crown its strongholds on Lake Champlain.

Now, however, a scheme was set on foot to withdraw the Grants from the hated jurisdiction of New York by erecting them, and that part of New York east of the Hudson, into a separate royal government. Colonel Philip Skene, who lived in considerable state in Skenesborough House on his estate at the head of Lake Champlain, was engaged in it, probably with a view to the governorship of the new province, and he went to England to further the project. Whatever his success may have been, it came to nothing with the breaking out of the Revolution.[1]

The people of the Grants maintained their attitude of defiance and resistance. The stinging imprint of the beech seal was still set as relentlessly on the backs of justices who yet dared to act under the authority of New York, and their stern judges sent them " toward the City of New York, or to the westward of the Grants," with duly signed certificates that they had received full punishment for their crimes.

Lieutenant-Governor Colden, now acting governor, as Tryon "had been called home to give Lights on the Points in dispute," applied to General Gage at Boston for a force of 200 men to aid the civil officers in the county of Charlotte, but Gage declined, as Haldimand had done ; and the attempts of New York to enforce its authority continued as futile as ever, while the Rob Roys of the new world Highlands as boldly went their way as if no price was set upon their heads.

[1] Williams's *History;* Thompson's *Vermont.*

CHAPTER VI.

THE WESTMINSTER MASSACRE.

WHILE the western portion of the New Hampshire Grants was involved in this turmoil of incipient warfare, most of the settlers to the eastward of the Green Mountains held aloof from the strife, for many of them had surrendered their original charters, taking new ones under New York and submitting quietly to its jurisdiction. Yet they were not lacking in the spirit of patriotism that was now warming all their countrymen into a new life, and presently there came an event which welded them into closer affiliation with their brethren of the western grants, and brought them into active opposition to the imperious government of New York.

On the 16th of May, 1774, a committee of correspondence was formed in the city of New York, with the object of learning the sentiments of the people concerning the measures of the British government respecting its American colonies. A letter, addressed by its chairman to the supervisors of Cumberland County, was kept secret by them, and no action taken upon it at their June session; but its receipt in some way became known to Dr. Jones of Rockingham and Captain Wright of Westminster, who notified their towns ; and a committee for the purpose being appointed in each, the supervisors were called on at their September session for any papers received by them which should be laid before the towns of the county. The letter was unwillingly produced, a copy was sent to each town, and a county convention was called to meet at Westminster on the 19th of October. Delegates from twelve towns met accordingly, and passed resolutions similar in spirit to those of the Continental Congress. When the action of Congress in declaring the rights of the colonies, and in adopting the "Articles of Association," became known, another convention was called, which met at Westminster on the 30th of October, "and did adopt all the resolves of the Continental Congress as their resolves, promising religiously to adhere to that agreement or association." But a motion to choose a "committee of inspection" to observe whether any person violated the Articles of Association was defeated by the opposition of two Tory members. The town of Dummerston, however, whose good people, "tired of diving after redress in a Legal way," had set Lieutenant Spaulding free from the jail to which he had been committed on a charge of high treason for saying that, "if the king had signed the Quebec bill, it was his opinion he had broken his coronation oath," at a town-meeting held in January following chose such a committee. This body removed two assessors from office for refusing to execute an order of the town to assess a tax, payable in potash salts, for the purpose of procuring 100 pounds of powder, 200 pounds of lead, and 300 flints, for the town use ; suspended another town officer till by his conduct he proved himself a Whig; and disarmed a suspected Tory. The example of this town was generally followed by others, without waiting the action of a convention.

The General Assembly of New York had refused to adopt the resolves and Articles of Association of the Continental Congress, and the courts of justice were continued in that province, while elsewhere they were almost universally suspended.

Affairs were at this pass, causing great dissatisfaction among the patriots of the Grants, when the time for the session of the King's Court of Cumberland County, to be holden at Westminster the 14th of March, 1775, drew near. A deputation of forty citizens of the county waited upon the chief judge, Colonel Chandler, at Chester, and endeavored to dissuade him from holding the court. He admitted that it would be better to hold no court in the present state of affairs, but said there was a case of murder which it was necessary to try, after which, if not agreeable to the people, no other cases should come on. In answer to the objections of one of their number, that the sheriff would be present with an armed posse and there would be bloodshed, he assured them that no arms should be brought against them, and dismissed them with thanks for their civility. After considerable discussion of methods to prevent the sitting of the court, it was decided that it should be permitted to come together, when the objections to its proceeding should be laid before it, " thinking," says the " Relation of the Proceedings," " they were men of such sense that they would hear them." [1] It presently became known that the court intended to take possession of the court-house the day before its session was to begin, and hold it with a strong guard against the intrusion of those opposed to its opening. To forestall this purpose, about 100 men, armed only with clubs that the stalwart men of Rockingham took from a neighboring woodpile, entered the court-house late in the afternoon of that day, with the intention of holding it till the judges should hear their grievances. They had not been long within it when the sheriff, with a strong posse of armed men and attended by the officers of the court, came marching up the level street of the little town. Halting near the door, he demanded entrance, but received no answer. He then read the king's proclamation in a loud voice, commanding all persons unlawfully assembled to disperse, adding with an oath that, if they did not do so within fifteen minutes, " he would blow a lane through them." They answered that they would not disperse, but would admit the sheriff and the others if they would lay aside their arms, and asked if they had come for war; declaring they themselves had come for peace, and would be glad to hold a parley with them. Upon this the clerk of

[1] *Governor and Council*, vol. i. p. 332.

the court drew his pistol, and, holding it up, swore that " only by it would he hold parley with such damned rascals," and would give no more friendly reply to any overtures. Judge Chandler, however, came to them when the sheriff's posse had gone for refreshments, and declared that the arms were brought without his consent, and said that those who held the house might continue to do so undisturbed till morning, when the court should come in without arms, and hear what they had to say before it.

With little fear of molestation now, yet taking the precaution to post a sentry at the door, the garrison of the court-house held the place. The curving crest of hills that half encircle the town, touching the river above and below it, grew dim against the darkening sky, and the last gleam of daylight faded from the ice-bound reaches of the broad Connecticut. The pallid dusk of the starless winter night blurred houses and threshold trees into indistinct forms, and fused the half-surrounding wall of forest-clad hills with the sky, till they seemed a part of it creeping down upon the little hamlet. One by one the lights went out, save where some housewife waited her husband's coming, and where the glare of the inn's hospitable fire fell in broad bars of flickering light across the snowy street. The sentinel at the door paced his short beat. Of those whose guard he kept, some fell asleep on the hard benches, some gathered in groups to listen to the discourse of oracular politicians, or discuss the all-absorbing topic of the hour. Some of the younger men crowded into the charmed circle wherein some gray and garrulous veteran of the old wars discoursed of bush fights and Indian ambuscades, the siege of Number Four or Ticonderoga's woeful day of slaughter and defeat, where he fought so hotly for the sovereign whom he now denounced. Some sat apart silently brooding, and taking no heed of the buzz of conversation, but grimly awaited the struggle they felt was impending. All became suddenly alert when, about midnight, the sentinel discovered armed men approaching, and gave the word to man the doors. The sheriff and his men were coming, with courage reinforced by potations of flip and fiery rum.

They marched to within ten rods of the door and halted. In a moment the order was given to fire, and three shots were reluctantly delivered. The order was repeated with curses, which incited the posse to a deadlier volley that killed William French almost outright, fatally wounded Daniel Houghton, and severely injured several others. The assailants then rushed in on the men, who had only clubs to defend themselves with, made several prisoners and took them to the jail. One of these was the dying man, whom " they dragged as one would a dog, and would mock at as he lay gasping," and " did wish there were forty more in the same case." Lying on the jail-room floor, his five wounds undressed, French, not yet twenty-two, died in the early morning of the 14th. Houghton survived his wounds nine days.

Thus in a remote frontier town was shed the first blood of the momentous conflict that gave birth to a nation.

In the darkness and confusion all the rest of the Whigs escaped, some fighting their way out with their clubs ; one, Philip Safford, laying about him so lustily that eight or ten of the sheriff's posse went down beneath the blows of his cudgel.

The court party came out of the mêlée victorious for the present, and without serious injury to any of their number, though in the "State of the Facts," prepared next day by the judges and other officers of the court, two were reported as wounded by pistol shots, which, if indeed so, must have been fired by their friends, for the others declared that they had not so much as a pistol among them, having come with the expectation of gaining their object without violence. Some did now go home for their guns, but did not return to renew the fray. More hastened away to carry the woeful tidings of bloodshed to the Whigs of all the country around, and with such dispatch was this done that, before noon of the next day, two hundred armed men had arrived from New Hampshire. Before night every one known to have been concerned in the killing of French was seized and kept under strong guard. The next day an inquest was held, and a verdict given that French came to his death at the hands of the sheriff, and certain others of his posse. Armed men continued to come from the southern part of the county and from Massachusetts, till by the fol-

lowing morning five hundred "good martial soldiers, well equipped for war," thronged the one
street of the little town.

On that day all the people who had come assembled, and voted to choose a large committee to act
for the whole, to be composed in part of citizens of
Cumberland County, and in part of those residing
outside its limits. After an examination of the
evidence, this committee voted to commit those
most implicated in the killing of French to the jail
at Northampton, Mass., there to await a fair trial,
while those who seemed less guilty should be put
under bonds to appear at the next court. The
bonds of those admitted to bail were taken next
day, and the others were conducted under a strong
guard to Northampton jail, but it does not appear
that any of them were ever brought to trial, these
cases being lost sight of in the thickening whirl of
Revolutionary events.

Such is substantially the account of the affair as
given by the committee chosen by the people. The
accounts given by the officers of the court in their
"State of the Facts," and by members of the sheriff's posse in their deposition, make it appear that
the so-called rioters were the first violent aggressors, beating the sheriff with clubs when he first
attempted to force his way in ; that three shots
were then fired by his order above the heads of
those who held the court-house, who at once returned the fire by a discharge of guns and pistols,
one pistol-shot being fired at such close quarters

that the powder burned a large hole in the breast of his coat, and yet the wearer was not hurt ; that only four or five shots were fired into the court-house by the sheriff's party, and yet by this volley French was struck by five bullets, Houghton received a fatal wound, and several others were hurt. According to these accounts, Robert Cockran and others proposed such atrocities as burning the court - house and all within it, or firing volleys through it, and were only restrained by the New Hampshire men from doing so.[1] But there is nothing of this in the relation of the committee, which is quite as likely to impress the unbiased inquirer with its truthfulness. Governor Colden, in his report to Lord Dartmouth of what he calls this "dangerous insurrection," does not attribute it to any dispute concerning land titles, but only to the example of Massachusetts ; nor does he charge the Bennington rioters with being implicated in it, though he foresaw that it would draw to the common cause of resistance to New York the people of the eastern Grants with their brethren of the western. He wrote to General Gage of this affair in Cumberland, and hoped that by his assistance he might soon be able to hold a court of oyer and terminer in that county ; but the British general had weightier affairs upon his hands at Boston, and could give him no help.

In a convention held at Westminster on the 11th of April, it was voted " that it is the duty of the

[1] *Doc. Hist. N. Y.* vol. iv. pp. 547, 549.

inhabitants to wholly renounce and resist the administration of the government of New York till such time as the lives and property of these inhabitants may be secured by it, or till such time as they can have opportunity to lay their grievances before his most gracious Majesty in council," with an humble petition " to be taken out of so offensive jurisdiction, and either annexed to some other government or erected and incorporated into a new one, as may appear best to said inhabitants, to the Royal wisdom and clemency, and till such time as his Majesty shall settle this controversy." Colonel John Hazletine, Charles Phelps, and Colonel Ethan Allen were appointed to prepare the remonstrance and petition that were to be presented.

Never again did any representative body of the Grants give an expression of loyalty to the king. Not many days later came the news of Lexington fight, and presently the mountaineers were all in as open revolt against King George as any had ever been against his royal government of the province of New York. Men grown so accustomed to resistance of the tyranny of the lesser power, as were the persecuted settlers of the western Grants, were not apt to be laggards in opposing the greater when its encroachments became as unendurable, and for a time the petty warfare of provincial bounds and jurisdiction was hidden from their sight in the overspreading cloud of the grander struggle that involved the liberties of every American.

CHAPTER VII.

TICONDEROGA.

THOSE ruthless destroyers, time and man, have wrought sad havoc on the once formidable fortress of Ticonderoga. One wall of solid masonry has withstood their assaults, and still rears its sharp-cut angles and massive front, gray with age and scaled with lichens of a century, as grimly now as in the days of yore, above the broad expanse of fields that stretch away to the southwest.

Across the neck of the peninsula, in the shadow of great oaks that were but saplings then, may be seen the well-preserved breastworks against which the storm of Abercrombie's assault so vainly beat, and within them green mounds show the position of old outworks. But the fort itself is a desolate ruin. Ditches choked with brambles and rubbish, grass-grown ramparts, crumbling bastion, and barrack walls, fallen-in bomb-proof and magazine, mark the site of a stronghold once deemed worth the blood and treasure of nations to hold or gain.

Amherst's useless fort of Crown Point, built with lavish expense, has not suffered such complete decay. The barracks are in ruin, but the almost unbroken ramparts rear their walled and grassy steeps high above the long incline of the shrub-grown glacis, and the hoary walls of the outworks have stoutly withstood the ravages of almost seven-score years. The older French fort of St. Fred-eric; its citadel within whose walls commandant, priest, and fierce Waubanakee plotted raids on the frontier hamlets of the heretics, in whose dungeons English captives languished; its chapel, where masses were said in celebration of savage deeds, while white-coated soldier of France, rough-clad habitant, and painted Indian knelt together before the black-robed priest; its water-gate, bastions, scarps, and counter-scarps, — all have fallen into the desolation of utter ruin.

The conquest of Canada accomplished, it was no longer of vital importance that the forts on Lake Champlain should be maintained; conse-quently the elaborately planned fortifications of Crown Point were never completed, and they, with those of Ticonderoga, fell into such neglect that in September, 1773, the first one was reported by General Haldimand to be entirely destroyed, and the other in a most ruinous state. And though it does not appear that they were dismantled or quite abandoned, for years they were held by garrisons too insignificant to defend them against any vigor-ous attack. In such defenseless condition they continued, as if too remote from the great centres of revolt to be of consequence to England, while the threatening attitude of her American colonies daily grew more menacing. But while the appeal to arms was yet impending, the importance of these posts became apparent to some active patriots of the New England colonies. In March, 1775, John Brown of Pittsfield, Massachusetts, who had recently passed through the New Hampshire Grants on a secret mission to Canada, wrote from Montreal to Samuel Adams and Dr. Warren, the Committee of Correspondence in Boston, mentioning one thing to be kept a profound secret. " The fort at Ticonderoga must be seized as soon as possible, should hostilities be committed by the king's troops. The people in the New Hampshire Grants have engaged to do this business, and in my opinion they are the most proper persons for this job. This will effectually curb this province, and all the troops that may be sent here." Thus it appears that so early as February, 1775, the capture of the fort was contemplated by the leaders of the Green Mountain Boys, and that they were committed to the enterprise.

Yet, when confronted by the actual outbreak of war, they were sorely perplexed. Self-interest inclined them to hold aloof from a rupture with the mother country when king and privy council were considering, with apparent favor to them, their controversy with New York; while on the other hand the ties of birth strongly bound them to their brethren of New England, and every impulse of patriotism impelled them to espouse the cause of their common country.

Soon after receiving the news of the battle of

Lexington, which Ethan Allen says almost distracted them, the principal officers of the Green Mountain Boys, and other prominent leaders, met at Bennington, and in the council chamber of the Catamount Tavern " attempted to explore futurity ; " though they " found it to be unfathomable," [1] they resolved to unite with their countrymen, whom they doubted not would, in the event of a successful issue of the conflict, freely accord to them the rights which they demanded.

Without any knowledge of what was already brewing in the Grants, some gentlemen of Connecticut, who on the 26th of April met Benedict Arnold on his way to Cambridge with a company of volunteers, learned from him the defenseless condition of Ticonderoga and the great number of cannon there, and at once formed a plan for its capture. To carry it out, they procured £300 from the treasury of Connecticut. This was given to Noah Phelps and Bernard Romans, who immediately set forward toward the Grants, where it was thought best most of the men should be raised. Just after their departure, Captain Mott arrived at Hartford and proposed the same enterprise, to procure artillery and stores for the people of Boston, and being apprised of what was already on foot, agreed to join in the expedition. He set forth next day with five others, and at Salisbury was joined by eleven more. Arrived at Pittsfield it was determined, by the advice of Colonel Easton

[1] Ethan Allen.

and John Brown, just returned from his Canadian mission, to raise a number of men before reaching the Grants, where it was thought the scarcity of provisions and the poverty of the inhabitants would make it difficult to raise and equip a sufficient number. Accordingly about forty men were recruited and made ready to march, in Jericho and Williamstown, by Colonel Easton and Captain Mott, while the others went on to Bennington When, after this service, Easton and Mott were on their way to the same place, they were met in the evening by an express from their people with the news that Ticonderoga was reinforced and its garrison alert, and with the advice that, as it could not be surprised, the men recruited would better be dismissed. The news was discredited, the advice unheeded, and the colonel and the captain held forward for Bennington, rejoining their companions and finding the leading men of the Grants there in conclave. Captain Mott told his hesitating friends that the "account they had would not do to go back with and tell in Hartford;" and his friends Mr. Halsey and Mr. Bull declared they would go back for no story till they had seen the fort for themselves.[1] It was decided that the attempt to capture the fort should not be abandoned.

Two agents were dispatched to Albany to purchase and forward provisions for the troops, and trusty men were sent to waylay all the roads leading from the Grants to Skenesborough, Lake

[1] Mott's Journal in Chittenden's *Capture of Ticonderoga.*

George, and the Champlain forts, to prevent any intelligence of the movement from reaching those points. Then, going on to Castleton, the committee, of which Captain Mott was chairman, arranged there the plan of operations.

A party of thirty men under Captain Herrick were to go to Skenesborough and capture Major Skene and his men, and go down the lake in the night with his boats to Shoreham to transport the men assembled there across the water; while Captain Douglass was sent to Crown Point to concoct a scheme with his brother-in-law, who lived there, to hire the king's boats, on some plausible pretense, to assist in getting the men over to the New York shore.

Meanwhile Captain Phelps of Connecticut had gone to spy out the condition of Ticonderoga. In the guise of a simple backwoodsman, he easily gained admission to the fort on the pretext of getting shaved, and, after taking careful note of all that could be seen in the place, returned to Castleton and reported to his friends.

Agreeably to a promise made to the men when engaged that they should be commanded by their own officers, Colonel Ethan Allen was given the command of the force which was to attack Ticonderoga. After receiving his orders from the committee, and dispatching Major Gershom Beach of Rutland to rally the Green Mountain Boys, he went on to Shoreham, where they were to assemble.

Major Beach performed the almost incredible

feat of making on foot the journey of sixty miles in twenty-four hours, over rough by-paths marked only by blazed trees, and along the wretched roads of the new country. The forest-walled highway led him to the hamlets of Rutland, Pittsford, Brandon, and Middlebury, whose fighting men were quickly summoned. Along its course, he turned aside here and there to warn an isolated settler, to whose betterments he was guided by the songs of the earliest bobolink rejoicing over the discovery of a new meadow, by the sound of axe-strokes, by the drift of smoke climbing through the greening tree-tops from log-heap or potashery. Each man, as summoned, left his task unfinished, — the chopper his axe struck deep in the half-felled tree ; the grimy logger his smoking pile ; the sawyer his silenced mill with the saw stopped in its half-gnawed course through the great log ; the potash-maker left the fire to smoulder out beneath the big kettles ; and the farmer, though hickory leaves as large as a squirrel's foot calendared the time of corn-planting, exchanged the hoe for the gun. Each took his firelock, bullet pouch, and powder horn from their hooks above the fireplace, and, bidding brief farewell to homefolk, set forth to the appointed meeting place. In little bands, by threes and twos and singly, scarred and grizzled veterans who had scouted the Wilderness with Rogers, Putnam, and Stark, men in their prime who had seen no service but in raids on the Yorkers, and beardless boys hot with untried youthful valor, took their way

toward the lake. Most of them plodded the unmistakable course of the muddy highways till they
struck Amherst's road leading to Crown Point;
but some, with consummate faith in their woodcraft,
took the shortest ways through the forest, now
breasting the eastern slope of ledges whose dun incline of last year's leaves was dappled thick with
the white bloom of moose-flowers and green tufts
of fresh forest verdure, now scrambling down the
sheer western wall of diluvian shores, now wading
the mire of a gloomy morass, and now thridding
the intricate tangle of a windfall.

On the evening of the 9th of May, 1775, they
had come to the appointed place of meeting, a little cove about two miles north of Ticonderoga,
where the mustering force was quite hidden from
the observation of voyagers along the lake, and
where the camp-fires might blaze behind the wide
screen of newly leafing woods unseen by the garrisons of the two forts. Here the Green Mountain
Boys were met by their adored leader, and awaited
the arrival of the boats and their comrades coming
from the southward.

Allen had just left Castleton when Benedict Arnold arrived there, and demanded the command of
the expedition by authority of a colonel's commission just received from the Massachusetts Committee of Safety, with orders to raise 400 men
for the reduction of Ticonderoga. The committee in charge of the enterprise, in consideration of
the conditions under which the men had engaged,

refused to give him the command. But he persisted in demanding it, and at once set forward to overtake Allen, whom he found no more disposed to yield to his demand than the committee had been, nor would his men consent to follow another leader. Upon this, Arnold joined the force as a volunteer.

By the evening of the 9th, 270 men, all but forty of whom were Green Mountain Boys, had assembled on the shore of the little creek in Shoreham now known as Hand's Cove, which is in summer a level expanse of sedgy marsh threaded by a narrow sluggish channel, but during the spring floods is a broad cove of the lake, its waters overrunning the roots of the trees that grow upon the banks. Here the force anxiously awaited transportation, for the seemingly well-laid plans for securing boats had not proved successful. It was not till near morning that the watchers, often deceived by the cries of strange waterfowl, the sudden plunge of the muskrat, or his long wake gleaming in the light of the camp-fires, at last heard the unmistakable splash of oars, and saw the boats coming in among buttressed trunks of the great elms and water-maples that stood ankle-deep in the spring flood. When scows, skiffs, dugouts, and yawls had crushed through the drift of dead waterweeds and made a landing, it was found that there were not enough of the motley craft collected to transport half the force.

Allen, Easton, Arnold, and eighty others at once

embarked, and, crossing the lake, landed a little north of Willow Point, on the New York shore, when the boats returned to bring over those who, under Warner, remained at the cove. Day was now dawning, the rugged horizon line of forest and mountain becoming each moment more distinct against the eastern sky, and it became evident that, if the attack was much longer delayed, there would be no chance of surprising the garrison.

Allen, therefore, determined to move forward at once, without waiting to be joined by those who remained on the other shore. Briefly addressing his men, who were drawn up in three ranks, he called on those who would voluntarily follow him to poise their firelocks. Every musket was poised, the order was given to right face, and Allen placed himself at the head of the centre file ; but when he gave the order to march, Arnold again asserted his right to take command, and swore that he would be first to enter the fort. Allen as stoutly maintained his right, and, when the dispute waxed hotter, turned to one of his officers and asked, " What shall I do with the damned rascal ? Shall I put him under guard ? " The officer, Amos Callender of Shoreham, advised them to compromise the untimely dispute by agreeing to enter the fort side by side, to which they both assented, and the little column at once moved forward in silence, guided by a youth named Beeman, who, living near by, and having spent many of his idle hours in the fort, was well acquainted with the entrances and all the interior appointments.

Captain Delaplace and his little garrison of a lieutenant and forty-two uncommissioned officers and privates [1] were sleeping in careless security, not dreaming of an enemy near, while two or three sentinels kept listless guard. The drowsy sentry at the sallyport, now come upon so suddenly by the attacking party that he forgot to challenge or give an alarm, aimed his musket at the leader and pulled trigger. The piece missed fire, and, Allen running toward him with raised sword, the soldier retreated into the parade, when he gave a loud halloo and ran under a bomb-proof. The Green Mountain Boys now swiftly entered the fort, and, forming in the parade in two ranks facing the east and west rows of barracks, gave three lusty cheers. A sentry made a thrust with his bayonet at one of the officers, and Allen dealt him a sword-cut on the head that would have killed him, had not the force of the blow been broken by a comb which kept his hair in place. [2]

He threw down his gun and asked for quarter.

---

[1] Allen's own accounts of the number do not agree. In his report to the Albany committee he gives the number of prisoners taken as one captain and a lieutenant and forty-two men, while in his *Narrative* it " consisted of the said commander, a lieutenant, Feltham, a conductor of artillery, a gunner, two sergeants, and forty-four rank and file." The first number, given in the report made on the day following the capture, is probably the correct one.

[2] Goodhue's *Hist. of Shoreham.*

Allen demanded to be shown the apartment of the commandant, and was directed to a flight of stairs leading to the second story of the west row of barracks. Mounting to the door at their head, Allen ordered Captain Delaplace to " come forth instantly, or he would sacrifice the whole garrison." The bewildered commandant came to the door with his breeches in his hand, when Allen demanded the immediate surrender of the fort. " By whose authority do you demand it? " asked Delaplace, and Allen answered, " In the name of the great Jehovah and the Continental Congress." Delaplace attempted to parley, but Allen cut him short, and, with his drawn sword over his head, again demanded an immediate surrender. Having no choice but to comply, Captain Delaplace at once ordered his men to parade without arms, and Ticonderoga with all its cannon and military stores was surrendered to the Green Mountain Boys.

Warner presently arrived with the remainder of the force, and after some convivial celebration of the almost bloodless conquest was dispatched by Allen, with about one hundred men, to take possession of Crown Point, which was held by a sergeant and twelve men, and on the 12th Warner and Peleg Sunderland reported its capture on the previous day to the governor and council of Connecticut. Captain Remember Baker, who had received orders to come with his company from the Winooski and join the force, after meeting and capturing two small boats on their way to St.

John's with the alarming news of the surrender, arrived at Crown Point nearly at the same time with Colonel Warner.[1]   Skenesborough was taken possession of by Captain Herrick, Major Skene made prisoner, and his schooner seized.   Callender was sent with a small party to seize the fort at the head of Lake George, an exploit easily accomplished, as its sole occupants were a man and woman.

Thus, by no heroic feat of arms, but by well-laid plans so secretly and promptly executed that they remained unsuspected till their purpose was accomplished, the two strongholds that guarded the passage to the head of the lake fell into the hands of the Americans, with 200 cannon, some mortars and swivels, and a quantity of military stores, all of which were of incalculable value to the ill-supplied patriot army.

Allen at once sent a report of the capture of Ticonderoga to the Albany committee, and asked that provisions and a reinforcement of 500 men might be sent to the fort, as he was apprehensive that General Carleton would immediately attempt its recapture.   He also reported the capture to the Massachusetts government, and on the 12th sent the prisoners under guard to Connecticut, at the same time apprising Governor Trumbull of the preparations being made to take a British armed sloop then lying at St. John's.

Ticonderoga had not been many hours in possession of its captors when Arnold again attempted

[1] Ira Allen's *History of Vermont.*

to assume command, as no other officer had orders
to show. But the soldiers refused to serve under
him, declaring that they would go home rather than
do so. To settle the question of authority, the
committee issued a written order to Colonel Allen
directing him to keep the command of said garrison
for the use of the American colonies till further
orders from the colony of Connecticut or from the
Continental Congress.

The capture of the English sloop was now undertaken. Arnold, in command of the schooner taken
at Skenesborough and now armed with a few light
guns, and Allen of a batteau, set forth on this enterprise, favored by a brisk south wind, more propitious to Arnold than to his coadjutor, for it wafted
his schooner so much more swiftly onward that he
reached St. John's, made an easy capture of the
larger and more heavily armed sloop, made prisoners of a sergeant and twelve men, and still favored
by the wind, which now shifted to the north, was
well on his way up the lake with his prize when he
met Allen's sluggish craft, some distance south of
St. John's, and saluted him with a discharge of
cannon. After responding with a rattling volley
of small arms, Allen and his party went on board
the sloop, and further celebrated the successful
issue of the expedition by toasting Congress and the
cause of the colonies in bumpers furnished forth
from the ample stores of his Majesty's navy. The
vessels then pursued their way up the lake, past unfamiliar headlands and islands whose fringe of dark

cedars was now half veiled in the misty green of
the opening deciduous leaves, now sailing in mid-
channel with low shores on either hand, on this
La Motte and Grand Isle, on that the pine-clad
plains and Valcour, the scene of Arnold's future
desperate naval fight, and now, when the Isles of
the Four Winds and solitary Wajahose, far astern,
hung between lake and sky, they hugged the cleft
promontory of Sobapsqua[1] and the rugged walls
of the western shore, till Bullwagga Bay was
opened and the battlements of Crown Point arose
before them and their present voyage ended.

The Americans now had complete control of the
lake, the only armed vessels afloat upon its waters,
and all the forts except St. John's. Yet for a time
a greater value seemed to be attached to the cannon and stores received than to the military importance of the forts taken. After the capture of Ticonderoga and Crown Point, more than a month
passed in a wrangle of the commanders for the
supremacy, and dissatisfaction and insubordination
of the men, before the garrisons were effectively
strengthened by a force of a thousand men under
Colonel Hinman, who was put in command of the
posts by the government of Connecticut, to which,
in the division of affairs, this quarter had been
relegated.

---

[1] "Pass through the Rock," Split Rock.

CHAPTER VIII.

GREEN MOUNTAIN BOYS IN CANADA.

On the 23d of June, 1775, the Continental Congress, recognizing the services of Allen and his associates, voted to pay the men who had been employed in the taking and garrisoning of Crown Point and Ticonderoga, and " recommended to the Convention of New York that they, consulting with General Schuyler, employ in the army to be raised for the defense of America, those called Green Mountain Boys, under such officers as said Green Mountain Boys shall choose." With a copy of these resolutions, and a letter from John Hancock in his official capacity as President of Congress, Allen and Warner presented themselves before the convention on the 4th of July. They were admitted in spite of the opposition of their old enemies, the speculators. Acting upon this recommendation of Congress, the convention ordered that an independent body of troops, not exceeding five hundred men including officers, be forthwith raised of those called Green Mountain Boys, under officers of their own election.

When this order, forwarded by General Schuyler, was received in the Grants, a convention of the town committees was called, which met at the house of Mr. Cephas Kent, innholder, in the township of Dorset, on the 26th of July, and, after electing a chairman and clerk, at once proceeded to elect the officers of the regiment. Ethan Allen, who had previously proposed to the New York convention a list of officers in which his name appeared first, followed next by Warner's, now offered himself as a candidate for the lieutenant-colonelcy, which was the rank of the commander. But he received only five votes, while Warner was given forty-one. As may well be imagined, he was greatly mortified by the result, which he charged to the old farmers who did not incline to go to war, while with the young Green Mountain Boys he claimed to be a favorite.[1] Though it seemed like a slight to the acknowledged leader of the Green Mountain Boys to elect his junior and subordinate to the command of this regiment, if not an act of calm and dispassionate judgment, it was one of which future events proved the wisdom; for the less impetuous but no less brave Warner was the safer commander in regular military operations. It is noticeable that neither Baker, Cockran, nor Sunderland, Allen's intimate associates in resistance to New York, was elected by the Dorset convention, though they were on his list of proposed captains.

A copy of the proceedings was forwarded to General Schuyler, with a letter briefly setting forth that this action had been taken in compliance with the

[1] *Governor and Council*, vol. i. p. 6.

orders of Congress and General Schuyler's recommendation, in no wise acknowledging the authority of New York, but as independently as other colonies contributing a military force to the Continental army.

There were then no more regular troops in Canada than served to garrison the posts, and the governor, General Carleton, attempted to raise an army of Canadians and Indians for offensive operations, for the equipment of which 20,000 stand of arms had been sent from England. But the habitants had no stomach for fighting, and, though martial law was proclaimed, refused to arm for the invasion of the southern provinces, while they declared their willingness to defend their own. The governor urged the Bishop of Quebec to exercise his ecclesiastical authority to effect this purpose, but the prelate adroitly excused himself. An attempt was made, through the influence of the son of the late Sir William Johnson, to engage the Indians in the contest, but they prudently declined to take part in it. Of all the Canadians, only the French *noblesse* showed any willingness to support the governor, and they were too few to be of much account.

The Americans, apprised of these futile attempts, determined to invade Canada before reinforcements should arrive from England. Two thousand men were to be raised in New York and New England, and commanded by Generals Schuyler and Montgomery.

Among the prizes secured by the capture of Ticonderoga and Crown Point was a quantity of materials for boat-building, which now became available. With ready Yankee aptitude, the soldiers turned their hands to the construction of batteaux for the transportation of the troops down the lake, and the surrounding forests rang for many a summer day with the busy stroke of axe and hammer.

Montgomery reached Crown Point in August, and upon receiving news that Carleton was preparing for offensive operations, and had several armed vessels at St. John's ready to transport his forces up the lake, at once set forth with what troops had arrived. With sweep and sail, the lazy flotilla of batteaux was urged down the lake to Isle la Motte, where Montgomery was joined by Schuyler, who though ill had hastened on from Albany. They then moved on to Isle aux Noix, and there so disposed their forces as to prevent the passage of the enemy's vessels. From this point they issued a proclamation to the Canadians, assuring them that their army was not in any way directed against them, but against the British, and inviting them to join in the struggle for liberty.

Ethan Allen, whose patriotic ardor had not been cooled by his recent rebuff, had, by invitation of the generals, accompanied them to Isle aux Noix. He held no commission, but was considered as an officer, and was upon occasion to be given the command of detachments. He was now employed, with Major Brown and accompanied by interpreters, to distribute this proclamation among the Canadians, and satisfactorily performed the duties assigned him. On the 6th of September, the American army, not more than a thousand strong, advanced toward St. John's, and landed a mile and a half from the fort. This they found too strong to warrant an assault, and after a reconnoissance, in which they were attacked by a party of Indians, and suffered a slight loss while inflicting a somewhat greater one, they withdrew next morning to the Isle aux Noix, to await the arrival of artillery and reinforcements. It was during these operations that the brave Captain Remember Baker was killed. He was held in great esteem by his friends, and his death, being the first that occurred in the military operations in this quarter, created more stir, says Ira Allen, than the death of a thousand later in the war. Montgomery's reinforcements having arrived, he again moved upon St. John's on the 17th, and laid siege to the place, but, with his undisciplined troops and slender supply of ammunition, his progress was slow. Parties were sent out through the country, and were favorably received by the Canadians, who contributed men and provisions, the latter the more valuable contribution.

At this time, much against his wishes, for he would rather have taken part in the siege, Ethan Allen was dispatched by Montgomery on a mission similar to that in which he was previously

engaged. With a guard of about eighty men,
mostly Canadians, he passed through the parishes
on the Richelieu and up the St. Lawrence to Longueuil, "preaching politics," as he says, and meeting
"with good success as an itinerant." On his way
thence to La Prairie, he fell in with Major Brown,
who was out on the same errand, and now proposed
to Allen that they should attempt the capture of
Montreal. His plan was, that Allen should return
to Longueuil, and, there procuring canoes, cross his
men to the island of Montreal, a little below the
town; while Brown, with about 200 men, should
cross above it. Allen readily fell in with it, and,
making haste back to Longueuil, obtained a few
boats and collected about thirty recruits. In the
course of the night he got his party across the
river, and, setting a guard between his position and
the town, with orders to let no one pass, awaited
the signal which Brown was to give when he had
effected a crossing. Allen waited with growing
impatience, while daylight grew and sunrise came.
All the world began to be astir, and yet Brown
made no sign. Unsupported as he now found
himself, he was in sorry plight, and would have
recrossed the river, but he had only boats enough
to transport a third of his force at a time, and the
attempt would certainly result in the capture of
the other two thirds. He determined to maintain
his ground if possible, and that, in any event, all
should fare alike. He dispatched messengers to
Brown at La Prairie, and to L'Assomption, to a

Mr. Walker, who was in the interest of the Americans, urging them to hasten to his aid.

Montreal was already alarmed, and the governor and his party were preparing to retire on board the vessels of war, when a spy, who had escaped from Allen's guards, brought them information of Allen's condition. Upon this, Carleton marched out to attack the presumptuous invader, with forty regulars and "a mixed multitude" of Canadians, English, and Indians, numbering nearly 500, and Allen perceived that it would be a "day of trouble if not of rebuke." [1] About two o'clock in the afternoon, the British force began firing from the cover of woodpiles, ditches, and buildings, Allen's men returning the fusilade from positions quite as favorable, till near half the enemy began a flank movement on their right. Observing this, Allen dispatched half his force, under a volunteer named Dugan, to occupy a ditch on their flank; but Dugan took the opportunity to escape with his detachment, as did one Young, posted on the other flank with a small force, and Allen was left with only forty-five men, some of whom were wounded. He began a hopeless retreat, which was continued for a while. An officer pressing close upon the rear fired his gun at Allen, the ball whistling past his head. Allen's shot in turn missed his enemy, as both were out of breath with running. Allen now offered to surrender if assured of quarter for himself and his men, which was promised by this officer. Whereupon

---

[1] Allen's *Narrative.*

Allen gave up his sword and surrendered his party, dwindled to thirty-eight, seven of whom were wounded. A painted and half-naked Indian rushed toward them, and within a few yards aimed his gun at Allen, who, seizing the officer to whom he had delivered his sword, made a shield of him, and kept him spinning around, as the Indian swiftly circled about the two, in a vain attempt to fire a shot that should kill only the Green Mountain Boy. Another Indian then took part in the attack, and Allen's shrift would have been short, had not an Irishman and a Canadian come to his rescue. He was then well treated by his captors, walking to the town between a British officer and a French gentleman, who, though he had lost an eyebrow in the action, "was very merry and facetious." But when General Prescott, who throughout the war never missed an opportunity of exhibiting his brutality, met them at the barracks and learned that the prisoner was the captor of Ticonderoga, he showered a torrent of abuse upon him, while he shook his cane over his head. Allen shook his fist at the general, and told him "that was the beetle of mortality for him if he offered to strike." An officer whispered to Prescott that it was inconsistent with his honor to strike a prisoner. Prescott turned his wrath upon the Canadians, and ordered a sergeant's guard to kill thirteen of them; and when Allen had somewhat dramatically but successfully interposed to save their lives, Prescott roared at him, with an oath, " I will not execute you now, but you shall grace a halter at Tyburn ! " By Prescott's orders he was taken on board a vessel of war and manacled like a common felon, and presently, with other prisoners, was sent to England. Landing at Falmouth, clad in the fawn-skin jacket and red woolen cap that he wore when taken, his strange appearance excited a curiosity that not a little gratified him. From his capture till he was exchanged in 1778, he suffered on shipboard and in prison, with brief intervals of kinder treatment, a hard and cruel captivity, from which he emerged, however, with a spirit unsubdued, and unswerving loyalty to his country's cause. The attempt upon Montreal has generally been characterized as rash ; yet, if Brown had not, for some unexplained reason, failed to perform his part in it, it is more than probable the undertaking would have succeeded. It was one of those daring enterprises which if successful receive the highest praise, if unsuccessful are scouted as foolhardy.

Meanwhile the siege of St. John's progressed slowly, principally through lack of ammunition. But on the 18th of October the fort at Chambly, further down the river, and garrisoned by about 100 men of the British Seventh Regiment, surrendered to Majors Brown and Livingston, and among the most important of its captured stores were 120 barrels of gunpowder, which enabled Montgomery to push the siege with more vigor. As gratifying if not as useful was the capture of the colors of the regiment, the first trophy of the kind received by the Continental Congress.

General Carleton was making all possible efforts for the relief of St. John's, whose garrison of 500 regulars and about 200 other troops was bravely defending it. He had collected a force of 800 regulars, militia, and Indians, which he embarked at Montreal, with the design of landing at Longueuil and joining Colonel McLean at the mouth of the Richelieu, where that officer was posted with a few hundred Scotch emigrants and some Canadians. Colonel Seth Warner with 300 Green Mountain Boys was keeping close watch of Carleton's movements, and when the flotilla drew near the south shore of the St. Lawrence, the rangers poured upon it a destructive volley of small-arms and a shower of grapeshot from a four-pounder. Carleton's force retired in confusion, and when McLean's Canadians got news of the disaster they took French leave of him, and he with his Scotchmen retired in haste to Quebec. Left now without hope of relief, St. John's capitulated on the 3d of November, and a considerable number of cannon, a quantity of military stores, and 600 prisoners fell into the hands of the Americans. The prisoners were sent by way of Ticonderoga into the interior of New England.

Montgomery now marched to Montreal, which Carleton had secretly quitted the night before. The inhabitants proposed a capitulation, which Montgomery refused, as they were incapable of making any defense. Promising them perfect protection of person and property, he marched his army into the place, and took peaceable possession on the 13th.

Colonel Easton had been sent with a detachment to the mouth of the Richelieu, where he erected a battery of two guns, and, being reinforced by a gunboat from St. John's on the 17th, he captured, as they attempted to pass on their way to Quebec, eleven sail of armed vessels freighted with provisions and military stores, and having on board General Prescott and 120 officers and privates.

The term of enlistment of Warner's men having now expired, they presently returned to their homes, not long after to be recalled, with their leader, in the stress of the Northern winter, by the urgent appeal of the commander of the army in Canada.

During the occurrence of these events, Arnold was engaged in his memorable expedition against Quebec by way of the Kennebec. Arriving at the mouth of that river on the 20th of September, he set forth with an army of 1,100 men, embarked in heavy batteaux, to voyage up the wild stream where hitherto had floated only the light craft of the Indian, the scout, and the hunter. Battling with dogged persistence against the angry rush of rapids, and now dragging their bulky craft over portages of swamp or rugged steeps, they made their slow and weary progress through the heart of the pitiless wilderness at the rate, at best, of little more than four miles a day. Through constant strain of toil and hardship many fell sick, and in the passage of the rapids much of their provisions was lost, so that the horror of starvation was added to the heavy measure of their suffering. Men killed and ate their dogs, or gnawed their shoes and the leather of their cartouch boxes, to allay the pangs of hunger. When the head of the Kennebec was reached, Colonel Enos, who was ordered to send back the sick, himself went off with three companies, a council of his officers having decided that it was impossible to proceed, for lack of provisions. But Arnold, with his remaining force, held on his way with desperate determination, and, coming to the Chaudière, followed it till on the 3d of November they came to the first house that they had seen for a month, and there procured some supplies. At Sortigan, the first village reached, they were kindly received by the Canadians and bountifully supplied with provisions. A proclamation prepared by Washington was distributed among the Canadians. It invited them to join the Americans and assured them protection of person, property, and religion, and was well received by them. With the aid which these people afforded, Arnold made an easy march to Point Levi, arriving there on the 9th with about 700 men. Twenty-four hours passed before his coming was known in Quebec. There was such dissension among the British inhabitants in consequence of the opposition of the English merchants to the Quebec Bill, that the city was in no condition for defense. The French citizens had no inclination to take up arms against the Americans; and had Arnold the means of transportation across the broad St. Lawrence, it is probable that he might easily have taken the city. Three days later Colonel McLean arrived there with 170 of his regiment of Scotch emigrants, and at nine in the evening of the next day Arnold began embarking his men in canoes. By four in the morning 500 were landed at Wolfe's Cove, whence they marched to the Plains of Abraham. When Arnold's landing became known in the city, sailors were brought on shore from the ships to man the guns of the fortifications; the loyal citizens became more confident of making a successful defense, and when Arnold sent a flag with a summons to surrender, it was fired upon. He was not strong enough to strike; he could but menace; and when menace failed to intimidate the enemy, there was nothing for him but to retire. Therefore he withdrew to Point au Trembles, seven leagues above Quebec, on the left bank of the St. Lawrence. There, on the 1st of December, he was joined by Montgomery, who had marched his little force of 300 men with all possible celerity through the half-frozen mire of roads wretched at best, and in the blinding snowstorms of a winter already rigorous in that climate. Three armed schooners had also arrived with ammunition, clothing, and provisions. On the 5th the little army, less than a thousand strong, appeared before Quebec, now garrisoned by more than 1,500 men of McLean's regiment, regulars, seamen, marines, and militia. Montgomery opened an ineffectual fire on the town from two small batteries of mortar and cannon. An assault was determined upon, and on the last day of the year, under the thick veil of a downfall of snow, the troops made the assault in four columns at as many points. The attack of two columns was a feint against the upper town. Montgomery and Arnold led the actual assault of the other two against the lower town, and gained some advantages. Montgomery was killed, and his corps of 200 swept back by a storm of grape and musket balls poured upon them from the second barrier. Arnold was carried from the field with a leg shattered in a successful attack upon a battery, and his column of 300, after a desperate fight of three hours, was overwhelmed by the whole force of the British now turned upon it, and it was obliged to surrender.

The command now devolved upon Arnold, and the troops, reduced to 400, withdrew three miles from the city, and there maintained a partial blockade of it.[1] General Wooster, in command at Montreal, sent expresses to Washington, Schuyler, and Congress, and on the 6th of January wrote to Colonel Warner urging him to raise and send on the more readily available Green Mountain Boys, " by tens, twenties, thirties, forties, or fifties, as fast as they could be collected." The response

[1] Williams, vol. ii.

to his call was prompt. In eleven days Warner mustered his men, and despite the rigors of the northern winter, whose bitterness they had so often tasted, they marched in snow and pinching cold to the assistance of their brethren in Canada, and their alacrity called forth the approval of Washington and Schuyler.[1]

The offensive operations of the Americans in Canada were thereafter feeble and ineffectual. Reinforcements had arrived, but smallpox was raging in the camp, so that when General Thomas took command on the 14th of May there were less than 900 men fit for duty. In this condition, and with only three days' provisions remaining, an immediate retreat was decided upon by a council of war. This became precipitate when three English ships of war arrived and landed more than a thousand marines and regulars, and General Carleton marched out with 800 regulars against the Americans, already in retreat.

Artillery, stores, and baggage were abandoned, and the troops scattered in flight, the general being able to collect no more than 300 of them. By day and night they retreated nearly fifty miles before they halted, when, being beyond immediate reach of the enemy, they rested a few days and then marched to Sorel, in sorry plight, worn with disease, fatigue, and hunger.

For the most part, the Canadians proved but fair-weather friends, and gave them little aid now

[1] Hall's *Early History of Vermont.*

that the fortune of war no longer favored them. General Thomas died here of smallpox, and General Sullivan took command. After the cowardly surrender by Major Beadle of his force of nearly 400 posted at The Cedars, a small fort on the St. Lawrence, to Captain Foster, with a detachment of 40 regulars, 100 Canadians, and 500 Indians, without artillery, and the disastrous failure of General Thompson with 1,800 men to surprise the British advance at Trois Rivières, all the American troops began a retreat from Canada, where an army of 13,000 English and German troops were now arrived.

Arnold, who had been in command at Montreal since the 1st of April, crossed the St. Lawrence at Longueuil on the 15th of June, and marched to Chambly, whence the army continued its retreat in good order, first to Isle aux Noix and then to Crown Point.

During the withdrawal of the army from Canada, the services of Warner and his Green Mountain Boys again became conspicuous. Following in the rear, but little in advance of the pursuing enemy, he was chiefly employed in gathering up the sick and wounded. Some straggling in the woods, some sheltered in the garlick-reeking cabins of the least unfriendly habitants, he succeeded in bringing a great number of them to Isle aux Noix.

Thence embarked, in leaky open boats, the wretched invalids voyaged to Crown Point, their misery mocked by the brightness of the June skies, the beauty of the shores clad in the luxuriant leafage of early summer, and the glitter of the sunlit waters. The condition of the broken army gathered at Crown Point was miserable in the extreme. More than half of the 5,200 men were sick, and those reported fit for duty were weak and half clad, broken in spirit and discipline. A few were in tents, some in poor sheds, while the greater part had only the shelter of bush huts. Colonel Trumbull says: "I did not look into a tent or hut in which I did not find either a dead or dying man." More than 300 new-made graves marked the brief tarry of the troops at Crown Point. Those whom Colonel Warner did not succeed in bringing off, and who fell into General Carleton's hands, were treated by him with the greatest kindness.

So closed this unprofitable campaign, in whose prosecution such heroism had been expended in vain, such valuable lives wasted. Beginning with a series of successes, it ended in disaster, and was fortunate only in that it did not achieve the conquest of a province to hold which would have required the presence of an army that could ill be spared elsewhere, — a province which was chiefly peopled by a race alien in language and religion, too abject to strike for its own freedom, and so priest-ridden and steeped in ignorance that its incorporation with it could prove but a curse to the young republic.

CHAPTER IX.

LAKE CHAMPLAIN.

GENERAL GATES having been appointed to the command of the northern army, General Sullivan resigned it to him on the 12th of July, receiving the thanks of his officers and the approval of Congress for the ability with which he had conducted the retreat.

In conformity to the decision of a council of war, General Gates withdrew his troops from Crown Point, where not a cannon was mounted, to Ticonderoga, and began strengthening the works there and erecting new ones upon a hill on the opposite side of the lake. While this new work, a star fort, was in progress, news came of the Declaration of Independence, and in honor of the event the place was named Mount Independence. The smallpox patients were removed to a hospital at Fort George, and the recruits, now coming in considerable numbers, were assembled at Skenesborough.

The construction of vessels of war, wherewith to keep control of the lake, was now entered upon. In spite of the difficulties attending their construction in a place so remote from all supplies but timber, and that green in the forest, the work was pushed so vigorously that before the end of August one sloop, three schooners, and five gondolas were ready for service, mounting fifty five, twelve, nine, and six pounders and seventy swivels. These were manned by 395 men, old sea-dogs drifted to inland waters, and unsalted navigators of lakes and rivers, " a miserable set," Arnold wrote to Gates. In the latter part of August the fleet sailed down the lake under the command of Arnold, and, when soon after reinforced by a cutter, three galleys, and three gunboats, amounted to fifteen sail.

At the north end of the lake, the British were as busy in constructing and assembling a fleet. Six armed vessels, built in England especially for this service, could not be got over the rapids at Chambly, and were taken to pieces, transported above this obstruction, and reconstructed. The largest of these, the Intrepid, was completed in twenty-eight days from the laying of the keel. Several gondolas, — a sort of long, narrow, flat-bottomed craft,' — thirty longboats, and 400 batteaux were hauled up the rapids by the amphibious Canadians, with an immense expenditure of toil and vociferous jabber. By the 1st of October the fleet was ready to enter the lake, and consisted of the Inflexible, carrying eighteen guns; the schooners, Maria and Carleton, carrying fourteen and twelve respectively; and the Thunderer, a floating battery of raft-like construction, mounting six

twenty-fours, as many sixes, and two howitzers;
with a number of gondolas, gunboats, and longboats, each carrying one gun. It was manned
by 700 experienced seamen, and commanded by
Captain Pringle. In opposing this formidable
fleet, so vastly superior in all its appointments, in
everything but the bravery of officers and men,
the odds were fearfully against the Americans, but
the intrepid Arnold did not hesitate to accept the
chances.

The sails of the British squadron were whit-
ening the lake beyond Cumberland Head when
Arnold disposed his vessels behind the island of
Valcour, where, screened from sight of the main
channel by woods whose gorgeous leafage was yet
unthinned by the frosty touch that painted it, he
awaited the approach of the enemy. Sailing past
the island, the British discovered the little fleet of
the Americans, and, conscious of their own superi-
ority, at once advanced to the attack from the
southward; but the wind, which before had favored
them, was now against them. The flagship Inflexible, and some others of the larger vessels, could
not be brought into action, and the Carleton and
the gunboats took the brunt of the battle.

For four hours the fierce fight raged, sustained
with the utmost bravery by both combatants. The
forests were shaken with the unwonted thunder,
whose roar was heard at Crown Point, forty miles
away, and the autumnal haze grew thick with sulphurous smoke. General Waterbury, commanding

the Washington galley, was in the hottest of it, and only brought his shattered vessel out of the fight when all but two of his officers were killed or wounded. One of the American schooners was burnt, a gondola sunk, and several other vessels much injured; while the British had two gondolas sunk, and one blown up with sixty men on board. Toward nightfall, Captain Pringle withdrew the vessels engaged, and anchored his whole fleet across the channel to prevent the escape of the Americans. Escape was all that Arnold hoped for now, and in the darkness of night he silently got his vessels around the north end of Valcour,[1] and, making all speed southward, was out of sight of his enemy when daylight came.

The British gave chase, and overtaking the Americans at Split Rock, about noon of the 13th, at once began firing on them. The sorely crippled Washington was forced to strike her colors after receiving a few broadsides. Arnold fought his flagship, the Congress galley, with desperate courage, while, within musket-shot, the Inflexible poured broadsides into her, and two schooners raked her from astern. He effectually covered the

---

[1] There are conflicting statements concerning Arnold's course in eluding the British fleet. According to some authorities he slipped directly through the enemy's line under cover of thick darkness; others state circumstantially that he escaped around the north end of Valcour, and this unobstructed course certainly seems the one which would naturally be taken, instead of attempting the almost impossible feat of passing through a fleet that guarded the channel, barely half a mile in width.

retreat of his escaping vessels with the Congress and four gondolas, and then ran ashore in the shoal head of a little bay on the eastern side of the lake. He set fire to the vessels, and keeping his flag flying on the Congress, which he did not quit till she was enveloped in flames, got all his men landed but one wounded lieutenant, who, forgotten in the confusion, was blown up with his vessel. Of the American fleet, only two galleys, two schooners, a sloop, and gondola had escaped; and toward Ticonderoga, whither these had fled, Arnold retreated with his stranded crews, barely escaping an Indian ambuscade. Joined by the few and now defenseless settlers, they toiled along the rough forest road, behind them rolling the irregular boom of the cannon, exploding as the fire heated them, and at intervals the thunder of a bursting magazine. Throughout that long, unequal combat, as in many another in the same good cause, Arnold bore himself with cool, intrepid valor, still preserved by an unkind fate from honorable death to achieve everlasting infamy. The land-locked bay, where may yet be seen the oaken skeletons of his brave little craft,[1] bears his name, nowhere else honorably commemorated in all his native land.

General Carleton, who accompanied the British fleet, gave orders that the prisoners taken should

[1] Years afterward, a brass gun was raised from one of these wrecks, and played its part in gaining the naval victory at Plattsburgh.

be treated with the greatest kindness. He himself praised their bravery, and sent them home on parole. By this politic course he so won their esteem, that it was deemed impolitic to permit them to mingle with the troops at Ticonderoga, and they were sent on to Skenesborough.

Following close on the heels of the victorious fleet came the swarming transports bearing General Carleton's army, with the intention of moving at once upon Ticonderoga. Crown Point was no longer an obstacle, for when news of the disaster of their fleet was brought to that post, the Americans set fire to the place, destroyed everything that could not be removed, and withdrew to the main army holding Ticonderoga. But the wind, which had been a fickle ally of the English since they began this invasion, again turned against them from the south on the 14th, and held stiffly in that quarter for eight days. General Carleton's transports could make no headway against it up the narrow waterway, and he was obliged to land his forces at Crown Point. Thence he sent reconnoitring parties on both sides of the lake toward Ticonderoga, and some vessels up the channel, sounding it within cannon-shot of the fort.

Meanwhile Gates's army made most of the time given by the kindly autumnal gale. The works were strengthened and surrounded by an abatis. In these eight days, carriages were built for forty-seven pieces of cannon and the guns mounted; while reinforcements that came in, and sick men

recovered, swelled the army to 1,200 strong.
Carleton's opportunity for an easy conquest of
Ticonderoga was past, and his reconnoissances
gave him no encouragement to attempt an assault.
Therefore, after tarrying at the fire-scathed fortress
till past the middle of November, when the wild
geese were flying southward over the gray and
desolate forests, and the herbage of the clearings
was seared by the touch of many frosts, he reëmbarked his army and returned to Canada. General Gates at once dismissed the militia, active
military operations ceased in this quarter, and the
northern armies of America and Great Britain began their hibernation.

ARNOLD'S BAY, LAKE CHAMPLAIN—SCENE OF THE BATTLE OF OCTOBER 13, 1776.

[FROM A SKETCH BY MR. R. E. ROBINSON.]

CHAPTER X.

At the beginning of the Revolution, the people of the New Hampshire Grants were without a regular form of government, for the greater part of them had long refused to submit to the jurisdiction of the royal government of New York, and were now as little disposed to compromise their asserted rights by acknowledging the authority of that province when it had taken its place among the United Colonies in revolt against Great Britain. Such government as existed was vested in Committees of Safety, but these, whether of greater or lesser scope, were without recognized power to enforce their decrees upon the respectable minority which still adhered to New York.

Under these circumstances a convention, warned by the Committee of Safety of Arlington, met at Dorset, January 16, 1776, at the "house of Cephas Kent, innholder." Persons were appointed to represent the case of the Grants before Congress by a "Remonstrance and Petition." This stated that inhabitants of the Grants were willing, as heretofore, to do all in their power for the common cause, but were not willing to act under the authority of

New York, lest it might be deemed an acknowledgment of its claims and prejudicial to their own, and desired to perform military service as inhabitants of the Grants instead of New York.

Upon the return of Heman Allen, who duly presented the memorial to Congress, a second convention was held in July at the same place, thirty-two towns being represented by forty-nine delegates. Allen reported that Congress, after hearing their petition, ordered it to lie upon the table for further consideration, but that he withdrew it, lest the opposing New York delegates should bring the matter to final decision when no delegate from the Grants was present. Several members of Congress and other gentlemen, in private conversation, advised the people of the Grants to do their utmost to repel invasions of the enemy, but by no means to act under the authority of New York; while the committee of Congress to whom the matter was referred, while urging them to the same exertions, advised them, for the present, to submit to New York, saying this submission ought not to prejudice their right to the lands in question.

The convention resolved at once " That Application be made to the Inhabitants of said Grants, to form the same into a separate District." The convention laconically declared that " the Spirited Conflict," which had so long continued between the Grants and New York, rendered it " inconvenient in many respects to associate with that province." But, to prove their readiness to join in the common defense of America, they, with one exception only, subscribed to the following association : " We the subscribers inhabitants of that District of Land, commonly called and known by the name of the New Hampshire Grants, do voluntarily and Solemnly Engage under all the ties held sacred amongst Mankind at the Risque of our Lives and fortunes to Defend, by arms, the United American States against the Hostile attempts of the British Fleets and Armies, until the present unhappy Controversy between the two Countries shall be settled."

The convention invited all the inhabitants to subscribe to this "Association," and resolved that any who should unite with a similar one under the authority of New York should be deemed an enemy to the cause of the Grants. Persons were appointed to procure the signature of every male inhabitant of sixteen years upwards, both on the east and west sides of the Green Mountains. Thus the convention took the first formal steps toward severing the connection with New York, and uniting all the towns within the Grants in a common league.

Only one town on the east side of the mountains was represented in this meeting ; but pains were taken to confer with those inhabitants, and at the adjourned session, in September, ten eastern towns were represented. At this session it was voted that the inhabitants should be governed by the resolves of this or a similar convention " not repugnant to the resolves of Congress," and that in fu-

ture no law or direction received from New York
should be accepted or obeyed. The power was
assumed of regulating the militia, and furnishing
troops for the common defense. For the especial
safe-keeping of Tories, a jail was ordered to be
built at Manchester. It was to be constructed
with double walls of logs, eighteen inches apart,
the space to be filled with earth to the height of
seven feet, " floored with logs double." The convention appointed a " Committee of War," vested
with power to call out the militia for the defense
of the Grants or any part of the continent. Fines
were exacted from every officer and private who
should not comply with the orders of the convention ; and each non-commissioned officer and private was required to " provide himself with a suitable gun and one pound of powder, four pounds of
bullets fit for his gun, six flints, a powder horn,
cartouch box or bullet pouch, a sword, bayonet, or
tomahawk."

The convention adjourned to meet at Westminster on the 30th of October. When that day
arrived, the country was in great alarm from the
disaster to the American fleet on Lake Champlain,
and Carleton's advance toward Ticonderoga. The
militia was hurrying to the defense of that fortress,
and many delegates were kept at home by the
impending need of protection for their families.
Owing to these circumstances, the few who met
could not be informed of the minds of the people,
and it adjourned to the 15th of January, 1777.

During this interim, the popular sentiment had so rapidly ripened for the proposed separation that, when the convention met, little time was spent in debate before the adoption of a Declaration of the Independence of the New Hampshire Grants. As revised for publication it is as follows : " We will at all times hereafter, consider ourselves as a free and independent state, capable of regulating our internal police in all and every respect whatsoever, and that the people on said Grants have the sole and exclusive and inherent right of ruling and governing themselves in such manner and form as in their own wisdom they shall think proper, not inconsistent or repugnant to any resolve of the Honorable Continental Congress.

" Furthermore, we declare by all the ties which are held sacred among men, that we will firmly stand by and support one another in this our declaration of a State, and in endeavoring as much as in us lies to suppress all unlawful routs and disturbances whatever. Also we will endeavor to secure to every individual his life, peace, and property against all unlawful invaders of the same.

" Lastly, we hereby declare, that we are at all times ready, in conjunction with our brethren in the United States of America, to do our full proportion in maintaining and supporting the just war against the tyrannical invasions of the ministerial fleets and armies, as well as any other foreign enemies, sent with express purpose to murder our fellow brethren and with fire and sword to ravage our defenseless country.

"The said State hereafter to be called by the name of New Connecticut."

This bold and decisive act, by which a free and independent commonwealth was erected, was with eminent fitness consummated in the court-house at Westminster, a place already consecrated to the cause of liberty by the blood of William French, who, less than two years before, had fallen there in defense of the people's rights.

A "Declaration and Petition," announcing the step taken and asking that the new State might be "ranked among the free and independent American States," was prepared and sent to Congress. The action of the people of the Grants was received in a not unfriendly spirit by the New England States; but New York at once made an earnest protest to Congress against it, and demanded the recall of the commission of Colonel Warner authorizing him to raise a continental regiment in the disaffected district, emphasizing the demand by reminding Congress of Warner's outlawry by the "late government." Considering the attitude of Congress and all the colonies toward the royal source of the "late government" of New York, this seems an absurd argument for the recall of Warner's commission. Fortunately for the cause which that brave officer so faithfully and efficiently served, the insolent demand was not complied with.

The adjourned convention met at Windsor in June with seventy-two delegates from fifty towns. One of their earliest transactions was to relieve the young State from the ridiculous name which was first bestowed upon it. It was discovered that a district lying on the Susquehanna was already known as New Connecticut, whereupon the convention rechristened the infant State "Vermont." This most befitting name was suggested by Dr. Thomas Young of Philadelphia, a firm friend of the defenders of the Grants. In the previous April he had addressed a circular letter to them, advising them to act in accordance with a resolution of Congress passed in May, 1776, which recommended to the respective assemblies of the United Colonies, where no sufficient government had been established, to adopt such government as should appear to the representatives of the people most conducive to the happiness and safety of their constituents. He advised a general convention of delegates from all the towns to form a Constitution for the State, to choose a Committee of Safety, and also delegates to Congress, declaring Congress could not refuse to admit their delegates. "You have," said he, "as good a right to say how you will be governed, and by whom, as they had." Dr. Young's letter called forth another earnest protest from New York to Congress, and that body declared that the action of the people of the Grants was not countenanced by any of its acts. The petition of Vermont was dismissed, the commission of Warner apologized for, and Dr. Young censured for a "gross misrepresentation of the resolution of Congress" referred to in his letter. Dr. Young rec-

ommended to the new commonwealth, as a model
for a Constitution, that of Pennsylvania, an instrument whose essential features originated in Penn's
"Frame of Government" of that province.   His
advice was followed, and a very similar Constitution was adopted early in July, 1777.

When, for this purpose, after a short adjournment, the convention met at the Windsor meeting-
house, all Vermont was in alarm at the British invasion which was sweeping upon its western border.   Almost at first the attention of the delegates
was called to the impending peril of Ticonderoga
by an appeal for aid from Colonel Warner.   This
was at once forwarded to the Assembly of New
Hampshire, and such measures as seemed best,
which elicited the warm thanks of General St.
Clair, were taken by the convention for the relief
of the threatened fortress.   Some of the members,
among whom was the president, the patriotic Joseph
Bowker of Rutland, whose families were in exposed situations, were now anxious for an adjournment; but a furious thunder-storm came roaring
up the Connecticut valley, and the storm-bound convention took up its appointed work, reading and
adopting, one by one, the articles of the Constitution amid the turmoil of the tempest.

To the first section of the declaration of rights,
which announced that " glittering generality," the
natural rights of man to life, liberty, and the pursuit of happiness, this specific clause was added:
" Therefore no male person born in this country, or

brought from over sea, ought to be holden by law to serve any person as a servant, slave, or apprentice after he arrives to the age of twenty-one years, nor female in like manner after she arrives to the age of eighteen years, unless they are bound by their own consent after they arrive to such age, or bound by law for the payment of debts, damages, fines, costs, or the like."

"Vermont was thus the first of the States to prohibit slavery by constitutional provision, a fact of which Vermonters may well be proud," says Hiland Hall in his "Early History."

Religious freedom, freedom of speech and of the press, were also established. The form of government was thoroughly democratic. Every man of the full age of twenty-one years, who had resided in the State for one year, was given the elective franchise, and was eligible to any office in the State. The legislative power was vested in a single assembly of members chosen annually by ballot. Each town was to have one representative, and towns having more than eighty taxable inhabitants were entitled to two. The executive authority was in a governor, lieutenant-governor, and twelve councillors, elected annually by all the freemen in the State. They had no negative power, but it was provided that "all bills of a public nature should be laid before them, for their perusal and proposals of amendment," before they were finally debated in the General Assembly. Such bills were to be printed for the information of the people, and not to be enacted into laws until the next session of the assembly. "Temporary acts" in cases of "sudden emergency" might, however, be passed without this delay. Compliance with this article was found so difficult that nearly all laws were treated as temporary, and declared permanent at the next session. Bills could originate in the council as well as in the house of assembly; and in cases of disagreement between the two bodies upon any measure, it was usually discussed in grand committee composed of both, the governor presiding. The final disposition of a measure was according to the pleasure of the house, but the advisory power of the governor and council was a strong check upon hasty legislation. In 1786 the provision for printing and postponing the passage of laws was expunged, and the governor and council were authorized to suspend the operation of a bill until the next session of the legislature, when, to become a law, it must again be passed by the assembly. Judges of inferior courts, sheriffs, justices of the peace, and judges of probate were elected by the freemen of the respective counties, to hold office during good behavior, removable by the assembly on proof of maladministration. The mode of choosing judges of superior courts was left to the discretion of the legislature, and they were elected annually by joint ballot of the council and assembly. When the Constitution was revised in 1786, it was provided that county officers should be annually chosen in the same manner.

The Constitution provided for an election, by the freemen of the State, of a Council of Censors, consisting of thirteen members, first to be chosen on the last Wednesday of March, 1785, and thereafter on the same day in every seventh year. It was the duty of this body to inquire whether the Constitution had been preserved inviolate, and whether the legislature and executive branches of government had performed their duty as guardians of the people, or had assumed greater powers than they were constitutionally entitled to. They were to inquire whether public taxes had been justly laid and collected, in what manner the public moneys had been disposed of, and whether the laws had been duly executed. The council was also empowered to call a convention, to meet within two years after their sitting, if there appeared to them an absolute necessity of any change in the Constitution, the proposed changes to be promulgated at least six months before the election of such convention, for the previous consideration of the people. This provision of the Constitution, though useless if no worse, was nevertheless a great favorite of the people of Vermont, and remained a prominent and unique feature of that instrument till 1870, when it was abrogated by the last convention called by a Council of Censors.

"This frame of government," writes Hiland Hall of the early Constitution, "continued in operation long after the State had become a member of the Federal Union, furnishing the people with as much security for their persons and property as was enjoyed by those of other States, and allowing to each individual citizen all the liberty which was consistent with the welfare of others."

Such are the main features of the Vermont Constitution established by the Windsor convention. An election of state officers was ordered to be held in the ensuing December, to be followed by a meeting of the legislature in January, and a Council of Safety was appointed to manage the affairs of the State during the intervening time.

CHAPTER XI.

TICONDEROGA ; HUBBARDTON.

NOTWITHSTANDING all that Sir Guy Carleton had accomplished in driving the American army from Canada, and regaining control of Lake Champlain as far as Ticonderoga, his management of the campaigns had not fully satisfied the ministry. He was blamed for dismissing his Indian allies when he found it impossible to prevent their killing and scalping of prisoners ; and he was blamed that, with a well-appointed army of invincible Britons, he had not in one campaign utterly destroyed or dispersed the rabble rout of colonial rebels. Consequently the command of the army in Canada, designed for offensive operations, was given to Sir John Burgoyne, a court favorite ; while Carleton, the far abler general, was left in command only of the 3,700 troops reserved for the defense of the province.

In June, Burgoyne's army of more than 7,000 regular troops embarked at St. John's, and made undisputed progress up the lake to the mouth of the Bouquet. Here it encamped on the deserted estate of William Gilliland, who had bought an immense tract in this region and made a settlement at the falls of the Bouquet in 1765, but was obliged to abandon it during the war. At this place the Indians were assembled, Iroquois and Waubanakees gathered under one banner, and alike hungry for scalps and plunder. Burgoyne addressed them in a grandiloquent speech, modeled in the supposed style of aboriginal eloquence, exhorting them to deeds of valor, to be tempered with a humanity impossible to the savages, and was briefly answered by an old chief of the Iroquois.

Moving forward to Crown Point, the army briefly rested there before advancing upon Ticonderoga. The general issued a proclamation to the inhabitants, inviting all who would to join him, and offering protection to such as remained quietly at their homes, and in no way obstructed the operations of his army, or assisted his enemies; while those who did not accept his clemency were threatened with the horrors of Indian warfare. Having delivered himself of speech and proclamation, Burgoyne continued his advance on Ticonderoga.

The post was not in the best condition for defense, as General Schuyler, now commanding the Northern Department, discovered when visiting it while Burgoyne was airing his eloquence at the Bouquet. The old French lines had been somewhat strengthened, and block-houses built on the right and left of them. More labor had been expended on the defenses of Mount Independence, a water battery erected at the fort, and another battery

half way up the declivity. Communication between the forts was maintained by a bridge thrown
across the lake, consisting of twenty-two piers, connected by floats fifty feet long and twenty wide.
On the lower side, this bridge was protected by a
boom of immense timbers fastened together by
double chains of inch and a half square iron.   To
garrison these extensive works, General St. Clair,
now the commander of Ticonderoga, had but few
more than 2,500 Continental troops, and 900 poorly
armed and equipped militia.   He had been unwilling to call in more of the militia, for fear of
a failure of supplies.

   But a danger more potent than the weakness of
the garrison lurked in the silent heights of Sugar
Loaf Hill, now better known as Mount Defiance,
that, westward from Ticonderoga, and overlooking
it and all its outworks, bars the horizon with rugged
steeps of rock and sharp incline of woodland.
Colonel John Trumbull, of Revolutionary and ar-
tistic fame, had suggested to General Gates the ad-
visability of fortifying it, saying that it commanded
both Ticonderoga and Mount Independence.   The
idea was ridiculed, and he obtained leave to test
the truth of his assertion.   A shot from a twelve-
pounder on Mount Independence struck half way
up the mountain, and a six-pound shot fired from
the glacis of Ticonderoga struck near the summit.
Yet the Americans did not occupy it then, nor
now, though a consultation was held concerning
it.   It was decided that there were not men enough

to spare for the purpose from the fortifications already established. St. Clair hoped, moreover, that Burgoyne would choose rather to assault than besiege his position, and an assault he thought he might successfully repel.

The General Convention now sitting at Windsor sent Colonel Mead, James Mead, Ira Allen, and Captain Salisbury to consult with the commander of Ticonderoga on the defense of the frontier. While this committee was there, General Burgoyne advanced up the lake, and during his stay at Crown Point sent a force of 300, most of whom were Indians, to the mouth of Otter Creek to raid upon the settlers. The committee was refused any troops for the defense of the frontiers, but Colonel Warner was allowed to go with them, and presently raised men enough to repel this invasion.

On the 1st of July Warner wrote from Rutland to the convention that the enemy had come up the lake with seventeen or eighteen gunboats, two large ships, and other craft, and an attack was expected every hour; that he was ordered to call out the militia of Vermont, Massachusetts, and New Hampshire, to join him as soon as possible, and desired them to call out the militia on the east side of the mountain, and to send forty or fifty head of beef cattle for Ticonderoga. "I shall be glad," he writes in conclusion, "if a few hills of corn unhoed should not be a motive sufficient to detain men at home, considering the loss of such an important post might be irretrievable." In

view of the impending invasion of the British, the
convention appointed a day of fasting and prayer,
but this pious measure had no apparent effect on
the movements of the enemy, and Burgoyne continued to advance.

His army moved forward on either side of the
lake, the war-craft to an anchorage just out of range
of the guns of Ticonderoga and Mount Independence. The Americans abandoned and set on fire
the block-houses and sawmills towards Lake George,
with which the communications were now cut off.

On the 2d of July a British force of 500, commanded by Frazier, attacked and drove in the
American pickets, and, the right wing moving
up, took possession of Mount Hope. St. Clair expected an assault, and ordered his men to conceal
themselves behind the breastworks, and reserve
their fire. Frazier's force, not perceiving the position of the Americans, screened as it was by bushes,
continued to advance till an American soldier fired
his musket, when the whole line delivered a ran-
dom volley, followed by a thunderous discharge of
artillery, all without orders, and without effect but
to kill one of the assailants, and raise a cloud of
smoke that hung in the hot, breathless air till the
assailants had escaped behind it out of range.

The possibilities of Mount Defiance had not escaped the eyes of the British engineers, and they
were at once accepted. General Phillips set himself to the task of making a road up the rocky de-
clivities, over which heavy siege guns were already

being hauled. When, on the morning of the 5th of
July, the sun's first rays shot far above the shadowed valley, they lighted to a ruddier glow the
scarlet uniforms of a swarm of British soldiers on
the bald summit, busy in the construction of a battery.

St. Clair called a council of his officers, and it
was decided that it was impossibile to hold the
place, and the only safety of the army was in immediate evacuation. This was undertaken that
night. The baggage, stores, and all the artillery
that could be got away, embarked on 200 batteaux,
set forth for Skenesborough under the convoy of
five galleys. The main army was to march to
Castleton, and thence to Skenesborough. At two
o'clock on the morning of the 6th of July, St.
Clair moved out of Ticonderoga. Sorrowfully the
Green Mountain Boys relinquished, with almost
as little bloodshed as two years before they had
gained it, the fortress that guarded the frontier of
their country.

The troops fled across the bridge in silence to
the eastern shore, and an hour later the garrison
of Mount Independence began moving out. So
far, the doleful work of evacuation had progressed
with such secrecy that the British were unaware
of any movement. Just then a French officer of
the garrison, zealous to destroy what he could not
save, set fire to his house. The sun-dried wooden
structure was ablaze in an instant, lighting up with
a lurid glare all the works of the place, the hurry-

ing troops, the forest border with ghastly ranks of
towering tree-trunks, the bridge still undulating
with the tread of just-departed marching columns,
and the slow throb of waves pulsing across the
empty anchorage and breaking against deserted
shores.

All was revealed to the British on the heights
of Mount Defiance, and this sudden discovery of
their movements threw the Americans into great
confusion, many hurrying away in disorderly retreat. But about four o'clock Colonel Francis of
Massachusetts brought off the rear in good order,
and some of the other regiments were soon recovered from the panic into which they had fallen.

At Hubbardton the army halted for a rest of
two hours, during which time many stragglers came
in, then St. Clair with the main body pressed on
to Castleton, six miles distant. On that same day
Hubbardton had already been raided by Captain
Sherwood and a party of Indians and Tories. Of
the nine families that composed the entire population of the town, most of the men had been taken
prisoners, and the defenseless women and children
left to whatever fate might befall them in their
plundered homes, or to make their forlorn way
through the wilderness to the shelter of the older
settlements. To Warner was again committed the
covering of a retreat. He was here put in command of the rear-guard, consisting of his own,
Francis's, and Hale's regiments, with orders to remain till all stragglers should have come in, and

then follow a mile and a half in the rear of the main army.

When the retreat of the Americans was discovered, General Frazier set forth in hot pursuit with his brigade, presently followed by General Riedesel with the greater part of the Brunswickers. Frazier kept his force on the march all through the hot summer day, in burning sunshine and breathless shade of the woods till nightfall, when, learning that the American rear was not far in advance, he ordered a halt till morning. Pushing forward again at daybreak, he came up with his enemy at five o'clock, and advanced to within sixty yards of the American line of battle, formed across the road and in the adjacent fields. Colonel Hale of New Hampshire, with Falstaffian valor, had prudently withdrawn his regiment, leaving Warner and Francis with not more than 800 men, to bear the brunt of the impending battle.

The action began at seven with a volley delivered by these two regiments upon the British, who returned it as hotly. The men of the Massachusetts border and the mountaineers of Vermont had no lead to waste in aimless firing, and held rifle and musket straight on the advancing columns of the enemy. Trained to cut off a partridge's head with a single ball at thirty yards, they did not often miss the burly form of a Briton at twice the distance, and their volleys made frightful gaps in the scarlet line. It wavered and broke. Warner and Francis cheered on their men, Francis still

leading his regiment after a ball had struck him
in the right arm. The British line closed up, and
charged upon the Americans, throwing them into
disorder till Warner rallied them, and checked the
British advance. While the fluctuating chances
of the fight favored the Americans, Francis fell,
pierced by a bullet in the breast, and, seeing him
fall, his men faltered and began to retreat. When
Warner saw them scattering in disorderly flight,
he was overcome with wrath. He dropped upon
a log, and poured forth a storm of curses upon the
fugitives.[1] But it did not stop them, nor, if it had,
would it have availed to avert defeat. Riedesel
came up with his Brunswickers, who had toiled
onward in the burning heat for nine hours as
bravely as if they were conquering the country for
themselves. They at once engaged in the action,
and the Americans were everywhere routed, fleeing
across a little brook, and scattering in the shelter
of the woods beyond it.

Collecting most of his regiment, with his accustomed cool intrepidity, Warner retreated to Castleton. The others made their way to Fort Edward.
Hale in his retreat had fallen in with a small detachment of the enemy, to which he surrendered
with a number of his regiment without firing a
shot. Learning that he was charged with cowardice, he asked to be exchanged, that he might have
an opportunity to disprove the charge, but he died
while a prisoner on Long Island. St. Clair sent

[1] Chipman's *Life of Warner.*

no assistance to his friends. Writing to General Schuyler of the affair, he said, "The rear-guard stopped rather imprudently six miles short of the main body," when in fact Warner remained at Hubbardton as ordered, while St. Clair himself advanced beyond supporting distance.

In this first battle of the Revolution on Vermont soil, the Americans lost Francis, an officer whose bravery was acknowledged by friend and foe, and whose early death was mourned by both. In killed, wounded, and prisoners, their loss was 324. The loss of the British force, — about 2,000 strong, — in killed and wounded, was not less than 183. Ethan Allen, in his narrative, sets the enemy's loss, as learned from confessions of their own officers, at 300. Among these was the brave Major Grant, who, while reconnoitring the position of the Americans from the top of a stump, was picked off by a Yankee rifleman. "I heard them likewise complain that the Green Mountain Boys took sight," Allen tells us.

Meanwhile Burgoyne was busy on the lake. By nine o'clock on the morning of the evacuation, the unfinished boom and the bridge were cut asunder; the gunboats and the two frigates passed these obstructions, and, with several regiments on board, went up the channel in rapid pursuit of the American vessels. At three in the afternoon the gunboats got within range of the galleys, not far from Skenesborough, and opened fire upon them. This was returned with some warmth till the frigates were brought into action, when the galleys were abandoned, three were blown up, and the other two fell into the hands of the enemy. Having neither the men nor defenses here to offer any effectual opposition, the Americans set fire to the fort, mills, and batteaux, and fled up Wood Creek toward Fort Anne. They were pursued by Colonel Hill with the Ninth British Regiment, upon whom they turned, and attacked furiously in front with part of their force, while the other was sent to assail his rear. Hill withdrew to an eminence, whither the attack followed so hotly that his complete defeat seemed almost certain, when a large party of Indians came up. They made the woods ring with the terrible warwhoop, which the British answered with three lusty cheers, and the uproar of rejoicing convinced the Americans that a strong reinforcement was at hand; whereupon they drew off, and, again marking the course of their retreat with conflagration by setting fire to Fort Anne, retired to Fort Edward. On the 12th, here also St. Clair joined the main army under Schuyler, after a weary march over wretched roads.

England was exultant over the fall of famous Ticonderoga. The king rushed into the queen's apartments, shouting, "I have beaten them! I have beaten all the Americans!" and such was the universal feeling in the mother country. In America was as universal consternation, which only found relief in storms of abuse poured upon

St. Clair and upon Schuyler, who, as commander of the northern army, received his full share of blame, though both had done the best their circumstances permitted.

Yet it proved not such a disaster to the Americans, nor such an advantage to the British, as it then appeared to each. Burgoyne was obliged to weaken his army by leaving an eighth of it to garrison a post that proved to be of no especial value to him, when, after a rapid and an almost unopposed advance to the head of the lake, he began to encounter serious hindrances to his progress.

For some days he continued at Skenesborough, and issued thence a second proclamation to the people of the Grants, offering to those who should meet Colonel Skene at Castleton "terms by which the disobedient may yet be spared." Schuyler addressed a counter proclamation to the same people, warning them that, if they made terms with the enemy, they would be treated as traitors; and he continually urged them to remove all cattle and carriages beyond reach of the enemy.

Schuyler had two brigades of militia and Continentals busily employed in destroying bridges, and obstructing roads by felling huge trees across them, and, in all ways that expert axemen and woodsmen could devise, making difficult the passage of an army. Having accomplished this, Schuyler abandoned Fort Edward, which was in no condition for defense, and fell back to Stillwater, thirty miles above Albany.

When Burgoyne began to advance toward Fort Edward, his progress was slow and tedious. The obstructed channel of Wood Creek was cleared to Fort Anne, roads cleared and repaired, and forty bridges rebuilt, before, at the snail's pace of a mile in twenty-four hours, he reached Fort Edward. When, on the 30th of July, he established his headquarters here on the Hudson, there was great rejoicing in his army; for now it was thought all serious obstacles were past, and the safe and easy path to Albany lay open before them.

The fall of Ticonderoga and the almost unchecked invasion of their country created a panic among the settlers of western Vermont. Burgoyne's threat of turning loose his Indian allies upon the obdurate incensed most and alarmed all who were exposed to the horrors of such cruel warfare. A few half-hearted Whigs, who became known as Protectioners, — a name but little less opprobrious than Tory, — availed themselves of his proffered clemency, and sought the protection of his army; and a few Tories seized the opportunity now offered to take the side to which they had always inclined.

All the farms in the exposed region were abandoned, the owners carrying away such of their effects as could be hastily removed on horseback and in their few carts and wagons, and, driving their stock before them, hurried toward a place of refuge. The main highways leading southward — at fords, bridges, and the almost impassable mud·

holes that were common to the new-country roads
— were choked with horsemen, footmen, lumbering
vehicles heavily laden with women, children, and
house-gear, and with struggling and straying flocks
and herds.

CHAPTER XII.

BENNINGTON.

WHEN the convention adjourned at Windsor, July 8, 1777, Ticonderoga had fallen; Burgoyne's splendid army was advancing along the western border of Vermont; Warner had made his brave but ineffectual stand at Hubbardton, and was now with the remnant of his regiment at Manchester.

Hither the Council of Safety at once proceeded, and, with Thomas Chittenden as its president, began its important labors. It issued a call to all officers of militia to send on all the men they could possibly raise, as they had learned that a " large Scout of the Enemy are disposed to take a Tour to this Post," and their aim seemed to be the Continental stores at Bennington. On the same day, Ira Allen, as secretary, sent the alarming news to General Schuyler, with an appeal for aid; but Schuyler, as a Continental officer, declined to " notice a fourteenth State unknown to the Confederacy," and could send no men but the militia under Colonel Simmonds, whom he had ordered to join Colonel Warner at Manchester.

Allen also wrote to the New Hampshire Council of Safety for assistance in making a stand against

the enemy in Vermont, which might as well be
made there as in New Hampshire; for, "notwithstanding its infancy, the State was as well supplied
with provisions for victualling an army as any
country on the continent." Meshech Weare, president of that State, replied that New Hampshire
had already determined to send assistance, and
one fourth of her militia was to be formed into
three battalions, under command of Brigadier-General John Stark, and sent forthwith into Vermont.
President Weare requested the Convention of Vermont to send some suitable person to Number
Four, to confer with General Stark as to the route
and disposition of the troops; and two trusty persons were accordingly sent by Colonel Warner.
On the 19th, Stark received his orders to repair
to Number Four, and take command of the force
there mustering. Influenced by a miserable spirit
of jealousy or favoritism, Congress had slighted
this veteran of the late war, passing over him in
the list of promotions. Resenting such injustice,
he went home, but was now ready to unsheath his
sword in the service of his State, though he refused
to act under Continental officers.

Ira Allen, the secretary and youngest member
of the Vermont Council, strongly advocated the
raising of a regiment for the defense of the State,
while the majority could not see the way clear to
raise more than two companies of sixty men each;
nor could they, in the unorganized condition of the
new State, a third of whose inhabitants were in the

confusion of an exodus, see how more than this meagre force could be maintained, and the day was spent in fruitless discussion of the vexed question. At last a member moved that Allen be requested to devise means for paying the bounties and wages of his proposed regiment, and to report at sunrise on the morrow. The astute young secretary was equal to the occasion, and when the Council met next morning, at an hour that finds modern legislators in their first sleep, he was ready with his plan of support. This was, that Commissioners of Sequestration should be appointed, with authority to seize the goods and chattels of all persons who had joined or should join the common enemy; and that all property so seized should be sold at public vendue, and the proceeds be paid to the treasurer of the Council of Safety, for the purpose of paying the bounties and wages of a regiment forthwith to be raised for the defense of the State. "This was the first instance in America of seizing and selling the property of the enemies of American independence," says its originator, in his "History of Vermont." [1] These "turbulent sons of freedom," as Stark afterward termed them, were indeed foremost in many aggressive measures. The Council at once adopted the plan, and appointed a Commissioner of Sequestration. Samuel Herrick was appointed to the command of the regiment, his

[1] November 27, 1777, four months after the Vermont Council of Safety had adopted this measure, Congress recommended the same course to all the States. — *Journals of Congress,* vol. iii. p. 423.

commission being signed on the 15th of July by Thomas Chittenden, president. The men were enlisted and their bounties paid within fifteen days. The colonels of the state militia were ordered to march half their regiments to Bennington, "without a moment's Loss of Time," and the fugitives, who since the invasion had been removing their families to the southward, were exhorted to return and assist in the defense of the State.[1]

Stark was collecting his men at Charlestown, and sending them forward to Warner at Manchester as rapidly as they could be supplied with kettles, rum, and bullets. There was great lack of all three of these essentials of a campaign, especially of the last, for there was but one pair of bullet-moulds in the town, and there were frequent and urgent calls for lead. When the lead was forthcoming, the one pair of moulds was kept hot and busy. But at last, on the 7th of August, Stark was at the mountain-walled hamlet of Manchester with 1,400 New Hampshire men and Green Mountain Boys, ready to follow wherever the brave old ranger should lead.

Schuyler was anxious to concentrate all the available troops in front of Burgoyne, to prevent his advance upon Albany, and urged Stark to join him with his mountaineers; but, considering the terms on which he had engaged, Stark felt under no obligations to put himself under the orders of a Continental officer, and had, moreover, opinions of his

[1] *Hartford Courant,* August 17, 1777.

own as to the most effective method of retarding
Burgoyne's advance, which he thought might best
be done by falling upon his rear when an opportunity offered. Therefore he declined to comply
with Schuyler's demands, though he assured him
he would lay aside all personal resentment when
it seemed opposed to the public good, and would
join him when it was deemed a positive necessity.
Schuyler's Dutch name, honored as it was by his
own good deeds and those of his ancestors, had a
smack of New York patroonism that was unpleas-
ant to New England men, especially those of the
Grants, and he was no favorite with any of them.
They were jubilant when he was superseded in
command of the Northern Department by the incompetent Gates, who accomplished nothing himself, but managed to repose serenely on the laurels
that others had gathered. Schuyler complained to
Congress of Stark's refusal, and that body censured
him and the New Hampshire government under
which he was acting.

General Lincoln was at Manchester, whither he
had come on August 2d, to take command of the
eastern militia. The force of the enemy, which for
some time had remained at Castleton, menacing
Manchester and all the country to the eastward,
had marched to join Burgoyne on the Hudson; and
Stark moved forward to Bennington with the purpose, now, of joining Schuyler. He was accompanied by Colonel Warner, who left his regiment
at Manchester under command of Lieutenant-Colonel Safford.

At the earnest request of the Council, already at Bennington, who apprehended an attack on that place, Stark encamped his brigade there and awaited the movements of the enemy. The Council was established at Captain Fay's[1] famous " Catamount Tavern," and during these fateful days sat in the low-browed room above whose wide fireplace was carved the words " Council Chamber." Here these faithful guardians of the young commonwealth consulted with Stark and Warner, and sent forth orders to colonels of militia and appeals to the valiant men of Berkshire.

Provisions were becoming scant in the army of Burgoyne, and he determined to seize for his use the stores which the Americans had collected at Bennington. To accomplish this, he dispatched Colonel Baum, a German officer of tried valor, with 300 dismounted dragoons who had won reputation on European fields, and whom it was a part of the plan of operations to provide with horses. There were also a body of marksmen under Captain Frazer, Colonel Peters's corps of Tories, some Canadian volunteers, and 100 Indians, — in all amounting to nearly 800 men, with two light field-pieces. Colonel Skene accompanied the German colonel, by request of Burgoyne, to give him the benefit of his knowledge of the country, and to use his influence in drawing the supposedly numerous Loyalists to the support of the British.

[1] This same Landlord Fay had five sons in Bennington battle, one of whom was killed.

Lieutenant-Colonel Breyman was ready to support Baum, if occasion required, with a veteran force of Brunswickers, 620 strong, with two more field-pieces.

On the 13th of August Baum set forth with his "mixed multitude," and on the same day reached Cambridge, sixteen miles from Bennington, and next day arrived at Sancoick, on a branch of the Walloomsac River.

Here a party of Americans was posted in a mill, which they abandoned on his approach. The Brunswickers had had a sharp taste of the quality of Yankee valor at Hubbardton, yet Baum held his present adversaries in supreme contempt, and expected no serious opposition from them. He wrote to Burgoyne, on the head of a barrel in the mill, that prisoners taken agreed there were fifteen to eighteen hundred men at Bennington, "but are supposed to leave on our approach."

Being first apprised of the appearance of a party of Indians at Cambridge, General Stark sent Lieutenant-Colonel Gregg with 200 men to oppose them, but he was presently informed that a more formidable force was closely following the Indians and tending towards Bennington, and he sent at once to Manchester for Colonel Warner's regiment and all the militia of the adjacent country to come to his support.

Early on the morning of the 14th he set forward with his brigade, accompanied by Colonels Warner, Williams, Herrick, and Brush, and after marching

about five miles met Gregg retreating from Sancoick, closely pursued by the enemy. Stark formed
his troops in line of battle, but Baum, perceiving
the strength of the Americans, halted his force in
a commanding position on a hill, and Stark fell
back a mile to a farm, where he encamped.

Baum's position was on the west side of the
Walloomsac, a branch of the Hoosic, nearly everywhere fordable. Most of his Germans were posted
on a wooded hill north of the road, which here
crossed the river. For the defense of the bridge,
a breastwork was thrown up and one of the field-
pieces placed in it, and two smaller breastworks on
opposite sides of the road were manned by Frazer's
marksmen. The Canadians were posted in some
log-huts standing on both sides of the stream, the
Tories under Pfister on a hill east of the stream
and south of the wood, while near their position
was the other field-piece manned by German gren-
adiers. A hill hid the hostile encampments from
each other, though they were scarcely two miles
apart.

That night rain began falling, increasing to such
a steady downpour as often marks the capricious
weather of dogdays. Some of the Berkshire militia had come up under Colonel Simonds, and among
them was Parson Allen of Pittsfield, who complained to Stark that the Berkshire people had
often been called out to no purpose, and would not
turn out again if not allowed to fight now. Stark
asked if he would have them fall to, while it was

dark as pitch and raining buckets. " Not just at this moment," the parson admitted. " Then," said the old warrior, " as soon as the Lord sends us sunshine, if I do not give you fighting enough, I 'll never ask you to come out again." All the next day the rain continued to pour down from the leaden sky. Baum employed the time in strengthening his position, keeping his men busy with axe and spade, piling higher and extending his works, in the drenching downfall. At the same time, Stark with his officers and the Council of Safety was planning an attack.

Next morning broke in splendor. Innumerable raindrops glittered on forest, grass-land, fields of corn, and ripening wheat; clouds of rising vapor were glorified in the level sunbeams that turned the turbid reaches of the swollen Walloomsac to a belt of gold. So quiet and peaceful was the scene that it seemed to Glich, a German officer who described it, as if there could be no enemy there to oppose them.

But the mountaineers were already astir. Three hundred under Nichols were making a wide circuit to the north of Baum's position, to attack his rear on the left; while Herrick with his rangers and Brush's militia made a similar movement to the rear of his right, and Hobart and Stickney with 300 of Stark's brigade were marching in the same direction. While these movements were in progress, Baum was diverted by a threatened attack in front.

At three in the afternoon Nichols had gained his desired position and began firing, quickly followed by Herrick, Stickney, and Hobart, while Stark assailed the Tory breastwork and the bridge with a portion of his brigade, the Berkshire and the Vermont militia. " Those redcoats are ours to-day, or Molly Stark's a widow!" he called to his mountaineers, and, following him, they dashed through the turbulent stream in pursuit of the scattering Tories and Canadians. The despised Yankee farmers, un-uniformed for the most part, wearing no badge but a cornhusk or a green twig in the hatband, fighting in their shirtsleeves, — for the sun poured down its scalding rays with intense fervor, — closed in on all sides and showered their well-aimed volleys upon the Brunswick veterans, who fought with intrepid but unavailing bravery.

The Indians fled in affright, stealing away in single file, thankful to get off with their own scalps and without plunder, for " the woods were full of Yankees," they said. Parson Allen, mounting a stump, exhorted the enemy to lay down their arms, but received only the spiteful response of musketry. Clambering down from his perch, he exchanged his Bible for a gun, and his gunpowder proved more effective than his exhortations.

The fire was furious, and every musket and rifle shot, every thunderous roar of the rapidly served cannon, was repeated in multitudinous echoes by the hills. For two hours the roar of the conflict was, said Stark, " like a continuous clap of thunder." He had been in the storm of fire that swept down Abercrombie's assaulting columns at Ticonderoga, had fought at Bunker Hill, Trenton, and Princeton, yet he declared that this fight was the hottest he had ever seen. Warner, who was in the thickest of it with him, well knew every foot of the ground they were fighting over, and the value of his aid and advice was generously acknowledged by Stark. The cannoneers were shot down and the guns taken; an ammunition wagon exploded and the assailing Yankees swarmed over the breastworks, charging with bayonetless guns upon the valiant Brunswickers, many of whom were killed, many taken prisoners, while a few escaped.

The victory of the Americans was complete, and when the prisoners had been sent to Bennington town under a sufficient guard, the militia dispersed over the blood-stained field in quest of spoil.

But they were soon brought together again by the alarm that another British force was coming up, and was only two miles away. The rattle of their drums and the screech of their fifes could be heard shaking and piercing the sultry air. It was Breyman's force of German veterans. Early in the fight, Baum had sent an express to hasten Breyman's advance, which had been delayed by the violent rain-storm of the preceding day, and the consequent wretched condition of the roads, now continuous wallows of mire; but they were close at hand, and the scattered militiamen were ill-prepared to oppose them. Fortunately, the rem-

nant of Warner's regiment, from Manchester, just
then came up, led by Lieutenant-Colonel Safford.
There were only 140 of them, but they were a
host in steadfast valor, and they took a position
in front, forming a rallying point for the militia
which now came hurrying in. The Americans fell
back slowly before Breyman, who advanced up the
road, firing his field-pieces with more noise than
effect, till a body of militia of sufficient strength to
make a stand was collected. Then the Germans
were attacked in front and flank, the deadliest fire
raining upon them from a wooded hill on their left.
The engagement was hotly maintained till after
sunset, when, having lost many men and his artillery horses, Breyman abandoned his cannon and
beat a precipitate retreat. Stark pushed the pursuit till it was impossible to aim a gun or distinguish friend from foe in the gathering gloom, and
then withdrew his men. In his official report he
said, " With one hour more of daylight, we should
have captured the whole body." As it was, Breyman escaped with less than 100 men.

The present fruits of the double victory were four
brass field-pieces, 1,000 stand of arms, four ammunition wagons, 250 sabres, and more than 650 prisoners. Among these were Baum and Pfister, both
of whom received mortal wounds and died a few
days later, and 207 were left dead on the field.

The American loss was 30 killed and 40 wounded.
Its more important results were the inspiriting
effect upon the whole country, and the depressing

influence of the defeat upon the enemy. Washington considered it decisive of the fate of Burgoyne, who four days later wrote a gloomy account to the British minister of his situation resulting from this disaster. He had lost faith in the Tories, and said, "The great bulk of the country is undoubtedly with the Congress. . . . Their measures are executed with a secrecy and dispatch that are not to be equaled. Wherever the King's forces point, militia to the amount of three or four thousand assemble in twenty-four hours. They bring with them their subsistence; the alarm over, they return to their farms. The Hampshire Grants in particular, a country unpeopled and almost unknown in the last war, now abounds in the most active and most rebellious race of the continent, and hangs like a gathering storm on my left."

Congress hastened to revoke its censure of the insubordinate New Hampshire colonel, and made him a brigadier of the army. In Stark's report of the battle to Gates he says: "Too much honor cannot be given to the brave officers and soldiers for gallant behavior; they fought through the midst of fire and smoke, mounted two breastworks that were well fortified and supported with cannon. I cannot particularize any officer, as they all behaved with the greatest spirit and bravery. Colonel Warner's superior skill in the action was of extraordinary service to me." He gave the "Honorable Council the honor of exerting themselves in the most spirited manner in that most critical time," and he presented that body " a Hessian gun with bayonet, a Brass Berriled Drum, a Grenadier's Cap, and a Hessian Broad Sword," to be kept in the Council Chamber as a " Memorial in Commemoration of the Glorious action fought at Walloomsaik, August 16, 1777, in which case the exertions of said Council was found to be Exceedingly Serviceable." [1] Two of the cannon taken from the Hessians stand in the vestibule of the capitol at Montpelier.

[1] Williams's *History of Vermont;* Hiland Hall's *History of Vermont;* Ira Allen's *History of Vermont; Account of Battle of Bennington,* by Glich; *Ibid.,* by Breyman; *Official Reports, Historical Soc. Coll.* vol. i.; *Centennial Exercises,* 1877.

CHAPTER XIII.

GENERAL LINCOLN determined to make a demonstration in Burgoyne's rear, and moved forward from Manchester to Pawlet. On the 13th of September he dispatched Colonel Brown [1] with Herrick's regiment and some militia to cross the lake, and take the outposts of Ticonderoga and the works on Lake George. Colonel Warner was ordered to move toward Mount Independence with a detachment of Massachusetts militia, and Colonel Woodbridge, with another detachment, was sent against Skenesborough and Fort Anne. Captain Ebenezer Allen, with a party of rangers, was to take Mount Defiance, and then rejoin Brown and Herrick to attack Ticonderoga together with Warner.

Brown crossed the lake in the night, and pushed over the mountain to the foot of Lake George, arriving there the day before the contemplated attack. Here he captured an armed sloop, 200 longboats, and several gunboats, with 293 soldiers and 100 American prisoners taken at Hubbardton.

[1] The same officer who so unaccountably failed Ethan Allen at Montreal. He was one of the first to plan the capture of Ticonderoga, an ardent patriot, and an officer of unquestioned bravery.

These were provided with arms just captured, and they took their places in the ranks of their compatriots. As the Americans moved forward in the darkness of the following evening, they were guided by three hoots of an owl, repeated at intervals from various points. This was the preconcerted signal of the sentinels, who so well simulated the mournful notes of the bird of night that the British sentries only wondered why so many were abroad, and the noiselessly moving troops sometimes thought the owls had conspired to lead them astray. Brown gained possession of Mount Hope and a block-house near the old French lines.

Captain Allen and his men scaled the steeps of Mount Defiance till a cliff was reached which they could not climb. Allen ordered one of his men to stoop, and, stepping on his back, got to the top, where only eight men could stand without being discovered by the enemy. His men swarmed after him "like a stream of hornets to the charge," he wrote, and all the garrison fled but one man, who attempted to discharge a cannon at the storming-party. "Kill the gunner, damn him!" shouted Allen, and the man fled, match in hand, with his comrades down the mountain road, and all were captured by Major Wait, posted at the foot to intercept them. Allen, who had never fired a cannon, now tried his hand and eye at this unaccustomed warfare, with good effect. He trained a piece of ordnance on a distant barrack and killed a man, then drove a ship from its moorings in the lake, and proclaimed himself commander of Mount Defiance.

Colonel Warner reached the neighborhood of Mount Independence early next morning.[1] Joining his force with Brown's, they demanded the surrender of Ticonderoga, but the comander, General Powel, declared his determination to defend it to the last. The Americans opened fire upon the fort, and for four days ineffectually hammered the walls with cannon-shot. It is not easy to understand why the position they had gained on Mount Defiance did not prove as advantageous to them as it had been to the British. They withdrew to the foot of Lake George, and then, embarking on the captured gunboats, attacked Diamond Island, where a quantity of stores was guarded by two companies of British regulars and several gunboats. The Americans were repulsed with some loss. They retreated to the east shore, where they burned their boats, and then crossed the mountains to Lake Champlain, and presently rejoined Lincoln at Pawlet.

Until the regular organization of the government of the State in the following March, the Council of Safety, in whom rested all the authority of the State, attended faithfully to the varied necessities that arose during those troubled times. It was diligent in forwarding to the generals of the army all information, received through scouts and spies, of the condition and movements of the enemy,

---

[1] Ira Allen, who never misses the chance of a fling at his brave kinsman, says, "He moved so extremely slow that he saved his own men, and hurt none of the enemy."

and always, by word and deed, was ready to aid
the common cause by every means in its power.
When General Gates urged reinforcements, his
letter was dispatched by expresses to all parts of
the State where men could be raised, and in response the recruits flocked in to swell the force
which was encircling the doomed army of Burgoyne.   September 24, President Chittenden wrote
Gates: "Several companies have passed this place
this Morning on their March to your assistance,"
and desired to be informed of any wants the council might relieve.

The British army was at Saratoga, ill-supplied
with provisions, and unable to advance or retreat.
Without hope of relief, on the 13th of October
Burgoyne made overtures to General Gates which
resulted on the 17th in the surrender of his entire
army, reduced since its departure from Canada to
less than 6,500 men, including more than 500 sick
and wounded.

When the news reached Ticonderoga, the troops
stationed there at once prepared to retreat to
Canada.   The barracks and houses there and at
Mount Independence were burned.   All the boats
not needed for the embarkation of the troops were
sunk with their cargoes, and the cannon spiked or
broken.   It was gloomy autumnal weather when,
in a few open boats, the garrison slunk back
through the "Gate of the Country."   The present
plight of the poor remnant of Burgoyne's splendid
army was a sorry contrast to the proud advance of

the gallant host that had passed these portals in the brightness of summer. No beat of drum nor strain of martial music now marked their passage, but in silent haste they pursued their way, in constant fear of attack whenever they approached the shores, that now were as sombre in their scant and faded leafage as the dreary November sky that overhung them.

The doughty and aggressive Captain Ebenezer Allen harassed their rear whenever opportunity was given for striking a blow. With a little force of fifty men of Herrick's Rangers, he took forty-nine prisoners, more than a hundred horses, twelve yokes of oxen, three boats, and a considerable quantity of stores.

Among the chattels taken by him were a slave woman, Dinah Mattis, and her child. Faithful to his convictions of the injustice of slavery, he set them free, having first obtained the consent of his Green Mountain Boys, among whom all captured property was to be divided.

Herrick's regiment was dismissed with the thanks of the council for " good services to this and the United States," and warm acknowledgment of its services from General Gates. Warner and his Continental regiment were on the Hudson with Gates's army, and Vermont was again without an armed force.

Ticonderoga, during the abortive planning of a Canadian invasion, was occupied for a time by a small garrison under Colonel Udney Hay. Otherwise the dismantled fortress remained for months in the desolation of ruin and desertion.

No longer menaced by the presence of the enemy, the inhabitants of Vermont, who had fled on Burgoyne's approach, returned to their homes, and made a late harvest of such crops as had not been destroyed, gathering, in almost winter weather, the scant remnants of their corn and hay.

The people who had been driven from their homes were so destitute of grain, both for food and for seed, that the council prohibited, under heavy penalties, the transportation of any wheat, rye, Indian corn, flour, or meal out of the State without a permit, excepting Continental stores.

Suffering privations that can now be scarcely understood, these people struggled through the long and bitter winter, never losing hope nor courage, though the gaunt wolf of hunger was often at their doors, and the future was as vague as the storm-veiled border of the encircling forest.

The Council of Safety was kept busily employed in providing for the defense of the frontier; in passing judgment upon Tories who were imprisoned, banished, or fined; in issuing orders for the disposal of their property, and permits to persons under suspicion to remain on their farms, or to visit certain points and return, — to some who had taken "the Oath of Fidellity," the liberty of the town, or a permit to pass to another place, they "to Behave as Becometh." "Comfort Canfield is permitted to go to Arlington to see his sick wife and return in thirty hours;" another is to go and "take care of his children and to return within six days;" Henry Batterman, a German soldier, is allowed to go to Colonel Simonds till further orders; Henry Bulls, who had joined the enemy in "Infamous Captain Samuel Adams's company," is permitted, on taking the oath of allegiance to the States of America, to pass to his farm in Manchester, there to remain, "he behaving as becometh a friend to his Country." There are orders to procure sides of leather from "Marshes Fratts;"[1] to transport "berrils of flour" to Colonel Herrick's regiment; to the Commissioners of Sequestration to seize the property of "Enimical Persons," and sell the same at vendue. Mary Reynolds is permitted to send for her "Gray horse and keep him till further orders." The wives of Captain Adams and Captain Sherwood are allowed to pass to their husbands at Ticonderoga, "necessary clothing and beds" allowed. Captain Nathan Smith is to "march to Pawlet on horseback with the men under his command and there receive a horse Load of Flours to Each man and horse;" and Captain Wood is ordered to take charge of the same, and "without one minute's loss of time" proceed to Pawlet and thence to Colonel Warner. When he returns he is to take "especial Care that the Horses and Bags be returned to their proper owners." It appears that two of the men did not return the horses, and were apprehended for horse-stealing, and were sentenced by

[1] Vats.

the council to be made a public example of, "to Deter people from such vicious practices," each to receive thirty-nine lashes on the naked back, at the liberty pole. This sentence was revoked and a fine substituted upon their making restitution. Five teams are dispatched to bring off the plunder secured by Colonel Brown. Colonel Herrick receives the thanks of the council for his spirited behavior in "his late noble enterprise," and in the same letter is informed there are thirty pairs of shoes ready for him at Shaftsbury. One order directs Benjamin Fassett to repair to Pownal, and bring from some of the Tories who had gone to the enemy, or otherwise proved themselves enemies of the country, "a Load of Saus for the use of the Hundred prisoners" at Bennington. He is "to leave sufficient for their families," and it appears that the Tories were generally treated with quite as much leniency as they deserved. Among the many curious orders is one issued in January, 1778, on application of General Stark to Captain Samuel Robinson, Overseer of Tories, "to detail ten effective men under proper officers, to march in Two Distinct files from this place through the Green Mountains to Col. Wm. Williams Dwelling-house in Draper Alias Wilmington within this State who are to March & Tread the Snow in s^d Road to suitable width for a Sleigh or Sleighs with a Span of Horses on Each Sleigh, and order them to return Marching in the Same manner to this place with all convenient Speed." [1]

[1] *Governor and Council,* by E. P. Walton.

A midwinter invasion of Canada was contemplated by Gates, to be commanded by General Lafayette. The Vermont Council of Safety took active measures to raise 300 men for this expedition, or one to act in conjunction with it under General Stark. A bounty or " encouragement " of ten dollars was offered to each man enlisting to serve till the last day of April following unless sooner discharged. Colonel Herrick was to command the force, and the officers were to be from those who had served in his regiment of Rangers. The council also engaged to furnish twenty-five sleighs for the use of the expedition, and to afford every assistance in its power in " Collecting Hay, Provisions and Transporting Flour." But while the unrecognized State of Vermont responded so promptly to the call, the project fell through for lack of men. Not more than 1,200 could be collected, most of whom were poorly clad and as poorly armed.

When the news of its abandonment was received by the council, orders were issued to stop enlistments; yet those already engaged were requested to " Take a Short Tour for the defense of the frontiers; " and almost the last act of the council was to instruct Captain Ebenezer Allen " to take post with such recruits at New Haven Fort,[1] to keep out proper Scouts to reconoitre the woods, to watch the movement of the enemy and Report them to this Council or officer Commanding the Troops in the Northern Department."

[1] The block-house built by Ethan Allen at the lower falls on Otter Creek in 1773.

On the 12th of March, 1778, while the Council of Safety was holding its last session, a brave little band of Green Mountain Boys was defending a block-house in Shelburne against the attack of a party of Indians commanded by a British captain named Larama. There were but sixteen of the Vermonters, including their captain, Thomas Sawyer, and Moses Pierson, to protect whose possessions here they had marched ninety miles through the wintry wilderness, while their assailants numbered fifty-seven. The block-house was set on fire by the enemy, but Lieutenant Barnabas Barnum went outside and extinguished the flames, though the daring act cost him his life. One of the defenders, who was struck in the arm by a ball, was so exasperated by the hurt that, when he had bound up the wound with a handkerchief and again taken his place at a loophole, he would at every discharge of his gun give it a spiteful push, as if to accelerate the speed of the ball, while he roared, " Take that for my arm ! " After a hot fight of two hours, the enemy retreated, were pursued, and two of them captured. Twelve were killed, among whom were the British captain and an Indian chief ; and three of the Vermonters fell in the gallant defense.

CHAPTER XIV.

THE UNIONS.

Owing to the continual disturbance and partial depopulation of the State caused by the presence of the enemy, the election of state officers was deferred by a convention in December till the 12th of March, 1778. It was held on that day, and the government took regular form under the Constitution.

Thomas Chittenden, who had for some time been prominent in the political affairs of the forming commonwealth, was elected governor. He was born in Guilford, Conn., in 1730. In early manhood he began pioneer life in Salisbury, Conn., where he lived twenty-six years, prosperous, and a man of consequence in the town. Then the pioneer spirit, that lusty begetter of new states, again laid hold of him, and he purchased a tract in the wilderness lying upon the fertile borders of the Winooski, in the town of Williston. In 1774 he took his family to this wild region, but was scarcely established when the retreat of the American army from Canada left the northern settlers exposed to the enemy, and they retired to the southern part of the Grants. Living at times in Danby, Pownal,

and Arlington, Chittenden remained till 1787, when
he returned to Williston. He had not long been
an inhabitant of the Grants when he naturally took
his place among the leading men of the district.
He was one of the committee that drafted the Vermont Declaration of Independence, and of the one
that framed the government, and was president of
that Council of Safety which exercised all the
powers of the government until it was constitutionally organized, when he was elected governor, in
which office, with the exception of one year, he was
continued for eighteen years. His educational advantages had been slight, but he was possessed of
a natural sagacity which enabled him to penetrate
the character and designs of others, and to per-
ceive, without the process of reasoning, the best
course to pursue in any emergency. He was a
masterful man, yet carried his points without appearing to force them, and seemed to fall into the
ways of others while in fact he led them imper-
ceptibly into his own. His calm, strong features
expressed the kindness of heart that his acts were
full of, such as refusing to sell for cash the abundant yield of his acres, but reserving it for the
relief of the people in a foreseen time of need.
Among the people with whom he had cast his lot,
his lack of polished manners was no discredit.
Hearty friendship was a better key to their affec-
tions, and his tall, athletic figure commended him
to the favor of the stalwart Green Mountain Boys.[1]

[1] They were so proud of their stature, it was sometimes re-

Governor Chittenden was eminently fitted for the times upon which he fell, and for the place to which he was appointed, and he wisely guided the young State through its turbulent infancy.

The first legislature met at Windsor in March, 1778, when a new trouble arose. Sixteen towns east of Connecticut River applied for admission to the new State of Vermont, on the frivolous plea that as New Hampshire, under the original grant to John Mason, extended only sixty miles inland from the sea, and its extension to the westward of this line had been made by royal commissions to the governor of that province, the royal authority being now overthrown, the people of the region were at liberty to elect what jurisdiction they would be under; but, as afterward became evident, the real object was to establish the seat of government on the Connecticut River. At first there was little disposition to accede to this petition, but it was also warmly urged by some of the Vermont river towns, that threatened in case of refusal to unite with the New Hampshire towns in establishing a new State. Whereupon the legislature submitted the subject to the consideration of the people, who should instruct their representatives how to act upon it at the adjourned session of the assembly to be held at Bennington in June.

corded on their tombstones. The epitaph of Benjamin Carpenter, one of the founders of the State, sets forth that "He left this world and 146 persons of lineal posterity, March 29, 1804, aged 78 yrs. 10 mos. 12 days, with a strong mind and full faith of a more glorious hereafter. Stature about six feet, weight 200. Death had no terror."

A few days before this session, Ethan Allen arrived at Bennington, his once burly form gaunt and worn by the cruel captivity from which he had just been released, but his bold spirit as robust as ever. The people thronged into the little hamlet to greet their old leader, and, though powder was scarce and precious, the rusty old cannon that had been brought from Hoosic Fort years before to repel the rumored invasion of Governor Tryon, was roundly charged, and thundered forth a welcoming salute of thirteen guns for the United States, and one for young Vermont. In response to a letter from Washington, commending Allen's unabated zeal in the cause of his country, Congress conferred upon him a brevet commission of colonel. But he appears to have thought his services more needed by his State than by the country, for he found the land speculators of New York as rapacious under the republican Governor Clinton as they were under the royal governors; and, after his return, he took no active part in the military operations of the United States. He was made brigadier-general of the militia of Vermont, a position that he held till 1780, when, being accused of traitorous correspondence with the enemy, he indignantly resigned it, at the same time declaring his willingness to render the State any service within his power, a promise he faithfully fulfilled during the few remaining years of his eventful life.

In the time afforded by the adjournment of the

assembly, the friends of the proposed union managed to secure a majority of the legislature, and when it met at Bennington thirty-seven of the forty-nine towns represented were found in favor of the union. An act was passed authorizing the sixteen towns to elect members to the assembly, and it was resolved that other towns might be similarly admitted.

New Hampshire protested to Governor Chittenden against the union, and instructed her delegates in Congress to seek the aid of that body in opposing it. At the same time Vermont sent Ethan Allen to Congress to learn its views concerning the union. He reported the proceeding was regarded with such disapprobation that, if Vermont did not at once recede, the whole power of Congress would be exerted to annihilate her, and establish the rights of New Hampshire.

Thus Vermont became aware that she had not only incurred the enmity of the New Hampshire government, until now so friendly that it tacitly acknowledged the independence of the young State, but had also strengthened the unfavorable feeling of Congress toward her. If the wily politicians of New York had intrigued to accomplish these ends, they could hardly have devised a more successful method. The action of the succeeding legislature was unfriendly to the union, and in February, 1779, it was finally dissolved.

As all the Continental troops were withdrawn from Vermont, and as the State was unable of itself to maintain a force sufficient to guard its extended frontier, the frontier line was established at Pittsford, and Castleton, where Forts Warren and Vengeance were held by small garrisons. Fort Ranger at Rutland was more strongly garrisoned, and made the headquarters of the state forces, and the inhabitants to the northward on Otter Creek were directed to come within this frontier line. When a captain of militia was called upon to furnish a certain number of men for guarding the frontier or for other duty, it was provided by law that he should divide his company into as many classes as there were men required. Each class was obliged to furnish one man ; and if it failed to do so, the captain was empowered to hire one, and each member of the class was obliged to bear his proportion of the expense. This method met with general approval, but in the southeast part of the State there were many malcontents, always unfriendly to the government of Vermont. They were in constant correspondence with Governor Clinton, who urged them to maintain a "firm and prudent resistance to the draughting of men, the raising of taxes, and the exercise of any acts of government under the ideal Vermont State." He issued commissions for the formation of a regiment, in which about 500 men were enlisted.

In response to a request from General James Clinton, commanding the Northern Department, the Board of War[1] ordered a levy of men "for

[1] The governor and council.

service of the State and the United States in guarding the frontier." Writing to General Washington concerning this levy, Governor Chittenden calls his attention to the destitute condition of the families of the soldiers. In consequence of the late encroachments of the enemy, they had been unable to harvest the crops already grown, or to sow the " Winter Grain on which they have ever had their Greatest dependence since the first settlement of this part of the Country. They are therefore principally reduced to an Indian Cake in Scant proportion to the number of their Families, & by the destruction of their Sheep by the Enemy, their loss of them otherwise as well as their flax, their backs & their bellies have become Co Sufferers. In this deplorable situation," he continues, " they remain firm and unshaken, and ready on the Shortest Notice to face their inveterate foe Undaunted ; " but considering their circumstances, he hopes they may not be kept in service during the summer.

In compliance with the order of the Board of War, the captain of a company in Putney divided his men into classes, in one of which was comprised Captain James Clay and two others, all known to be active partisans of New York. They refused to furnish their man, or the sum required to pay the man obtained to represent them. Upon this the sergeant of the company, having the proper warrant, seized two cows belonging to these persons, and posted them for sale. On the day of sale, a hundred of the adherents of New York, under the lead of their colonel, rescued the cattle, and returned them to their owners. The colonel soon learned that news of the affair had gone to the council at Arlington, and apprehended that Ethan Allen and his Green Mountain Boys might be sent to enforce the authority of the State, and he wrote to Governor Clinton for advice and aid. The governor gave the one, and made promises of the other, but never fulfilled them. Indeed, it would have been very difficult to raise a military force for that purpose among the inhabitants of the New York border, who were more in sympathy with the people of Vermont than with their own aristocratic government. The men who refused to submit to the rule of Vermont had not been called on by New York to render any military service, nor to pay for any. If they were exempted from service under Vermont, they would contribute nothing to the common cause, and their exemption would encourage all who wished to escape these burdens to join the opponents of Vermont, thus weakening it and the whole country. Vermont acted promptly in the matter. Ethan Allen was ordered to raise 100 men in Bennington County, and march to the county of Cumberland, there to join his force with the militia of that county under Colonel Fletcher, and assist the sheriff in enforcing the law. The order was duly executed. Most of the leaders of the opposition to Vermont in the county, and the principal officers of the New York regiment, were arrested, taken to Westminster, where the court was in session, and tried as rioters. Most of them were fined, and upon payment of the fines, which were light, and satisfying the costs, were soon discharged.

Complaint was, of course, made to Governor Clinton, and he in turned complained to Congress; and while New York was pressing upon that body its grievances, and its claims to the Grants, New Hampshire presented a counter-claim to the same region. Congress appointed a committee of five to visit the district, to confer with the people and learn their reasons for refusing to submit to the claiming States, and to promote an amicable adjustment of the dispute. Only two of the committee visited Vermont, and though they conferred with Governor Chittenden, and exerted themselves to bring about a reconciliation, their report to Congress was not acted upon, as they did not constitute a quorum of the committee.

Massachusetts now set up a claim to the southern portion of Vermont, founded on an ancient grant of the Plymouth Company. Congress urged the three contesting States to submit the matter to itself for adjustment, though Vermont, whose very life was at stake, was to have a hearing, but no voice in the settlement of the difficulty. Its unacknowledged government was enjoined to make no more grants of unoccupied lands, and to exercise no authority over those inhabitants who did not recognize it, while it patiently and silently awaited such dismemberment of its territory as Congress should decree. New Hampshire and New York promptly passed acts submitting the matter to Congress, but Massachusetts failed to take such action.

Vermont refused to submit to the jurisdiction of the three claiming States, and to an arbitrament that ignored her existence, but resolved to " Support their right to independence at Congress and to all the world," and to make grants of her unappropriated lands.

By direction of the governor and council, two pamphlets, strongly setting forth the right of Vermont to independence, were prepared and sent to leading men of the country, to generals of the army, and members of Congress. One was Ethan Allen's "Vindication of the Opposition of the Inhabitants of Vermont to the Government of New York, and their right to Form an Independent State." The other was " Vermont's Appeal to the Candid and Impartial World," by Stephen R. Bradley, in which it is vigorously stated that Vermont could not submit to a plan believed to be started by neighboring States ; that Congress had no right to meddle with the internal government of Vermont ; that the State existed independent of any of the thirteen United States, and was not accountable to them for liberty, the gift of God ; that it was not represented in Congress, and could not submit to resolutions passed without its consent or knowledge when all of value to it was at stake ; that it was and ever had been ready to share the burdens of the war, but after four years of war with Great Britain, in which it had expended so much blood and treasure, "it was not so lost to all sense and honor as to now give up everything worth fighting for, the right of making their own laws and choosing their own form of government, to the arbitrament and determination of any man or body of men under heaven."

Ira Allen was sent to the legislatures of New Jersey, Pennsylvania, Delaware, and Maryland to interest them in favor of Vermont.

Though Congress in September, 1779, had resolved to hear and determine the dispute in the following February, when the time arrived this business was postponed, and so on various pretexts it was for a long time deferred. In fact, Congress did not dare to take a decided step concerning it in any direction, fearing that by the one it might incur the enmity of the claiming States, that by the other it might force the warlike Green Mountain Boys into armed opposition to its authority. To lose the support of the first, or to be obliged to spend the strength that could ill be spared to subdue the latter, would alike be ruinous to the common cause.

There is reason to believe that about this time a plot was brewing by New York and New Hampshire to divide the bone of contention when Congress should decide in favor of the first, as was confidently expected it would. The line of the Green Mountains was to be the boundary between these States ; but the plan fell through in the New York Assembly, where Mr. Townshend opposed it in behalf of those adherents of New York living east of the proposed line, who would thereby be placed beyond the limits of their chosen government.

On the 2d of June Congress resolved that the acts of " the people of the Grants were highly unwarrantable, and subversive of the peace and welfare of the United States, and that they be strictly required to forbear from any acts of authority over those of the people who professed allegiance to other States.

In reply to these resolutions, Vermont declared that they were subversive of her rights, and incompatible with the principles on which Congress grounded the right of the United States to independence, and tended to endanger the liberties of America; that Vermont as an independent State denied the authority of Congress to judge of her jurisdiction, and boldly declared that, as she was refused a place among the United States, she was at liberty, if necessitated, to offer or accept terms of a cessation of hostilities with Great Britain, with whom she had no motive to continue hostilities and maintain an important frontier for the benefit of the United States, if she were not to be one of them, but only to be divided between her covetous neighbors. Thus was foreshadowed the policy which Vermont was soon forced to adopt for her own preservation. The declaration closed with saying that, " from a principle of virtue, and a close attachment, to the cause of liberty, she was induced once more to offer union with the United States of America."

In September some attempt was made in Congress to decide the contest. New Hampshire and New York presented their claims, denying the right of Vermont to independence. Ira Allen and Stephen R. Bradley were present as agents of Vermont, but were not treated by Congress as representatives of a State, or of a people invested with legislative authority. They were permitted to attend Congress on the hearing of the question, and protested against the manner of investigation which gave Vermont no hearing as a State. They declared her readiness to submit this dispute to the legislatures of one or more disinterested States, but protested Congress had no right to determine it by virtue of authority derived from the acts of one or more States who were but one party in the controversy. Congress heard the evidence of both New York and New Hampshire, and again postponed consideration of the troublesome question.

But the action of Congress did not discourage or intimidate the young commonwealth. She now assumed as aggressive an attitude as her neighbors had borne towards her. Reaching to the eastward, she again drew to herself that portion of New Hampshire whose people still desired the union which Vermont on the disapproval of Congress had dissolved. Then she stretched forth a welcoming hand to the people of that part of New York lying east of the Hudson, who, left defenseless by their own government, desired the better protection afforded by that of Vermont. This bold grasp on the territory of New Hampshire and New York enlarged her own to twice the extent Vermont had originally claimed, and correspondingly increased her importance.

Furthermore, with supreme disregard of the injunctions of Congress, Vermont was strengthening her position by the disposal of her unappropriated lands to the citizens of other States, who thus became interested in the establishment of her independence.

Her importance was also augmented by the negotiations which she was now known to be conducting with General Haldimand, lieutenant-governor of the Province of Quebec. Although the object of these secret negotiations was not known to any but the parties engaged in them, Congress and the country were greatly alarmed by fears of the possible result. A succinct account of this correspondence is given in the following chapter.

CHAPTER XV.

THE English government having determined to attempt making terms with the Americans, commissioners were appointed for that purpose, and arrived in America in June, 1778. They addressed a letter to the president of Congress, inclosing their commission from the crown. Their propositions were objected to by Congress, on the ground that they were founded on dependence, which was utterly inadmissible. Congress was inclined to peace, but it could only be treated for upon an acknowledgment of the independence of the States, or the withdrawal of the king's fleets and armies.

The commissioners were empowered to treat with such bodies politic or corporate, assemblies of men, person or persons, as they should think meet and sufficient for the purpose of considering the grievances supposed to exist in the government of any of the colonies respectively; to order and proclaim a cessation of hostilities on the part of the king's forces, as they should think fit; and also to appoint governors of provinces. These powers were to be transferred to Sir Henry Clinton in case Sir William Howe, one of the commissioners, should be disabled from exercising them. This did occur, and Sir Henry Clinton acted as a peace commissioner for a time beyond the limitation of the first commission, which was June, 1779.

Having failed with Congress, the commissioners appealed to the public in a manifesto offering to the colonies at large or separately a general or separate peace, with the revival of their ancient governments, secured against any future infringement, and protected forever from taxation by Great Britain.

The geographical situation of Vermont, bordering on the great thoroughfare from Canada southward, her controversy with the neighboring colonies, and the unfriendly attitude of Congress toward her, especially invited the overtures of the British agents.

In March, 1779, Lord George Germaine, Secretary of Colonial Affairs, wrote to General Haldimand: "The minister says, the separation of the Inhabitants of the country they style Vermont from the Provinces in which it was formerly included is a Circumstance from which much advantage might be derived, and sees no objection to giving them reason to expect, the King will erect their country into a Province."

The first overture was made, under the direction of Sir Henry Clinton, by Colonel Beverly Robinson, afterward engaged in the plot with Arnold. In March, 1780, he wrote to Ethan Allen, to whom the letter was delivered in July in the streets of Arlington by a British soldier disguised as a Yankee farmer. Robinson began by saying that he had been informed that Allen and most of the inhabitants of Vermont were opposed to the wild and chimerical schemes of the Americans in attempting to separate the continent from Great Britain, and that they would willingly assist in uniting America again to the mother country. He invited Allen to communicate freely whatever proposals he wished to make, and thought that upon his taking an active part, and embodying the inhabitants of Vermont in favor of the crown, they might obtain a separate government under the king, and the men be formed into regiments under such officers as Allen should recommend.

Allen at once laid the letter before Governor Chittenden and a few of the leading men, who all agreed that it was best to return no answer.

In September following, Governor Chittenden wrote to General Haldimand asking a cartel for the exchange of some prisoners who had been captured in the spring by scouting parties from Canada. In October a large British force came up the lake to Crown Point, and the commander, Major Carleton, brought an answer to Chittenden's letter, and wrote to Ethan Allen, commanding the Vermont troops, acquainting him that he had appointed Captain Sherwood to treat with him and Governor Chittenden on the subject of an exchange; also that no hostilities should be committed by the British on posts or scouts within the boundaries of Vermont during the negotiations, while Allen would be expected to observe the same, " and recall his scouts to prevent the appearance of not adhering to the above."

Allen asked that the cessation of hostilities might be extended to the northern posts and frontiers of New York, to which, after some demur, Carleton finally agreed. The Vermont militia returned to their homes, much to the surprise of the New York militia serving on their borders, and the British retired to winter quarters in Canada without making any hostile demonstration against Vermont.

Ira Allen and Joseph Fay were appointed on the part of Vermont to confer with the British commissioners, Captain Sherwood and Dr. Smyth, both Tories, on the subject of a cartel, and all proceeded together from Crown Point toward Canada. An early winter was coming on; and as they made their way down the lake, its waters were steaming like a cauldron, and lofty columns of vapor swept past the boats like an army of gigantic spectres. The passage of the boats was soon opposed by a more material obstacle in the rapidly forming ice, and as the men were breaking the way through this, Ira Allen says, "much political conversation and exhibit of papers took place." After some days of battling with the ice, the Vermont commissioners abandoned the struggle and went home, promising that they or other commissioners should visit Canada as soon as possible.

This Dr. Jonas Fay undertook in the winter, and went as far as Split Rock, where he found the ice still an enemy, now refusing to bear him further, and he was obliged to abandon the journey.

On the 23d of February, 1781, Ethan Allen received a second letter from Beverly Robinson, inclosing a copy of the first, which he feared had miscarried. He now confidently assured Allen that the terms mentioned in the first letter might be obtained, provided he and the people of Vermont took an active part with Great Britain. Allen returned no answer, but transmitted both letters, with one from himself, to Congress. His letter closed with bold and characteristic words : "I am confident that Congress will not dispute my sincere attachment to the cause of my country, though, I do not hesitate to say, I am fully grounded in opinion that Vermont has an indubitable right to agree on terms of cessation of hostilities with Great Britain, provided the United States persist in rejecting her application for a union with them ; for Vermont, of all people, would be most miserable were she obliged to defend the independence of the United claiming States, and they at the same time at full liberty to overturn and ruin the independence of Vermont. I am persuaded, when Congress considers the circumstances of this State, they will be more surprised that I have transmitted them the inclosed letters than that I have kept them in custody so long, for I am as resolutely determined to defend the inde-

pendence of Vermont as Congress are that of the
United States, and rather than fail will retire with
hardy Green Mountain Boys into the desolate cav-
erns of the mountains, and wage war with human
nature at large."

On the 1st of May, which being his birthday
he deemed propitious, Ira Allen, as sole commissioner, set forth for Isle aux Noix in considerable state, being attended by a guard consisting of
a lieutenant, two sergeants, and sixteen privates.
Afterward, when the British were again in force
upon the lake, General Haldimand objected to the
agents of Vermont being attended by so large a
retinue, and forbade more than five persons being
received. Allen was treated with great politeness
by the commander, Major Dundas, who was empowered to act only in the exchange of prisoners.
On the second day, as Sherwood and Allen were
walking in the gray of the soft spring morning
beneath the wide ramage of the nut-trees that gave
the island its name, the Tory captain informed
the handsome young colonel that he and Dr.
Smyth were to settle the armistice with him, and
concert measures to establish Vermont as a royal
colony. For his better opportunities of conducting them, the negotiations with Vermont had been
committed to General Haldimand's management,
and he had given his instructions to Sherwood
and Smyth on the 20th of the preceding December. These instructions authorized " positive assurances that their country will be erected into a

separate province, independent and unconnected with every government in America, and will be entitled to every prerogative and immunity which is promised to other provinces in the proclamation of the King's commissioners." It was proposed to raise two Vermont battalions of ten companies each, of which Haldimand should be colonel, but all other officers should be Vermonters, and entitled to half pay. The instructions still further state, "I am so much convinced of the present infatuation of these people, . . . I agree that this negotiation should cease, and any step that leads to it be forgotten, provided the Congress shall grant the State of Vermont a seat in their assembly, and acknowledge its independency." Sherwood said the reception of the British overtures during the ice-bound voyage on the lake was such that they had great hope of success. This hope it was the policy of Vermont to encourage, in order to secure the safety of the people, since all the Continental troops had been ordered out of the State, the New York troops withdrawn from Skenesborough, and Vermont had no adequate force wherewith to oppose the British force of 7,000 men in Canada. Thus abandoned, as it appeared to them designedly, that they might be forced into submission to New York, the leaders saw no hope of safety for the State but in an adroit management, to their own advantage, of these attempts of the British.

In his interviews with the commissioners, Allen was non-commital, and "very cautious and intri-

cate," as they reported. He would make no proposals, nor talk of anything beyond the neutrality
of Vermont during the war, at the close of which
it must, as a separate government, be subject to the
ruling power, if that power would give the State a
free charter.

A cartel for the exchange of prisoners was arranged, and a verbal agreement made that hostilities should cease between the British forces and
those of Vermont until after the session of the
legislature of the State, and longer " if prospects
were satisfactory to the commander-in-chief." After seventeen days the present negotiations ended,
and, with expressions of his satisfaction with the
treatment he had received, Allen departed with
his attendants, voyaging homeward past green for-
ested shores, above which, far to the eastward, the
Crouching Lion, hoary with yet unmelted snows,
reared his majestic front, as if guarding the beloved
land of the Green Mountain Boys.

In compliance with a request of the assembly,
Ira Allen appeared before them in June, and gave
a report of his mission to Canada to arrange a cartel, in which he had happily succeeded. He also
stated that he had " discovered among the British
officers a fervent wish for peace," but disclosed
nothing concerning the overtures made to him.[1]
These were then known to but ten persons, and

---

[1] A British spy who was in Bennington at the time gave a report of the proceedings rather unfavorable to the success of the
British cause.

were never disclosed to but few. That all might share alike the dangers and responsibilities of these negotiations, a paper giving approval of Colonel Ira Allen's policy by feigning or endeavoring to make them believe that the State of Vermont had a desire to negotiate a treaty of peace with Great Britain, and stating it " to be a necessary political manœuvre to save the frontiers of this State," was signed by Jonas Fay, Samuel Safford, Samuel Robinson, Joseph Fay, Thomas Chittenden, Moses Robinson, Timothy Brownson, and John Fassett, eight of the most ardent patriots of the State, who then and ever afterwards enjoyed the full confidence of the people. In the exposed and dangerous condition of the State, they deemed it justifiable to resort to stratagem, always practiced in war to ward off the blows of an enemy.

In July, Major Fay was sent to the enemy on Lake Champlain, to complete the exchange of prisoners, and was received on board the Royal George. The British found him as unprepared as Colonel Allen had been to close with the proffered terms, but wishing to continue the negotiations till November. The British agents suspected that the Vermonters were procrastinating to save themselves from an invasion by king or Congress. " Upon the whole," they said, " it appears to us that interest, not loyalty, induces the leading men of Vermont to unite with Canada. One fifth of the people wish it from the same motive, near another fifth from principles of loyalty, and the remainder are mad rebels."

Yet the hope of drawing such a rebellious people to the king's cause was not abandoned, and the correspondence continued.

Emissaries from Canada came now and then to Ethan Allen and his brother Ira. Unmolested if not undiscovered, they made their stealthy journeys between Canada and the Vermont settlements. Gliding in light canoes along the lake in the shadow of cedar-clad shores, up the solitude of wooded streams where only the silent flight of the disturbed heron heralded their approach, and stealing along the byways of almost forgotten Indian trails, they found at last safe hiding during their brief tarries, delivered in the dusk their precious packets, received others, and then returned by the ways they had come.

In July, Ira Allen wrote to General Haldimand that he and two others had been appointed agents to Congress, with full powers to make and receive proposals for articles of union between the United States and Vermont. "It is expected that the said agents will make proposals to Congress that will not be accepted, and show that Congress means nothing more than to keep this State in suspense till the end of the war, and then divide the territory among the claiming States." Yet when, soon afterward, Allen was acting as agent to Congress, he so far yielded the claim of Vermont to her east and west unions that the boundaries proposed by him through a member from Connecticut were at once accepted by Congress, though afterward rejected by Vermont on the ground that the proposals had not

been officially made by her agents. This shows
that his real preferences were not such as he would
lead Haldimand to believe.

A letter from Lord George Germaine to Sir
Henry Clinton, which had been intercepted by the
French and taken to Paris, was received by Congress, to whom it had been sent by Dr. Franklin.
" The return of the people of Vermont to their allegiance," it said, " is an event of the utmost importance to the king's affairs, and at this time, if
the French and Washington really meditate an irruption into Canada, may be considered as opposing an insurmountable bar to the attempt. General Haldimand, who has the same instructions with
you to draw over those people and give them support, will, I doubt not, push up a body of troops
to act in conjunction with them to secure all the
avenues through their country to Canada." This
letter had an immediate effect upon the action of
Congress, for a committee was at once appointed
by that body to confer with persons to be appointed
by the people of the Grants, who should have full
power to agree upon and ratify terms and articles
of union and confederation with the United States
of America.

Ira Allen, who with Jonas Fay and Bezaleel
Woodward had in June been appointed agents to
Congress, and were now on their way to Philadelphia, says : " This information had greater influence
on the wisdom and virtue of Congress than all the
exertions of Vermont in taking Ticonderoga, Crown

Point, and the two divisions from General Burgoyne's army, or their petition to be admitted as a State in the general confederation, and offers to pay their proportion of the expenses of the war."

In September, 1781, there were further negotiations at Skenesborough between the British commissioners and Colonel Allen and Major Joseph Fay, acting for Vermont. The plan of government for Vermont was considered, and it was agreed it should be essentially the same as that established by her Constitution, excepting the governor should be appointed by the king in council.

The commissioners proposed to make prisoners of several persons in Vermont who were most opposed to the negotiations, and insisted that Vermont should declare itself a British colony, and proposed an expedition against Albany. By uniting with the British troops, they said, the Vermonters would be able to defend themselves against the other States, and declared that something effectual must be determined on before they parted, or the armistice must cease, for the commander-in-chief would not lose this campaign by inactivity.

The agents of Vermont would not consent to the first proposal, which would make active enemies of those who should be conciliated. Against the others they set forth the extent of the frontier of Vermont, which it would be impossible for the king's troops to defend in winter, when, unsupported by them, their friends in Vermont would be overpowered ; that there were many zealous

Whigs among the inhabitants who might better be conciliated than openly opposed; that, by continuing the truce, other unions than those already existing might be established; and that, by the pursuit of the present policy, better results might be attained by the British than by those proposed by the commissioners. The commissioners took down in writing the heads of these objections, and then suggested an instruction, which they could not deviate from without putting an end to the armistice, which was, that General Haldimand should, in pursuance of full powers vested in him by his Majesty in council, issue a proclamation offering to confirm Vermont as a colony under the crown; that an army should come up the lake in October with said proclamations and distribute them while the legislature was in session, which must accept them, and with the British take measures for common defense. The agents strengthened their previous arguments by saying that, considering the climate and bad roads, and the absence of all necessary preparations, the season was too far advanced for such operations; that one winter would have great effect in changing the minds of the people for a new order of things. But if, in spite of these reasons, the general should still insist on such a proclamation, they trusted that he would learn the temper of the people before issuing it. With this understanding they consented to the proclamation rather than break the armistice.

Small chance was there of the acceptance of such

a proclamation by a legislature chosen from a people three fifths of whom were known to be "mad rebels," to cure whose madness it does not appear that any attempt had been made by the men who on the part of Vermont were conducting these negotiations. The conference now ended, and the agents departed, leaving the British commissioners very hopeful of success.

In October, while the legislature was in session at Charlestown, in the eastern union, General St. Leger came up the lake to Ticonderoga with a force so large that the narrow channel was black with the swarming armament. About the 25th a small scouting party, sent out for appearance' sake by the commander of the Vermont troops, General Enos,[1] who was in the secret of the negotiations, was fired upon while watching the movements of the British, and the leader, Sergeant Tupper, was killed. His body was buried with military honors, and his clothes, with an open letter expressing regret for his death, were sent by St. Leger to General Enos at Castleton. These being publicly delivered, considerable stir was caused among the troops, and no less in Charlestown when the news arrived there by a messenger bearing letters from General Enos to Governor Chittenden. These letters related as well to the private negotiations with the British as to public affairs; and while the governor, sitting with others in a public room, was acquainting himself

---

[1] When Ethan Allen resigned, General Enos was appointed in his place.

with their contents, Major Reynolds, commanding New Hampshire troops there, came in and demanded of Colonel Allen why a British general should be sorry for the death of an enemy. Allen answered that he did not know, unless that good men were sorry when good men were killed. Angry words ensued ; and while the spectators were agog to hear the quarrel, copies of the letters were made, excluding all that pertained to the negotiations. These were publicly read in place of the original letters, and the people were quieted. Ira Allen wrote to the commissioners, now with General St. Leger, reporting rumors of Cornwallis's surrender, which, whether true or not, had the same effect on the people, and advised that in the present situation the proclamation would best be withheld for a while. He also sent a list of the members of the new legislature, representing that the changes were favorable to the success of the negotiations. The letter was delivered at Ticonderoga about ten o'clock in the morning, and an hour afterward an express arrived from the south with tidings of the surrender of Cornwallis.

Before evening, St. Leger began the embarkation of his stores and troops, and, with a favoring wind, set forth toward Canada. The campaign had ended with barren results to the English, and no injury to Vermont but the death of poor Sergeant Tupper, perhaps slain only to " try the temper of the people." The commissioners flattered themselves that this affair had resulted very favorably to them.

There is no record of any subsequent interview of the agents of Vermont and the British commissioners, though there were frequent communications passing between them during the next year. One of the commissioners wrote to Ira Allen in February, 1782, expressing his anxiety to know what effect the surrender of Cornwallis had made upon the people of Vermont. He reminded Allen that it was well to consider the many chances and vicissitudes of war; that, however brilliant the last campaign might appear, the next might wear a very different aspect; and of the probability of the ruin of Vermont by her " haughty neighbors, elated by what they call a signal victory; " and hoped that Allen might see, as he did, that it was more than ever the interest of Vermont to unite with those who would make her a free and happy government.

In April General Haldimand wrote to Sir Henry Clinton that " coercion alone must now decide the part Vermont will take; " that it had made concessions to Congress by relinquishing its claims to the east and west unions, the confirmation of which had been promised by him.

In June Ethan Allen wrote to Haldimand that " the last refusal of Congress to admit the State into the union has done more to awaken common people to a sense of their interest and resentment of their conduct than all which they had done before. By their own account, they declare that Vermont does not and shall not belong to their confederacy; the consequence is, that they may fight their own battles. It is liberty which they are after, but they will not extend it to Vermont; therefore Vermont does not belong to the confederacy or the controversy, but are a neutral republic." He offers to meet General Haldimand on any part of Lake Champlain, and closes in bitterness of spirit: "There is a majority in Congress, and a number of the principal officers of the Continental army continually planning against me. I shall do everything in my power to render this State a British province."

Ira Allen was again sent to Canada early in July with a request from Governor Chittenden for the release of two Vermont officers then prisoners in Canada, a request which was granted. About this time a letter attributed to Ira Allen, though it was a wide departure from his cautious practice of making only verbal communications on such delicate affairs, was written from Quebec to General Haldimand. It begins with the request that a supposed charter to Philip Skene, for a government comprehending Vermonters with the tract of country called the " Western Union," might be produced, as the limits of Vermont would thereby be established according to an act of Congress confirming all royal charters and government lines established before the Declaration of Independence. The writer represents that the people of the Western Union " are mostly in favor of government, and would be of great use in bringing about the wished-for revolution." If General Haldimand advised it, the Vermont leaders would endeavor to raise a regiment or two from the other provinces, to consist of the most loyal or at least moderate men, with no officers but known and tried friends of government, to be stationed in Vermont under pretense of protecting the frontiers; such regiments to be supplied by the king, and always ready to act in or out of Vermont as ordered. "Thus far," he says, "I have not deviated from the principles of my employers, the ruling men of Vermont." But now, unauthorized, he proposes an immediate recognition of Vermont under government; that the principal gentlemen of Vermont promised to abide by any agreement he should enter into, provided it should be kept a profound secret till the British government could protect and assist them; and that they should not be obliged to go out of Vermont to make war with the other States; but if other colonies should invade Canada, they would oppose them as much as possible, but could not consistently go to Canada for its defense and leave their own State exposed to ruin; and also promised never to take arms again in opposition to British government, or assist Congress on any pretense whatever. In conclusion, the writer intimates that some of the king's money will be necessary to carry out these plans. There is only circumstantial evidence that Ira Allen was the author of this letter; although it is probable that he was, yet it contains contradictions hardly consistent with his usual shrewdness. Later in the same month General Haldimand wrote to Sir Guy Carleton: "I have brought it [the negotiation] to a very embarrassing crisis with regard to myself, having urged the people to the declaration in favor of government by a long series of persuasion, and the strongest assurances of support and reward. Uninformed as I am of the intentions of administration, except in general terms that they are pacific, I can no longer act with Vermont upon any certain grounds until I receive instructions for that purpose. In the mean time I shall amuse the messenger, who is very pressing for answers to his proposals, in the best way I can." In August he writes to Governor Chittenden: "You may rest assured that I shall give such orders as will effectually prevent hostilities of any kind being exercised in the district of Vermont until a breach on your part, or some general event, may make the contrary my duty."

After the signing of the preliminary articles of peace between Great Britain and the United States, but before Washington had proclaimed the cessation of hostilities, or the news of the peace, though expected, had reached Canada, General Haldimand dispatched his last letter to Vermont. "While," says this letter, "his Excellency sincerely regrets the happy moment which, it is much to be feared, cannot be recalled, of restoring to you the blessings of the British government, and views with concern the fatal consequences approaching which he had so long and so frequently predicted from your procrastination, he derives some satisfaction from a consciousness of not having omitted a circumstance which could tend to your persuasion and adoption of his desired purpose. If the report now prevailing has any foundation, a very short time will determine the fate of Vermont. Should anything favorable present, you may still depend on his Excellency's utmost endeavor for your salvation."

This closed the negotiations which had been continued for three years between the Vermont leaders and the British in Canada, and which, during that period, had saved the State from invasion on the one hand and disruption on the other. While it may be conceded that in the conduct of 'this policy the Vermonters did not exhibit the most exalted devotion to the faithless Congress,[1] though in it they did indeed serve it well, it must also be conceded that it was the only course by which they could preserve the autonomy of their State. This, antedating by eight years that of any other colony, could but be more precious to them than mere existence as a part or parts of other colonies, one of whom, and the principal claimant of their territory, had been, and still continued to be, more tyrannical and oppressive than Great Britain.

They had rendered a most valuable service to the cause of America in the capture of Ticonderoga and Crown Point, the first offensive operations of

---

[1] Winsor says in his *Critical History*, vol. vii. p. 188: "These tergiversations of Congress were not inducive of steadfast patriotism in the new State."

the Americans; on their own soil had fought their country's battles, one of which was largely instru. mental in the defeat of Burgoyne; and had contributed a regiment of Green Mountain Boys to the Continental army. But when, after they had declared the independence which they had so long maintained, they asked to be admitted to a union with the sister States, Congress turned a deaf ear to their appeal, and listened only to the dissentient voices of New York and New Hampshire, greedy for spoil, and to the Southern States, jealous even so early of a preponderance of Northern commonwealths.

Abandoned by those to whom they naturally looked for aid when threatened by the common enemy, whose advance upon their wide frontier they were too feeble to oppose, they took advantage of the attempts of that enemy to corrupt them to procure a cessation of hostilities, which saved not only their own State but the frontiers of New York from invasion. If, at any time, they really contemplated more than this, and a wholesome admonition to Congress to respect their rights, they never sought to work injury to the Confederation from which they were excluded; and in the very beginning General Haldimand promised, if Vermont should be admitted an independent State in that Confederation, the "negotiation should cease, and any step that leads to it be forgotten."

There was no treason. The Vermonters could

plot no treason against a government in which they had no part. As independent as the United States, their right was as absolute to make terms with Great Britain, even to becoming a province under it, as they boldly declared to Congress they would do rather than submit to the government of New York. Ira Allen did not scruple to carry misrepresentation beyond even the vaguely defined limits of diplomacy, and to him is chiefly due any doubts of the integrity of his associates, the wise and patriotic fathers of the State.

In the necessarily secret conduct of the policy adopted, they incurred the suspicions of friends and foes alike. Their own Warner and Stark, who had led the Green Mountain Boys to victory, suspected them, and General Haldimand complained of treachery; but they steadfastly pursued their course, to the accomplishment of all they desired.[1]

---

[1] *Vt. Hist. Soc. Collections*, vol. ii.; *Governor and Council*, vol. ii.; *Early History of Vermont*, Hiland Hall; *History of Vermont*, Ira Allen; Williams's *History*, vol. ii.; Thompson's *Vermont*.

The Haldimand correspondence, in a voluminous cipher, was obtained from the British Archives and sent to the distinguished antiquarian, Henry Stevens, of Barnet. These papers, now in the office of the secretary of state, were published in full by the Vermont Historical Society in 1871.

CHAPTER XVI.

UNIONS DISSOLVED.

VERMONT kept small garrisons in the forts at Rutland, Castleton, and Pittsford, and the militia in readiness to turn out in force when required, while two companies of rangers patrolled the frontier to watch the movements of the enemy. Her troops responded promptly to calls to act against the common enemy, as was proved when, to intercept the marauding force of Sir John Johnson, which had been ravaging the Mohawk Valley, Governor Clinton marched with the militia of Albany to Lake George, and sent an express to the commanding officer at Castleton to meet him at Ticonderoga with such force as he could muster. A day later, Ebenezer Allen, now major of the Vermont rangers, sent him word that he had arrived at Mount Independence with more than two hundred men, and was expecting a hundred more to join him, trusting that the governor would furnish boats to transport them across the lake. Johnson slipped by to the northward and escaped, but Clinton wrote to the New York delegates in Congress that the punctuality of the "militia of the Grants in complying with his request with 240 men did them great honor."

When, early in October, 1780, the British, as already stated, came up the lake with eight large vessels and more than a thousand men, their designs were against New York and not against Vermont, as the British policy was then to favor Vermont, with a view to future operations. Fort Anne was taken, and Fort George shared the same fate after the greater part of its garrison, consisting of eighty men of Warner's Continental Regiment under Captain Chipman, had been killed or captured by a superior force of the enemy, which they encountered when expecting to meet only a scout that had driven in one of their messengers sent to Fort Edward.

Marking its course with destruction, this invasion of the enemy created such a panic on the New York frontier that but few men could be raised there to oppose it. In this alarm, Governor Clinton so far acknowledged the existence of the "ideal Vermont State" as to direct an officer to write to Governor Chittenden for assistance.[1] He was immediately answered that the militia of the State were at the North, but the militia of Berkshire, which had been sent for, would be forwarded on their arrival.

Before the pacific intentions of the British were known, the militia of Vermont were called out. They immediately mustered at Castleton under General Ethan Allen, and the assembly, then in

[1] Clinton afterwards denied giving any authority to this demand on the State of Vermont.

session at Bennington, adjourned, that the members
might take the field. Vermont, late in October,
agreed to the truce, when her militia were dismissed,
save a small force of scouts.

During the progress of this invasion occurred
the last important incursion of the Indians within
the limits of Vermont. While Carleton's force
swept with purposed harmlessness past the western border of Vermont, an expedition set forth
against Newbury, on the Connecticut, with the pu-
tative object of capturing a Lieutenant Whitcomb,
who, while scouting on the Richelieu some years
before, had mortally wounded and then robbed
the British General Gordon. The force was commanded by Lieutenant Horton of the British army,
seconded by a Canadian named La Motte, aided
by one Hamilton, an escaped prisoner of war, who
had been in Newbury and Royalton on parole of
honor during the previous summer. It consisted
of 300 men,[1] all but seven of whom were Indians.
It is probable, from this preponderance of the savage element in its composition, that the real purpose of the expedition was the rapine which it so
successfully accomplished.

Guided by old warriors, who had often followed
this ancient warpath of their people in the days
when their onslaughts were the constant dread of
the New England frontiers, the party took its way
up the Winooski, past tenantless houses and deserted farms, on whose broad intervale meadows

[1] H. Hall, Z. Steele's *Indian Captive.*

the timid deer now grazed undisturbed. Then it came to where the wild stream wound through the unbroken wilderness; now among the frost-painted forest of deciduous trees, and now in the black shade of evergreens. Among the great pines that then clad the narrow valley, where now stands the capital of the State, they overtook and made prisoners two hunters from Newbury. These told the leaders that the people of their town were expecting an attack, and were prepared for it. Upon this they turned southward, and, following a branch of White River, on the 16th of October fell upon Royalton and neighboring towns.

The attack was at first conducted in perfect silence, till the alarm of it spread among the inhabitants; then the infernal clamor of the warwhoop resounded among the hills that had so long been strangers to its echoes, giving to the panic another terror.

Burning, pillaging, and making prisoners as they swooped with the celerity of falcons upon one and another isolated homestead or defenseless hamlet, they killed four persons, captured twenty-five others, and destroyed quantities of stock and garnered harvests.

As they drew off with prisoners and booty, Mrs. Hendee, the brave young wife of a settler, followed them, so earnestly pleading for the release of her little son that he was restored to her; and, upon her further entreaty, nine other small lads were set free.

The alarm soon reached the settlements on the Connecticut, and a force of 250 men were mustered, and, under command of Captain House, began a vigorous pursuit of the enemy in the night. Before daybreak they came up with the rear-guard of the marauders, who fired upon them, wounding one man. The fire was returned with better effect, killing one Indian and wounding another. The Indians then sent a prisoner to House with a threat that, if they persisted in the attack, the captives would all be immediately killed.

While the pursuers were deliberating on this message, the enemy retreated to the Winooski, and, following the river to its mouth, there embarked for Canada, whither they went unmolested. When they arrived at Montreal, the prisoners were "sold for a half Joe each," says Zadock Steele in his "Indian Captive." Most of them were exchanged and returned to their homes in the following summer, but Steele, who was imprisoned with others taken elsewhere, did not escape until two years after his capture. After three weeks of starved and weary wandering through the wilderness, first on the western shore of Lake Champlain, then crossing at Split Rock on a raft, and then along the eastern shore and up Otter Creek, he and his two comrades reached the fort at Pittsford.

Other towns, during the war, were visited by small bands of British and Indians that did little injury, and during the Haldimand negotiations they probably had orders from the British generals not to molest the inhabitants.

Late in the fall of 1780, Vermont endeavored to form a union with the neighboring States for the mutual defense of the frontiers, as well as to secure from them an acknowledgment of her independence. Governor Chittenden, in November, wrote to Governor Clinton, making a formal demand on New York to relinquish her claim to the jurisdiction of Vermont, at the same time proposing that New York should unite with Vermont against the British forces, especially such as should invade the frontiers of the two States from Canada. A similar letter was sent to each of the other claiming States. Massachusetts complied with the request. New Hampshire took no definite action ; and when Governor Clinton acquainted the legislature with this demand, he characterized it as "insolent in its nature, and derogatory to the honor of the State." The legislature, however, was disposed to adjust a quarrel which it was evidently useless to prolong. Resolutions were reported, which, though affirming the right of New York to the control of Vermont, declared it was inexpedient to further insist on such right, and provided for the appointment of commissioners to confer with commissioners from Vermont, with full powers to adjust terms for the cession of the territory to Vermont. The report was adopted by the Senate with but one dissenting vote, and the question of considering the resolutions received the affirmative vote of the House. Upon this, a message was received from Governor Clinton threatening to prorogue the House if it should agree to carry these resolutions into effect. This threat put a stop to the proceedings, which promised to end the long and bitter controversy. General Schuyler was a member of the Senate, and, convinced of the futility of attempting to coerce Vermont into submission to New York, and that Congress would not come to a decision in favor of his State, he took an active part in forwarding the conciliatory measures. Governor Clinton's obstinate opposition to them, against the calm judgment of the wise and patriotic Schuyler and the desire of the legislature of his State, can only be accounted for by his bitter enmity to the intensely democratic people of Vermont, and the fact that he and members of his family were claimants under New York of grants of large tracts in the disputed territory.

Vermont had already appointed agents to wait upon the legislators of New York, to agree upon and establish the line between the two States; but when news of the failure of the pacific measures was received, the council decided neither to send the agents to Albany nor to " write any further to the General Assembly of New York at present."

The intercepted letter from Lord George Germain afforded evidence that the British ministry were making overtures to the people of Vermont, and were somehow persuaded that they were disposed to accept them. Alarmed by this aspect of the affair, Congress was stirred to some favorable action, but made it an indispensable preliminary to the recognition of Vermont's independence and her admission to the Union that she relinquish her claims to lands and jurisdiction beyond her original limits.

Vermont, having formed the unions, her legislature being in session at Charlestown,[1] and her newly elected lieutenant-governor being a resident of the East Union, refused to break the compact, or submit the question of her independence to any power, but was willing to refer the question of her boundaries to commissioners mutually chosen, and when admitted to the Federal Union would submit any such dispute to Congress. The action of Congress called forth a protest from New York, and her delegates were instructed to oppose all such measures.

There now arose imminent danger of serious collisions in both unions. There was a probability that the government of New Hampshire was about to take measures to compel the submission to its authority of those who had joined Vermont; and Governor Chittenden wrote to General Paine, the lieutenant-governor, to call out the militia east of the Green Mountains to assist the sheriff, and, if New Hampshire made an attack with an armed force, to repel force by force. General Paine sent a copy of his orders to the president of New Hampshire, and informed him that he should carry them out if New Hampshire began hostilities; at the same time commissioners were sent to the Assem-

[1] *New Hampshire in the East Union.*

bly of New Hampshire to attempt an amicable arrangement of the matter. New Hampshire gave her revolted citizens forty days in which to return to her, and thus armed conflict was averted.

At the same time there were more serious disturbances in the Western Union. Colonel Van Rensselaer of Sancoik, acting under authority of New York, had arrested at New City (now Lansingburg) a colonel of the Vermont militia, who presently escaped. Not long afterwards Van Rensselaer himself was arrested and taken to Bennington, where, according to his own statement, he was well treated and soon discharged. Other arrests were made by both parties, all of whom were residents of the union, and who, gathering in arms near Sancoik, for a while threatened each other. The adherents of Vermont so greatly outnumbered those of New York — only about eighty strong — that the latter did not dare to attack them, and the New York commander, Colonel Yates, applied in December, 1781, to General Gansevoort at Albany for reinforcements. Governor Chittenden now called out the militia of the original territory of Vermont, and Colonel Walbridge marched from Bennington with his regiment to Sancoik. Colonel Yates at once withdrew his force, and, on his retreat, met General Gansevoort, who, after an unsuccessful endeavor to obtain a detachment from General Stark at Saratoga, was marching into the disturbed region with eighty men, all that he had been able to raise from four regiments, one of which furnished only the colonel and one private. General Gansevoort demanded by what authority and for what purpose Colonel Walbridge invaded the territory of New York; and Walbridge answered that he had come to protect those who held allegiance to Vermont, and, though he did not desire warfare, he would not be answerable for the consequences if the liberty and property of such persons were interfered with. Finding his insignificant and indifferent force confronted by 500 Green Mountain Boys, who were very much in earnest, General Gansevoort wisely withdrew, and left "those turbulent sons of freedom" masters of the bloodless field.

Thus, most fortunately, no actual hostilities in either quarter resulted from these threatening demonstrations. But the fire was only covered, not quenched, and its smouldering embers were ready to burst into a blaze of fratricidal war whenever fanned by the first mischievous wind. That this did not happen was due to the wise and kindly advice given by Washington in a letter to Governor Chittenden, dated January 1, 1782. Admitting that Congress had virtually acknowledged the right of Vermont to independence in its late action, and its willingness to confirm it, provided the new State was confined to her originally claimed limits, he strongly urged the relinquishment of Vermont's claims to the East and West Unions. "You have nothing to do but withdraw your jurisdiction to the confines of your own limits, and obtain an acknowledgment of independence and sovereignty."

When the Vermont Assembly met at Bennington in February, Washington's letter was laid before it and had the immediate effect of bringing about the measure which it advised. On the 22d the claims of Vermont to jurisdiction beyond the original limits of the New Hampshire Grants were formally relinquished, and, having made such compliance with the resolutions of Congress, four delegates were appointed by the assembly to negotiate the admission of the State, two of the delegates being empowered to take seats in Congress as representatives of Vermont upon her admission.

Before Congress was apprised of this action, resolutions were proposed in that body that if, within one month after notification, Vermont complied with the resolutions of August, she should at once be admitted into the Union, but that non-compliance with them would be considered a manifest indication of her hostility to the United States, whose forces should then be employed against her inhabitants, and her territory be divided by the line of the Green Mountains between New Hampshire and New York. But the resolutions were not adopted, and the Vermont delegates presently arriving at Philadelphia officially informed Congress of the action of the legislature.

The matter was referred to a committee of five, which reported on the 17th of April. Its sense was that, as Vermont had fully complied with the requirements of Congress, her recognition and admission had become " necessary to be performed ; " and it submitted a resolution recognizing and acknowledging Vermont as a free, sovereign, and independent State, and authorizing the appointment of a committee to treat with the Vermont delegates upon the terms of admission.

Notwithstanding all this, Congress again resorted to the policy of delay by which it had so long evaded a settlement of this controversy, and motions to consider the report were successively made and rejected.

The Vermont delegates were indignant at such treatment, and after addressing a letter to the president of Congress stating the confident hope of recognition which had induced Vermont to relinquish her unions, expressing their disappointment at the delay of Congress, and setting forth the critical situation in which Vermont was now placed, left unaided to oppose invasions of the enemy from Canada, they shook the dust of Philadelphia from their feet, " expecting to be officially acquainted when their attendance would be necessary."

There was a universal feeling in Vermont that the legislature had been duped by Congress into weakening the State. The people lost faith in the promises and resolutions of Congress, and there were frequent expressions of bitter feeling against it. A member of the legislature, gossiping with neighbors at the mill while their grists were grinding, declared that Congress had no business to interfere with the unions of Vermont; and when a noted adherent of New York expressed a different opinion, he cursed Congress roundly. " Curse Congress ! Have n't we waited long enough on them ? A pox on them ! I wish they would come to the mill now. I would put them between the millstones or under the water-wheel ! They have sold us like an old horse ! They have no business with our affairs. We know no such body of men ! " Another prominent worthy, who was in the secret of the Haldimand correspondence, said, " We 're fixin' up a pill that 'll make the Yorkers hum." Another declared in a public house that, " as long as the King and Parliament of Great Britain approved of and would maintain the State of Vermont, he was determined to drive it, and so were its leaders." [1]

There was a settled determination to maintain the independence of the State and to ask no favors of the vacillating Congress, though the legislature, that nothing might be wanting on their part, at its next session appointed agents empowered to arrange terms of admission to the Union.

[1] B. H. Hall's *Eastern Vermont.*

CHAPTER XVII.

"THE REPUBLIC OF THE GREEN MOUNTAINS."

FOR all its relinquishment of the unions, without which, according to the representations of some internal enemies, it had not the capacity to maintain inhabitants enough to support the "charges, honor, power, and dignity of an inland State," the commonwealth was constantly gaining strength by the rapid incoming of settlers from other States. These were chiefly from Connecticut, which had furnished so many of the founders and defenders of the State, and those who came now, being for the most part of the same mould and metal, gave a hearty support to the government under which they had chosen to live.

However, some disturbances occurred in the southeastern part of the State, where certain persons, encouraged to resistance by Governor Clinton, opposed the raising of troops by Vermont for the defense of the frontiers.

The town of Guilford was at that time the most populous in the State. A majority of the inhabitants were adherents of New York, and, having renounced the New Hampshire charter, had, while there was no actual government exercised in the

Grants, formed a little republic, not ill-governed by the decisions of town meetings. Here was the most active opposition to the levy of troops. The adherents of New York who were drafted refused to serve, and the sheriff of Windham County was directed to seize their goods and chattels to the amount expended by the State in hiring their substitutes. When the officer attempted to execute his warrant, a cow which he had seized was taken from him by a mob acting under a captain commissioned by New York. In levying on the property of Timothy Church, of Brattleboro, the sheriff was resisted by Church, and, when he attempted to arrest him, was prevented by three of Church's friends. Being unable to execute his warrants, the sheriff asked for a military force to assist him, whereupon, by the advice of the council, Governor Chittenden ordered Brigadier-General Ethan Allen to raise two hundred and fifty men, and march them into Windham County to support the civil authority.

Not many days passed before Allen led 200 mounted Green Mountain Boys into the rebellious region, making several arrests, and meeting with little opposition but from the tongue of a termagant, whose husband they were seeking, till they came to Guilford. Even here, where disaffection most rankly flourished, there was no serious resistance to the arrests, but when marching thence toward Brattleboro they were fired on by about fifty of the Guilford men, who ambuscaded the highway. Allen at once marched his force back to

Guilford, and made proclamation that if the people of that town did not peacefully submit to the authority of Vermont he would " lay it as desolate as Sodom and Gomorrah." Then, without further molestation, for the Yorkers "feared Ethan Allen more than the Devil," the prisoners, twenty in all, were conveyed to Westminster and lodged in jail. When brought to trial, fines were imposed on the lesser offenders, while four of the principal ones were sentenced to be forever banished from Vermont, not to return under pain of death, and their estates were forfeited to the State. Two had made themselves particularly odious by accepting commissions under New York after having sworn allegiance to Vermont. Timothy Church, who had borne a colonel's commission under New York, was one of them. He returned to the State, was taken, imprisoned for five months, and released upon taking the oath of fidelity to Vermont, but the faithless creature was presently as busily as ever plotting against the government which he had twice sworn to support. The banished men appealed to Governor Clinton, but he, always lavish of promises, yet niggardly of fulfillment, gave them no present comfort, but forwarded a representation of their case to Congress. The New York delegates, aided by Charles Phelps, the most active of the Vermont refugees, succeeded in bringing Congress into a certain degree of hostility to Vermont.

There were other reasons than the claims of New York, or the right of Vermont to independence, or the obligations of Congress to acknowledge it, that influenced the action of the different States. Those of New England, with the exception of New Hampshire, were inclined to favor Vermont from kinship and intimate relations with its people, " but principally," said Madison, " from the accession of weight they would derive from it in Congress." This " accession of weight " was as potent a reason for the opposition of the Southern States ; and another reason was the effect which a decision in favor of Vermont might have on the claims of Virginia, North and South Carolina, and Georgia to the vast tracts stretching westward to the Mississippi. For the same reason, Pennsylvania and Maryland inclined to favor Vermont, as did Delaware and New Jersey, from a desire to strengthen the interests of the small States.

On the 5th of December resolutions quite hostile to Vermont were adopted by a vote of seven States, among whom were New Hampshire and New York, though, by a previous resolution of Congress, both were forbidden to vote on any question relative to the decision of this matter. The action of Vermont toward her rebellious inhabitants was denounced, and " the people inhabiting said district, claiming to be independent," were required to make full restitution to the persons who had been condemned to banishment, or deprived of their property by confiscation or otherwise, since the first of September, and that they be not molested on returning to their homes. It was declared that the

United States would take effectual measures to enforce these resolutions in case they were disobeyed. Persons holding commissions under New York or the "district claiming to be independent" were forbidden to exercise authority over any inhabitants of said district, contrary to the resolutions of September 24, 1779, and June 2, 1780. A copy of these resolutions was transmitted to "Thomas Chittenden, Esq., of Bennington, in the district aforesaid, to be communicated to the people thereof." [1] A month later Governor Chittenden returned a forcible and spirited answer, reminding Congress of its solemn engagements to Vermont, and giving an extract from Washington's letter to him advising the restriction of the limits of Vermont, which advice had been complied with, in full reliance on the faith and honor of Congress to fulfill its agreement. The right of Congress to control the internal police of the State, from which it had never received any delegated power, was denied. If Congress attempted to carry out its threat of coercion, Vermont would probably appeal to General Washington, who, with most of the inhabitants of the contiguous States, favored the independence of the State. "Would it not, then," he asked, "be more prudent to refer this dispute to New York and Vermont than to embroil the confederacy of the United States therewith?" The course pursued toward the rebellious persons was

[1] For these resolutions see Slade's *State Papers*, p. 177; also Chittenden's reply, p. 178.

justified on the ground that nearly all of those banished or fined had taken the oath of allegiance to Vermont, and were, according to the resolutions of Congress itself, amenable to no laws or regulations but those of Vermont. The remonstrance closed by earnestly soliciting the admission of Vermont to the Union, "agreeable to the before cited preliminary agreement, which the committee of Congress have reported has become absolute and necessary on their part to be performed, and from which this State will not recede."

When the legislature met in February, Governor Chittenden laid before it the resolutions of Congress, which called forth a remonstrance quite as spirited as his own. It declared the willingness of Vermont to comply with every reasonable requirement of Congress; "but when Congress require us," it continues, "to abrogate our laws and reverse the solemn decisions of our courts of justice in favor of insurgents and disturbers of the public peace, we think ourselves justified to God and the world when we say we cannot comply with such their requisitions." "It would be licensing factious subjects to oppose government with impunity." "As we have, from the commencement of the war, braved every danger and hardship against the usurpations of Britain in common with the United States, as our inherent right of sovereignty and jurisdiction stands confessed upon the principles of the Revolution, and implied by the solemn transactions of Congress, we cannot but express our surprise at the reception of the late resolutions of Congress."

The remonstrance of Governor Chittenden was printed and extensively circulated, especially among the officers of the Continental army, to inform them of the merits of a controversy in which they might soon be called upon to take part. General Washington's letter being referred to in it, he laid it and the one to which it was an answer before Congress, and at the same time wrote to Mr. Jones, a member of that body, reminding him that the committee on these affairs, of which he was a member, had approved of the reply to Governor Chittenden. He was sure that Vermont had a powerful interest in the New England States, and with regard to the enforcement of the resolutions of Congress by the army he wrote: "Let me ask by whom that district of country is principally settled? And of whom is your present army (I do not confine the question to this part of it, but will extend it to the whole) composed? The answers are evident, — New England men. It has been the opinion of some that the appearance of force would awe those people into submission. If the General Assembly ratify and confirm what Mr. Chittenden and his council have done, I shall be of a very different sentiment, and, moreover, that it is not a trifling force that will subdue them, even supposing they derive no aid from the enemy in Canada; and that it would be a very arduous task indeed if they should, to say nothing of a diversion which may and doubtless would be made in their favor from New York if the war with Great Britain should continue." He could not say that there "would be any difficulty with the army if it were to be ordered on this service," but "should be exceedingly unhappy to see the experiment." There would be "a general unwillingness to imbrue their hands in the blood of their brethren."

The threat of Congress certainly had not the effect of awing Vermont into any compliance with its behests, and if more than a threat was ever intended, nothing beyond it was ever attempted.

No reparation was made to the offenders who had been so summarily dealt with; and when two of the banished men ventured to return, they were seized and imprisoned, but were released on their promise of submission to the laws of the State. When opposition was offered serious enough to require it, the militia was properly called out to enforce the civil authority; and the sturdy little commonwealth continued to exercise its jurisdiction unmolested by Congress, though the legislature of New York seethed with wrath and boiled over in protests and complaints.

Constable Oliver Waters had made himself particularly obnoxious to the New York party by his activity in making arrests, and while he was lodging at an inn in Brattleboro the house was attacked by twenty or thirty men. After firing through the doors and windows and wounding two of the inmates, they made forcible entry, and, seizing Waters, carried him into Massachusetts, intending to deliver him to Governor Clinton at Poughkeepsie, but he was taken from them by a rescue party and brought safely to Vermont. This affair was the cause of vigorous action against the insurgents, several hundred of the militia turning out to aid the state troops. Several of the ringleaders were taken, and several fled into Massachusetts, whither they were not pursued.

In February a new act was passed making punishable by death the levying of war against the State by any citizen thereof. At the same time the governor and council were given discretionary power to grant pardons, during the recess of the legislature, to offenders "who should appear penitent and desirous of returning to their duty." In the following month all active opposition to the jurisdiction of Vermont ceased, and the troops were gradually withdrawn from Windham County. Many of the disaffected persons were granted pardons and the restoration of their confiscated property on taking the oath of allegiance. Among these was Charles Phelps, who had been one of the most inveterate opponents of Vermont, but who now became a peaceable citizen of the State, and so continued during the remainder of his life. Many of the adherents of New York removed to lands on the Susquehanna, granted them by that State.

New York made complaint to Congress of the employment of troops by Vermont to reduce residents thereof who professed allegiance to New

York, and again urged the intervention of Congress. Being apprised of this, Governor Chittenden wrote a pungent letter to the president of Congress. "It seems they are willing Congress should settle this dispute," he says of New York, "as they have a mind, but not otherwise." Referring to the desire expressed by New York that she might not be blamed if blood was shed in the assertion of her authority : "As to this bloody proposition, the council of this State have only to remark that Vermont does not wish to enter into a war with the State of New York, but she will act on the defensive, and expect that Congress and the twelve States will observe strict neutrality, and let the two contending States settle their own controversy." Referring to the suppression of the malcontents, he wrote : "This matter has been managed by the wisdom of the legislature of this State, who consider themselves herein amenable to no earthly tribunal." Congress was reminded of the impropriety of permitting New York and New Hampshire to vote on any motion which came before it respecting Vermont, contrary to the express resolution of September, 1779, though it appeared they had ever since done so. In conclusion, the desire of Vermont for a confederation with the United States was reiterated. This letter was referred to the same committee to which the representation of New York, and other papers relating to Vermont, had been committed. On the 29th of May, 1783, it reported in favor of Vermont, reciting the resolutions of August, 1781, and offering one recognizing the independence of the State, and admitting it into the Union. A few days later the New York delegates moved the postponement of another matter that this report might be taken up, but only New York and New Hampshire voted in favor of the motion. This was the last action taken by the Continental Congress in relation to Vermont, with whose affairs it thenceforth offered no interference.

By the treaty of peace with Great Britain signed at Paris on the 3d of September, 1783, Vermont was included in the territory belonging to the United States. But she was in fact thenceforth, till her admission to the Union, what the legend[1] on her copper coins declared her to be, "The Republic of the Green Mountains," and independent of every other government.

A standard of weights and measures was prescribed, the value of coins regulated, and a postal service established, the rates of postage being the same as those of the United States, for the superintendence of which a postmaster-general was appointed, and the post-riders were given the exclusive right of carrying letters and packages. The mails were carried on horseback, and in their long and lonely routes the riders encountered much discomfort of storm and cold on roads always bad, often worse with blockades of snow or bottomless quagmires. The post-offices were for

[1] *Vermontensium Res Publica.*

the most part a shelf in the great tavern bar, inconspicuous among the array of bottles and decanters that were in more frequent demand ; or **a** drawer in the village store, into which the infrequent letters and few newspapers were promiscuously tumbled, to be searched through on demand of each inquirer. The furniture of one central office is still preserved, — a great chest of three drawers, each bearing in large letters the name of a town.

Being out of the Confederation, Vermont could not be called on to bear any part of the debt incurred by the war, by such general government as existed, and having made the taxes for the support of her own troops payable in provisions, which were always furnished, she herself owed no considerable debt, and this was in course of speedy liquidation by the sale of her lands, now in great demand by people of the neighboring States. Her bills of credit, issued in 1781, had suffered no depreciation, and were faithfully redeemed.

Under these circumstances, the people of the prosperous commonwealth were quite lukewarm concerning its admission to the Union, though they cultivated friendly relations with the neighboring States, and the legislature of the State enacted that all citizens of the United States should be equally entitled to all the privileges of law and justice with those of Vermont, and an annual election of delegates to Congress was provided for, though none had occasion to attend.

Contrasting their condition with that of the pioneers, these people might well be content with that which was now enjoyed. Those brave invaders of the wilderness had been opposed by all unkindly forces of nature, — unpropitious seasons, floods, the bitterness of almost arctic winters endured in miserable shelter with meagre fare, and by more cruel man, the prowling, murderous savage and his as relentless Christian allies ; and withal had borne the heavy loneliness of isolation, lightened only by toil save when Nature changed her mood and conversed in songs of familiar birds, voices of wind-swept trees and babble of streams whose torrential rage was spent, or smiled in sunshine from the little patch of sky, and in the bloom of innumerable flowers out of the border of the grim forest. The dangers and privations of pioneer life had now been passed through, and there were peace and abundance of all that simple lives required.

The " plumping-mill " — the rude device for pounding corn in a huge mortar, with a pestle hung from a spring-pole — went out of use, and the long journeys on foot or on horseback to the grist-mill forty miles away were no longer necessary. The wild streams were tamed to the turning of millstones, as well as to plying the saws that were incessantly gnawing into the heart of the woods.

The wild forest had receded and given place to broad fields of tilth, meadow land, and pastures, not now in the uncouth desolation of stumps and log-heaps, but dotted with herds and flocks. The jangle of the sheep-bell was as frequent as the note of the thrush in the half-wild upland pastures, for two shillings were deducted from the lists for each pound of wool raised during the year. Orchards were beginning to whiten hillsides with bloom and color them with fruitage, for every acre with forty growing trees was exempted from taxation.

But while Vermont continued very indifferent and almost inactive concerning the acknowledgment of her independence by Congress, her old enemy had come to desire what she had so long opposed. It had become apparent to New York that the admission of the State to the Union would be to her own advantage. The establishment of Vermont as a free and independent State was an accomplished fact; her interest in the affairs of the nation, were she an acknowledged part of it, would in the main accord with that of New York. There was, then, no good reason why New York should continue to oppose her admission merely in the selfish and insignificant interest of the land speculators, and in the blind lead of Governor Clinton's persistent enmity. In accordance with this wiser view, the legislature of New York, on the 15th of July, 1789, appointed commissioners with full power to acknowledge the independence of Vermont, and settle all matters of controversy with that State. In October Vermont appointed commissioners to treat with those of New York, and finally determine everything which obstructed the union of Vermont with the United States. The principal difficulty was the adjustment of the compensation for lands claimed by citizens of New York which had been re-granted by Vermont, but after two or three meetings the commissioners came to an amicable arrangement of this most troublesome question. In October, 1790, the commissioners of New York declared the consent of the legislature of that State to the admission of Vermont to the Union, and that upon such admission all claims of New York to jurisdiction within the limits of Vermont should cease; that the boundary line between the two States should be the western lines of towns granted by New Hampshire, and the mid-channel of Lake Champlain.

For the adjustment of the land claims, it was declared that if the legislature of Vermont should before the 1st of January, 1792, agree to pay to the State of New York the sum of $30,000 on or before the first day of January, 1794, all rights and titles to land granted by the colonial or state government of New York should cease, except those which had been made in confirmation of the grants of New Hampshire.

The legislature of Vermont at once acceded to this arrangement, and on the 28th of the same month passed an act directing the state treasurer to pay the sum named to the State of New York, and to accept the line proposed as a perpetual boundary between the two States.

Thus peaceably ended the controversy that for more than a quarter of a century had been an almost continual annoyance to the people of this district, and in its later stages a source of danger to the whole country.

The Assembly of Vermont called a convention to consider the expediency of joining the Federal Union. This convention met at Bennington, January 6, 1791, and though at first several members were not in favor of union, after a debate of three days the question was decided in the affirmative by a vote of 105 yeas to 3 nays. A few days later the assembly chose Nathaniel Chipman and Lewis R. Morris commissioners to negotiate with Congress for the admission of the State to the Union. The commissioners went immediately to Philadelphia, and laid before the president the proceedings of the legislature and convention.

On the eighteenth day of February, 1791, Congress, without debate or one dissenting vote, passed an act declaring that on the fourth day of March next, "the said State, by the name and style of the State of Vermont, shall be received into this Union as a new and entire member of the United States of America." So at last the star, that so long had shone apart, now added its constant ray to the lustre of the constellation.

CHAPTER XVIII.

THE NEW STATE.

WHEN Vermont had taken her place in the Union, her state government continued to run smoothly in its accustomed lines, still guided by the firm hand and wise counsel of her first governor. With unabated faith in the wisdom, integrity, and patriotism of Thomas Chittenden, the freemen of Vermont again and again reëlected him to the chief magistracy of the commonwealth after its admission, as with but one exception they had done in the twelve years preceding that event.

Notwithstanding the simplicity of home life in those days, "Election Day" was observed with a pomp and ceremony well befitting the occasion.

An old newspaper[1] of the day tells us that the morning was ushered in by beat of drums, and that the governor-elect, Thomas Chittenden, Esq., and Lieutenant-Governor Peter Olcott, accompanied by several members of the council, Jonas Fay, Samuel Safford, Walbridge, Bayley, and Strong, old associates in the stalwart band of Green Mountain Boys, were met at some distance from the town of

[1] *Vermont Journal*, October 18, 1791.

Windsor by a troop of horse, a company of artillery, and one of infantry, all in "most beautiful
uniforms," doubtless of the beloved Continental
buff and blue, glittering with great brass buttons,
whereon were inscribed the initials " G. W." and
the legend, " Long live the President."

As this corps, made up of veterans who had
smelled powder when it burned with deadly intent,
and of martial youths whose swords were yet un-
fleshed, marched proudly to the screech of fife and
beat of drum, the chronicler writes, their evolutions
and discipline would have gained the applause of
regular troops.   Upon the formal announcement of
the result of the election, the artillery company
fired a salute of fifteen guns, and then the governor
and council, the members of the house, and all the
good people there assembled, repaired to church,
and listened to the election sermon, delivered by
the Rev. Mr. Shuttleworth " with his usual energy
and pathos ; " and in the evening the happy occasion was further celebrated by an " elegant ball
given by a number of Gentlemen of this town to
a most brillant assembly of Gentlemen and Ladies,
of this and neighboring States."

The sessions of the legislature usually continued
about four weeks, and its business principally consisted in the granting of new townships, levying
a small tax, and the passage of necessary laws.
Frequent petitions were received, and many granted,
to establish lotteries to aid towns in the building
and repairing of bridges and roads ; to remove

obstructions in the channel of the Connecticut; to enable individuals to carry out private enterprises, such as the building of a malt and brew house; in one case to furnish a blind man means wherewith to go to Europe to have an operation performed on his eyes; and at least one petition was presented praying for the grant of a lottery to build a church!

Some of the statutes made for the government of the commonwealth in its turbulent infancy, and which were soon repealed, are curious enough to deserve mention.

Manslaughter was punishable by forfeiture of possessions, by whipping on the naked back, and by branding the letter "M." on the hand with a hot iron. Whoso was convicted of adultery was to be punished by whipping on the naked body not exceeding thirty-nine stripes, and "stigmatized or burnt on the forehead with the letter 'A' on a hot iron," and was to wear the letter ".A" on the back of the outside garment, in cloth of a different color, and as often as seen without it, on conviction thereof, to be whipped ten stripes. The counterfeiter was punished by having his right ear cut off, and by branding with the letter "C" and being kept at hard labor during life. Burglary and highway robbery were punished by branding with the letter "B" on the forehead, by having the right ear nailed to a post and cut off, and by whipping. A second offense entailed the loss of the other ear and the infliction of a severer whipping, and for the third offense the criminal was to be " put to death as being incorrigible."

Every town was obliged to maintain a good pair of stocks set in the most public place, and in these were exposed the convicted liar, the blasphemer, and the drunkard. In such place also must be maintained a sign-post, whereon all public notices were placed, with occasional ghastly garnishment of felons' ears.

Every town assigned a particular brand for its horse kind, each one of which was to be marked on the left shoulder by a regularly appointed brander, who should record a description of every horse branded. All owners of cattle, sheep, or swine were required to ear-mark or brand such animals, and cause their several marks to be registered in the town book. Many of these ear-marks may yet be seen described and rudely pictured in faded ink on the musty pages of old record-books.

There was a general revision of the laws in 1787, and a second revision ten years later, whereby the barbarous severity of the penal laws was considerably lessened.

After admission to the Union, Vermont was as faithful to the newly assumed bond as she had been steadfast and unflinching in the assertion of her independence of Congress when that body attempted to exercise its authority over the unrecognized commonwealth. She was not backward in furnishing soldiers for the common defense. In

1792, Captain William Eaton, who some years later won renown as the heroic leader of a bold and successful expedition against the city of Derne in Tripoli, raised a company for service against the Indians in the Northwest. There, in the fourth sub-legion of General Wayne's army, these brave men well sustained the valorous reputation of the Green Mountain Boys, bearing the evergreen sprig to its accustomed place in the battle-front. At the battle of Miami, of the eleven privates killed in the fourth sub-legion five were Vermonters. The patriotism of these three-years' volunteers was stimulated by a bounty of eight dollars, and a monthly wage of three dollars.

The pioneers of Vermont aged early under the constant strain of anxiety and hardship which their life entailed, and though most of the leaders were spared amid the dangers of the frontier, the perils of war, and intestine feuds, few reached the allotted term of man's life. Warner, whose vigorous constitution was sapped by the stress of continuous campaigns, died in 1785, aged only forty-two, six years before the State in whose defense he first drew his sword became a recognized member of the nation to whose service he unselfishly devoted the best years of his brave life. Neither was Ethan Allen permitted to see the admission of Vermont to the Union, but was suddenly stricken down by apoplexy, in the robust fullness of his strength, two years before that event. Noble and generous in his nature, bold, daring, and resolute,

"he possessed," says Zadoc Thompson, "an unusual degree of vigor both of body and mind, and
an unlimited confidence in his own abilities."

Vermont has given him the first place among
her heroes, has set his marble effigy in the national
capitol, in her own, and on the monument that
marks his grave ; yet to that brave and modest soldier, Seth Warner, the knightliest figure in her
romantic history, the State he served so well has
not given so much as a tablet to commemorate his
name and valorous deeds.   It is as if, in their
mouldering dust, the character of the living men
was preserved, the one still self-asserting, the other
as unpretentious in the eternal sleep as he was in
life.   Though Governor Chittenden's age was not
beyond that in which modern statesmen are still
active, infirmity and disease were upon him, ad-
monishing him that he could no longer bear the
fatigues of the office which for eighteen years he
had held.   In the summer of 1797 he announced
that he would not again be a candidate for the
governorship.   He had seen the State, which he
had been so largely instrumental in moulding out
of the crude material of scattered frontier settlements, and which his strong hand had defended
against covetous neighbors and a foreign enemy,
in the full enjoyment of an honorable place in the
sisterhood of commonwealths, and felt that his
work was done.   While still in office, a few weeks
later, his honorable life closed at his home in Williston, among the fertile fields that his hand had

wrought out of the primeval wilderness, and his death was sincerely mourned by the people whom he had so long ruled with patriarchal care.

At the next election, Isaac Tichenor was chosen governor. He was a native of New Jersey, and, becoming a resident of Vermont in 1777, he presently took an active part in the affairs of the State. For several years previous to his election to the first place in its gift, he had served it as a member of the council, chief justice, and United States senator. No choice was made by the people, though he received a plurality of the popular vote, and the election devolved upon the assembly. The Federalist party predominating therein, he was elected by a large majority. He was ten times reëlected, and, such faith had the people in him, several times after his party was a minority in the State, although the acrimony of party strife had begun to embitter its politics.

In the early part of Tichenor's administration, while the legislature was in session at Vergennes in the autumn of 1798, five chiefs of the Cognahwaghnahs presented a claim of their people to ancient hunting grounds in Vermont, bounded by a line extending from Ticonderoga to the Great Falls of Otter Creek, and in the same direction to the height of land dividing the streams between Lake Champlain and the river Connecticut, thence along the height of land opposite Missisque, and then down to the bay, and comprising about a third of the State. The Indians were handsomely entertained during their stay, and dismissed with a present of a hundred dollars, "well pleased with their own policy," says Williams, "and with that of the Assembly of Vermont, hoping that the game would prove still better another season."

An investigation of this claim resulted in a decision that, if any such right ever existed, it had been extinguished by the cession of the lands in question to the United States by Great Britain, whose allies these Indians were in the late war.

When, upon the passage of the alien and sedition laws by Congress, the legislatures of Virginia and Kentucky, in 1798, passed resolutions, which were sent to the legislatures of all the other States, declaring these acts null, the Assembly of Vermont made a firm, dignified, and forcible reply, denying the right of States to sit in judgment on the constitutionality of the acts of Congress, or to declare which of its acts should be accepted or which rejected. Considering the almost recent antagonism which had existed between Congress and the State of Vermont, the one by turns vacillating or threatening, the other boldly defiant and denying the right of interference with her affairs, it might be thought that the new commonwealth would be found arrayed among the extreme defenders of state rights rather than so stoutly opposing them.

Party spirit had begun to embitter the politics of the State, and the growing minority of Republicans was hotly arrayed against the still predominant Federalists. The Federal strength was further weakened by the imprisonment, under the sedition law, of Matthew Lyon, one of the Vermont members of Congress. His free expression of opinion concerning the conduct of the administration of President Adams would not now be considered very extravagant, but for it he was sentenced to four months' imprisonment, and to pay a fine of $1,000.

While in prison at Vergennes, he wrote letters which it was thought would cause his re-arrest before he could leave the State to take his seat in Congress, to which he had been reëlected while in prison. Measures were taken for the payment of his fine in indisputably legal tender, one citizen of the State providing the sum in silver dollars, and one ardent Republican of North Carolina coming all the way from that State on horseback with the amount in gold. But Lyon's many political friends desired to share the honor of paying his fine, and it was arranged that no person should pay more than one dollar. No sooner had he come forth from prison than his fine was paid, and he was placed in a sleigh and driven up the frozen current of Great Otter to Middlebury, attended, it is said, by an escort in sleighs, the train extending from the one town to the other, a distance of twelve miles. With half as many, he might boast of a greater following than had passed up the Indian Road under any leader since the bloody days of border warfare when Waubanakee chief or Canadian partisan led their marauding horde along the noble river.

Lyon was of Irish birth, and came to America at the age of thirteen under an indenture for his passage money. This was sold for a pair of steers to one of the founders of Danville, Vermont, and Lyon was wont to swear " By the bulls that redeemed me." He served in the Vermont troops in the Revolution, and for a time was paymaster in Warner's regiment. He was a member of the Dorset convention, and for several years took a prominent part in the politics of the State, of which he was an enterprising and useful citizen. His second wife was the daughter of Governor Thomas Chittenden. In 1801 he removed to Kentucky, and was eight years a member of Congress from that State. He died at the age of seventy-six, in the territory of Arkansas, soon after his election as delegate to Congress.

Four years after the arbitrary measures against Lyon by a Federalist majority in the legislature, the opposite party gained the ascendency in that body, though Tichenor had been reëlected by a majority of the freemen of the State.

The customary address of the governor, and the reply of the house thereto, was the occasion of a hot party debate, which was kept up for several days, and it was expected that the Republicans would use their newly acquired power to place adherents of their party in all the offices at their disposal. But the wise counsel of the first governor still prevailed, and there were but few removals for mere political causes. Though party spirit was rancorous enough, the elevation of men to office, more for their political views than for their fitness, did not obtain in the politics of Vermont till the bad example had for some years been set by the party in power at the seat of national government.

Until 1808, the legislature of Vermont wandered from town to town, like a homeless vagrant, having held its sessions in fifteen different towns, one of which, Charlestown, was outside the present limits of the commonwealth, though then in its Eastern Union. This year, as if partially fulfilling the threat of Ethan Allen, it gathered among the fastnesses of the mountains, and established a permanent seat at Montpelier, which town was chosen as the capital for being situated near the geographical centre of the State. A large wooden structure, three stories in height and of quaint fashion, was erected for a state house. The seats of the representatives' hall were of unpainted pine plank, which so invited the jackknives of the true-born Yankee legislators that in a quarter of a century they were literally whittled into uselessness. A handsome new state house of Vermont granite was built in 1835 on nearly the same ground. Twenty-two years later this was destroyed by fire, and replaced by a larger one of the same style and material.

Commercial intercourse with Canada had been established soon after the close of the war, principally by the people of western Vermont, to whom the gate of the country now opened the easiest exit for their products, the most of which were the lumber and potash that the slain forest yielded to axe and fire.

As early as 1784, steps were taken by the independent commonwealth to open free trade with the Province of Quebec, and a channel through it for such trade with Europe. Ira Allen, Joseph and Jonas Fay were appointed agents to negotiate this business. Only Ira Allen acted in this capacity, and in the following year he reported having succeeded so far as to procure a free exchange of produce and manufactures, except peltry and a few articles of foreign production.

These negotiations, occurring with the arrival of English troops in Nova Scotia, gave rise to alarming rumors that Vermont was taking measures to become a British dependency; but this freedom of commerce through Lake Champlain and the Richelieu, and exclusively confined thereto, was accorded by the Canadian government to the States already in the Union as well as to the independent republic of Vermont, though the latter derived the greater benefit from it. To further promote this commerce, Ira Allen proposed the cutting of a ship canal to navigably connect the waters of Lake Champlain with those of the St. Lawrence, and made a voyage to England with the object of engaging the British government in this work. He offered, under certain conditions, to cut the canal at his own expense, and continued, though unsuccessfully, to urge the government of his own State to aid him in the enterprise so late as 1809.

The great pines, that fifty years before had been reserved for the "masting of His Majesty's navy," were felled now by hardy yeomen who owed allegiance to no earthly king, and, gathered into enormous rafts, voyaged slowly down the lake, impelled by sail and sweep. They bore as their burden barrels of potash that had been condensed from the ashes of their slain brethren, whose giant trunks had burned away in grand conflagrations that made midnight hills and vales and skies bright with lurid flame. The crew of the raft lived on board, and the voyage, though always slow, was pleasant and easy when the south wind filled the bellying sail, wafting the ponderous craft past the shifting scene of level shore, rocky headland, and green islands. In calms or adverse winds, it was hard work to keep headway with the heavy sweeps, and the voyage grew dangerous when storms arose, and the leviathan heaved and surged on angry waves that threatened to sever its huge vertebræ and cast it piecemeal to the savage rocks.

Sloops, schooners, and square-sailed Canada boats plied to and fro, bearing that way cargoes of wheat and potash; this way, salt and merchandise from over-seas. After midwinter, the turbulent lake became a plain of ice, affording a highway for traffic in sleighs, long trains of which fared to Montreal with loads of produce to exchange for goods or coin.

The declaration of what was commonly called the land embargo in 1808, cutting off this busy commerce, and barring western Vermont from its most accessible market, caused great distress and dissatisfaction, and gave rise to an extensive contraband trade.

The Collector of the District of Vermont wrote to Mr. Gallatin, United States Secretary of the Treasury, that the law could not be enforced without military aid. Upon this, President Jefferson issued a proclamation, calling on the insurgents to disperse, and on all civil and military officers to aid in quelling all disturbances.

There is nothing in the newspapers of the day or in official documents to show any combination to oppose the law, and at a regularly called town meeting the citizens of St. Albans, through their selectmen, formally protested to the President "that no cause for such a proclamation existed." Nevertheless, the militia of Franklin County were called out by Governor Smith, a Republican, who had that year been elected over Tichenor. The troops were assigned to duty at Windmill Point in Alburgh, to prevent the passage of certain timber rafts, which, however, got safely past the post in the night. For this the Franklin County troops were unjustly blamed, and, to their great indignation, were sent to their homes, while militia from Rutland County and a small force of regulars were brought up to take their place.

The smugglers grew bold, plying their nefarious traffic by night in armed bands of such strength that the revenue officers seldom ventured to attack them. A notorious craft named the Black Snake had crept a few miles up the Winooski with a cargo of contraband goods, when she was seized by a party of militia. Twelve soldiers, under command of Lieutenant Farrington, were detailed to take her to the lake. The smugglers ambuscaded them, firing on them repeatedly from the willow-screened bank with a wall-piece charged with bullets, slugs, and buckshot, killing three of the party and wounding the lieutenant. The remainder of the militia hurried to the rescue of their comrades, and succeeded in taking eight of the smugglers, while two escaped who were afterwards captured. At a special term of the Supreme Court one of them was sentenced to death,[1] and three to ten years' imprisonment, after first standing in the pillory, and two of the smugglers to receive fifty lashes each.

The temper of both parties grew hotter under the existing conditions, but expended itself in violent language, and there was no further resistance to the laws. The Federalist party gained sufficient strength to reëlect Governor Tichenor at the ensuing election, but in the following year the Republicans elected their candidate, Jonas Galusha, who was continued in the office four years.

[1] This was the first instance of capital punishment since the organization of the State.

A.A. 1880

THE FARMER'S NEW YEAR'S CALLERS.—Drawn by R. E. Robinson.

own. You have him hooked; and if you deal gently with him, giving way to no rash impulse, he is yours to have and to hold in creel and in pan. In trolling for him a small spoon is best. When a Bass will take the fly, he affords a sport almost as noble as do the Salmon and Trout. A large fly is used, of a dark color for clear water, but more showy for turbid water. In whatever way taken with the hook, he is a hard fighter, throwing himself now two or three feet out of water, now running up the line at topmost speed, full of devices, and game to the last gasp, and it needs a cool head and a skillful hand to bring him to basket; and he who brings him there safely, and surely, and scientifically, may rightly feel a thrill of pride and satisfaction.

staggering o'er the swirling pools and rippling shal As drunk with sunshine, or giddy, dodging swallow s Then the bass bethinks him that this gay new-comer Naught but a blossom is of the air of summer, A chrysalis the bud, this the gandy flower. Drowning here its briefly blooming sunlit hour. Then up he darts to seize it with a sudden madness. Born part of hunger and part of that wild gladness Which moveth all things in this glorious season, Proving sometimes better, sometimes worse than rea But how this gay-clad insect his attack resenteth: With sting so sharp that none but fiend inventeth: No blundering bumble bee, no wasp nor buzzing horn Hath e'er so pierced his lip, nor e'er so torn it! Then he spies an angler on the brink above him, Intent upon him: does he hate or love him? Ah! The wand he holds nods to him, out restrains hi To its slender thread belongs the sting that pains him To the depths he plunges with his dear-bought treasu Wondering in this sport to whom belongs the pleasure The coolest desire, where he has had his life-long spo Afford him now no help in this his sorry sort. In vain he grinds his wounded jaw upon the gravel.

The spoon is used only for trolling from a boat with a hand-line or rod and reel, or walking along the shore or bank, when a rod must of course be used. Of all baits, the minnow is probably the most killing.

For bait fishing, a light rod and tackle must be used if sport is the object. The pot-fisherman may attain his end with a sapling and a line half as big as a pipe

CHAPTER XIX.

THE continued aggressions of Great Britain were gradually but surely tending to a declaration of war against the imperial mistress of the sea. To the impressment of our seamen, the search and seizure of our vessels, the wanton attack of the Leopard on the Chesapeake, and many other outrages, was added the insult of attempting the same policy toward all New England which years before England had pursued in the effort to draw Vermont to her allegiance.

To open communication with the leading men therein, and to ascertain the feeling of the New England States, in all of which, except Vermont, the party opposing the administration of Madison was in the ascendant, Sir James Craig, Governor-General of Canada, employed an adventurer named John Henry, a naturalized citizen of the United States. Coming from Canada, he passed through Vermont, tarrying awhile at Burlington and Windsor. From the first town he wrote an unwarranted favorable report to his employer, representing that Vermont would not sustain the government in case of war; but, on reaching Windsor, he was led to give a less favorable representation. He then journeyed through New Hampshire, and, at length arriving at Boston, wrote many letters in cipher to Sir James. He represented the opposition of the New England Federalists to the administration to be of so violent a nature that, in case of war, they would at least remain neutral, and probably would bring about a separation of those States from the Union, and their formation into a dependency of Great Britain. Having performed the duty assigned him, he received from the British government, as reward for his services, not the appointment he asked, but only compliments. In retaliation for this poor requital, he divulged the whole correspondence to President Madison, receiving therefor the sum of $50,000. In the manifesto of the causes of war, this attempt at disruption was declared to be an "act of greater malignity than any other."

On the 18th of June, 1812, an act was passed by Congress declaring war against Great Britain. A considerable proportion of the citizens of the United States were strongly opposed to a resort to arms, believing that all disputes might have been adjusted more certainly by further negotiations than by the arbitrament of war, for which the nation was so ill-prepared.

So it was in Vermont. Of the 207 members of the Assembly which was that year elected, seventy-nine were Federalists opposed to the war, who made earnest protest against a resolution of the majority, declaring that those who did not actively support this measure of the government "would identify themselves with the enemy, with no other difference than that of locality." But the overwhelming majority of Republicans, with a governor of their own politics, framed the laws to their own liking. An act was passed prohibiting all intercourse between the people of Vermont and Canada without permit from the governor, under a penalty of $1,000 fine and seven years' imprisonment at hard labor; also, an act exempting the bodies and property of officers and soldiers of the militia from attachment while in actual service, and levying a tax of one cent per acre on all lands, for arming and supporting the militia to defend the frontiers.

Soon after the declaration of war, recruiting offices were opened in the State, a cantonment for troops was established at Burlington, and small bodies of volunteers were stationed at several points on the northern frontier. On either side of the scattered settlers of this region lay the forest, — on this, the scarcely broken wilderness of northern Vermont; on that, the Canadian wilds, that still slept in almost primeval solitude. The old terror of Indian warfare laid hold of these people, and their imagination filled the gloomy stretch of northward forest with hordes of red warriors awaiting the first note of conflict to repeat here the horrors of the old border warfare. In some of these towns stockades were built, and from all came urgent appeals to the state and general government for arms to repel the expected invasion. One frontier town was obliged to borrow twenty muskets, and the selectmen were authorized to purchase twenty-five pounds of powder and one hundred pounds of lead on six months' credit, a circumstance which shows how poorly prepared Vermont was for war.

Two months before the declaration of war, Congress authorized the President to detach 100,000 militia to march at a minute's notice, to serve for six months after arriving at the place of rendezvous. Vermont's apportionment was 3,000, and was promptly raised.

In November an act was passed by the legislature for the raising of sixty-four companies of infantry, two of cavalry, and two of artillery, to hold themselves ready at a minute's notice to take the field.

It appears that this corps was formed almost exclusively from exempts from military service. In one company, says an old paper,[1] was a venerable patriarch who could still shoot and walk well, and who " was all animation at the sound of the drum."

As shown by the disbursements by the State for premiums to recruits, it appears that only the old and populous States of Massachusetts, New York, Pennsylvania, and Virginia furnished more men to the regular army than this young commonwealth, which was half a wilderness. The 30th and 31st regiments of infantry were composed entirely of

[1] *Niles' Register.*

Vermonters, as were largely the 11th and 26th.
The 3,000 detached Vermont militia were assembled at Plattsburgh in the fall of 1812. In
November General Dearborn marched from Plattsburgh to the lines with an army of 5,000 men,
2,000 of whom were militia. At the La Colle
he made an ill-planned and feebly conducted
attack upon a very inferior British force, and
then retired to Plattsburgh. A large number of
Vermonters shared the barren honors of this expedition under an incompetent leader. The militia
were presently disbanded, and four regiments of
regulars crossed the lake and took post at Burlington.

All along the lake, during the summer, there had
been a stir of busy preparation. Vessels of war
were built and fitted out to contest the supremacy
on the lake with the British naval force already
afloat. " Niles' Register " reports the arrival at
Plattsburgh [1] of the sloop of war President, and
a little later that of the smaller sloops, which, with
six gunboats, constituted at the time the American
force on Lake Champlain, all under the command
of Lieutenant Macdonough. But the belligerent
craft of either nation held aloof from more than
menace, while sullen autumn merged into the bitter
chill of northern winter, and the ships were locked
harmless in their ice-bound harbors.

When returning warm weather set them free,
some British gunboats crept up the lake, and on the

---

[1] October 27, 1812.

3d of June the Growler and Eagle went in pursuit of them, chasing them into the Richelieu. Having come in sight of the works on Isle aux Noix, the sloops put about and endeavored to make their way back to the open lake against the current of the river and a south wind. Three row-galleys now put out from the fort, and began playing on them with guns of longer range and heavier metal than those of the sloops, upon whom a galling fire of musketry was also rained from the river banks. The vessels poured a storm of grape and canister upon the green wall of leafage that hid the musketeers, and hurled ineffectual shot at the distant galleys, maintaining a gallant defense for more than four hours. Then a heavy shot from one of the galleys crushed through the hull of the Eagle below the water-line, sinking her instantly, but in shallow water, so that her men were rescued by boats from shore. Fifteen minutes later a shot carried away the forestay and main boom of the Growler, and being now unmanageable she was forced to strike. Only one of the Americans was killed, and nineteen were wounded, while the loss of the British was far greater, but the entire crews of both sloops were taken prisoners. Thus disastrously to the Americans resulted the first naval encounter of this war on these waters. The captured sloops were refitted, and, under the names of Finch and Chub, made a brave addition to the British fleet upon the lake.

The defenseless condition of the western shore in-

vited attack, and on the last day of July Colonel
Murray sailed up to Plattsburgh with two sloops,
three gunboats, and a number of longboats manned
by 1,400 men. Making an unopposed landing,
they destroyed the barracks and all other public
property there, and carried away eight thousand
dollars' worth of private property. During this
attack General Wade Hampton, recently appointed
to the command of this department, remained inert
at Burlington, only twenty miles distant, with 4,000
troops, although he had twenty-four hours' notice
of the expected attack, and received repeated calls
for aid.

Two gunboats and the longboats then proceeded
to Swanton, where they destroyed some old barracks and plundered several citizens, and committed
similar piratical depredations at several points on
the western shore.

The two sloops, late Growler and Eagle, now
sailed under changed names and colors up the lake,
accompanied by the other gunboats, and destroyed
several boats engaged in transporting stores. They
appeared before Burlington, firing a few shots upon
the town, which were briskly returned by the batteries. That night they cut out four sloops laden
with provisions, and burnt another with a cargo of
salt, and then bore away northward with their booty.

In September Macdonough sailed down the lake
with his little fleet and offered battle, but the British declined and sailed into the Richelieu, whither
the brave commodore would not follow to be en-

trapped as Lieutenant Smith had been. Again, in December, when some of the British vessels came up to Rouse's Point on a burning and plundering expedition, Macdonough endeavored to get within striking distance near Point au Fer, but they refused to engage, and retired to the same safe retreat.

In October Colonel Isaac Clark, a Vermonter and a veteran of the Revolution, made a brilliant dash with a detachment of his regiment, the 11th, on a British post at St. Armand, on Missisquoi Bay. With 102 riflemen he surprised the enemy, killing nine, wounding fourteen, and taking 101 prisoners in an engagement that lasted only ten minutes. In November he again visited St. Armand, securing fifty head of cattle which had been taken there from the Vermont side of the line. A Canadian journal was " glad to give the Devil his due," and credited him with having " behaved very honorably in this affair."

During the autumn General Wade Hampton amused himself and tired his troops with abortive meanderings along the line. In October he entered Canada, and made an attack on a small body of British troops, accomplishing nothing but the loss to himself of thirty-five men, killed and wounded. He refused to coöperate with General Wilkinson, who was advancing from Sackett's Harbor down the St. Lawrence, and desired Hampton to join him at St. Regis, the object being the capture of Montreal. Hampton's inglorious campaign ended with his retiring to winter quarters at Plattsburgh. Many Vermonters served under him, their hardships unrewarded by victory, or even vigorous endeavor to gain it.

Wilkinson's movements were as abortive, though when his flotilla reached the head of the Long Sault, a brigade of his army engaged a force of the enemy at Chrysler's Farm. The raw and undisciplined American troops, of whom the Vermonters in a battalion of the 11th formed a part, distinguished themselves by frequently repulsing some of the tried veterans of the English army. Neither side gained a victory, but the British remained in possession of the field, though they suffered the heavier loss in killed and wounded, and the flotilla continued its inconsequential voyage. Arriving at St. Regis, and learning that Hampton would not coöperate with him, Wilkinson abandoned the movement against Montreal, and went into winter quarters at French Mills.

On the last of December a British force made a succcessful raid on a depot of supplies at Derby, Vermont, destroying barracks and storehouses, and carrying away a considerable quantity of stores. In consequence of this, and some threatening demonstration on the Richelieu, Wilkinson removed his quarters to Lake Champlain. While this pretense was made of undertaking a conquest which might result in the annexation of Canada to the United States, and a consequent increase of power in the north, a result desired neither by the secre-

tary of war nor the generals here employed, hot
and earnest blows were falling on the enemy at the
westward.   On Lake Erie Perry had overcome the
British, and was master of that inland sea.   Har-
rison had vanquished the English and their Indian
allies at the battle of the Thames, and Michigan
was regained.

Meantime a storm of abuse raged between the
political parties of Vermont, each hurling at the
other the hard names of Tories, traitors, and enemies of their country, and neighborhoods and families were divided in the bitter contest.   The Federalist strength was so far increased by the growing
unpopularity of the war, and the irksomeness of
the restrictions on trade, that the party succeeded
at the election of 1813 in placing Martin Chittenden, son of the old governor, at the head of the
state government.

One of his earliest acts was to recall by proclamation a brigade of the state militia in service at
Plattsburgh.   In this the governor acted on the
ground that it was unconstitutional to call the
militia beyond the limits of the State without permission from the governor, their commander-in-
chief, a view of the case supported by the Supreme
Court of Massachusetts, and adhered to by most of
the other New England States ; and, further, that
the militia of Vermont were more needed for the
defense of their own State than for that of its
stronger sister commonwealth.   A number of the
Vermont officers returned a protest whose vigor was

weakened by its insolence. They refused to obey
the proclamation of their captain-general, but nev-
erthless the rank and file, tired of inaction, less
irksome to the officers, returned to their homes before the term, of enlistment expired, and the affair
passed without further notice.

The muskrats had long been housed in their
lodges on the frozen marshes, and all waterfowl
but the loons and mergansers had flown southward,
when Macdonough withdrew his fleet from the
stormy lake into Otter Creek, whose current was
already thick with drifting anchor-ice. The craft
were moored in a reach of the river known as the
Buttonwoods, three fourths of a mile above Dead
Creek, the ice closed around them, and they slept
inert until the return of spring.

The sap had scarcely begun to swell the forest
buds when Vergennes, eight miles upstream, where
the first fall bars navigation, was astir with the
building of other craft for the Champlain navy. A
throng of ship carpenters were busy on the narrow
flat by the waterside; the woods were noisy with
the thud of axes, the crash of falling trees, and the
bawling of teamsters; and the two furnaces were in
full blast casting cannon-shot for the fleet. Forty
days after the great oak which formed the keel of
the Saratoga had fallen from its stump, the vessel
was afloat and ready for its guns. Several gunboats were also built there, and early in May, their
sappy timbers yet reeking with woodsy odors, the
new craft dropped down the river to join the fleet
at the Buttonwoods.

The right bank of Otter Creek at its mouth is a rock-ribbed promontory, connected with the mainland, except at high water, by a narrow neck of low, alluvial soil. On the lakeward side of the point earthworks were thrown up, and mounted with several pieces of artillery, for the defense of the entrance against an expected attempt of the enemy to destroy the American fleet. The militia of Addison, Chittenden, and Franklin counties were put in readiness to turn out on the firing of signal guns, and a small detachment was posted at Hawley's Farm, near the mouth of Little Otter, to watch the approach of the army. About 1,000 of the militia were stationed at Vergennes. All the night of the 13th the officers of the neighboring towns were running bullets at their treasurer's, where powder and lead were stored for the militia at Vergennes.

On the 10th of May the British squadron passed Cumberland Head, and on the 14th eight of the galleys and a bomb-ketch appeared off the mouth of Great Otter, while a brig, four sloops, and several galleys were two miles to the northward. The galleys opened a fire on the battery, which was bravely defended by Captain Thornton of the artillery and Lieutenant Cassin of the navy. The rapid discharge of the guns, repeated in echoes from the rugged steeps of Split Rock Mountain till it became a continuous roar, for a time greatly alarmed the inhabitants of the adjacent country, but the assailants were beaten off after receiving considerable injury, while they inflicted on the defenders only the dismounting of one gun, and the slight wounding of two men. The British fleet sailed northward, and next day Macdonough's flotilla issued forth ready for battle, and sailed northward to Cumberland Bay.

The importance of this action has not had proper recognition. It is briefly, if at all, mentioned by historians. If the defense of the little battery which now bears the name of Fort Cassin, in honor of Macdonough's brave lieutenant, had been less gallant and successful, our fleet would in all probability have been destroyed before it could strike the blow which gained its commander imperishable renown. The British keenly felt the lost opportunity, for Captain Pring was charged by his superiors with cowardice and disobedience of orders in not having taken the battery and blockaded the American squadron.

The invasion of Canada again was the plan of the campaign for 1814. The two western armies were to move against the enemy on the upper lakes and at the Niagara frontier, while General Izard was to cut the communication on the St. Lawrence between Kingston and Montreal. The Vermonters of the 30th and 31st regiments, and part of the 11th, with the militia and volunteers raised in the vicinity of Lake Champlain were employed in this army, while the remainder of the 11th were in service on the Niagara frontier.

The contraband trade was not entirely suppressed all along the border. Many cunning devices were resorted to by the smugglers. One of the most notable was the fitting out of a pretended privateer by one John Banker of New York. Obtaining letters of marque from the collector of that city, he began cruising on the lake in a little vessel named the Lark, of less than one ton burden, and armed with three muskets. After evincing her warlike character by firing on the Essex ferry-boat, she ran down the lake to Rouse's Point, and there lay in wait for prizes. A barge heavily laden with merchandise presently fell a prey to the bold privateer; her cargo was conveyed to New York by Banker's confederate, and delivered to the owners. The government officials soon learned that the goods had not been received at the United States storehouse, the Lark was seized, and the brief career of privateering on these waters came to an end. In March, 1814, Colonel Clark of the 11th, with 1,100 Green Mountain Boys, took possession of the frontier from Lake Champlain to the Connecticut, establishing his headquarters at Missisquoi Bay, harassing the enemy as opportunity offered, and making vigilant efforts for the suppression of smuggling. After successfully accomplishing this, he joined Wilkinson at the La Colle.

In the brave but unsuccessful attack on the La Colle Mill, upon whose strong stone walls our two light pieces of artillery made no impression, Clark led the 600 Green Mountain Boys who composed the advance. Their loss was eleven of the thirteen killed, and one third of the 128 wounded. The Vermonters of this army had no further opportunity to distinguish themselves until September, but those of the 11th regiment gallantly bore their part in the bloody battles of Chippewa, Lundy's Lane, and Fort Erie. In the first, General Scott called on the 11th to charge upon the enemy, who had declared that the Americans " could not stand cold iron," and the regiment dashed impetuously upon the scarlet line and swept it back with their bayonets.

A formidable British army, 15,000 strong, largely composed of veterans, flushed with their European victories, was near the Richelieu, under command of Sir George Prevost, and their fleet had been strengthened by additional vessels.

Though there were at the time but about 6,000 troops fit for duty, to oppose the enemy's advance in this quarter, early in August the secretary of war ordered General Izard to march with 4,000 of them to the Niagara frontier. Protesting against an order which would leave the Champlain region so defenseless, Izard set forth from Champlain and Chazy with his army on the 29th, halting two days at Lake George in the hope that the order might yet be revoked.

On the 30th the British general Brisbane occupied Champlain, and four days later Sir George Prevost arrived there with his whole force; while Plattsburgh was held by the insignificant but undaunted army of the Americans under General

Macomb, abandoned to its fate by a government that did not desire the conquest of Canada. The three forts and block-house were strengthened, and the general made an urgent call on New York and Vermont for reinforcements, which was promptly responded to, while small parties were sent out to retard, as much as possible, the advance of the enemy. But the skirmishers were swept back by the overwhelming strength of the invading army, and retired across the Saranac, destroying the bridges behind them.

Governor Chittenden did not consider himself authorized to order the militia into service outside the State, but called for volunteers. There was a quick response. Veterans of the Revolution and their grandsons, exempt by age and youth from service, as well as the middle-aged, each with the evergreen badge of his State in his hat, turned out. With the old smooth-bores and rifles that had belched buckshot and bullet at Hubbardton and Bennington, and with muskets obtained from the town armories, they flocked towards the scene of impending battle, on foot, in wagons, singly, in squads, and by companies, crossing the lake at the most convenient points, of which Burlington was the principal one. General Strong was put in command of the Vermont volunteers. On the 10th of September he reported 1,812 at Plattsburgh, and on the 11th 2,500, while only 700 of the New York militia had arrived.

When the morning of the 11th of September

broke, the American army stood at bay on the south
bank of the Saranac. Fifteen hundred regulars
and about 3,200 hastily collected militia and volunteers, confronted by 14,000 of the best troops of
Great Britain, proudly wearing the laurels won in
the Napoleonic wars, and confident of victory over
the despised foe that now opposed them.

Early that morning the British fleet collected at
Isle La Motte weighed anchor, and sailed southward. At eight o'clock it rounded Cumberland
Head, and with sails gleaming in the sunlight,
swept down toward the American fleet like a white
cloud drifting across the blue lake.

Macdonough's vessels were anchored in a line
extending north from Crab Island and parallel
with the west shore, the Eagle, Captain Henly,
at the head of the line, next the Saratoga, Commodore Macdonough's flagship; the schooner Ticonderoga next; and at the south end of the line
the sloop Preble, so close to Crab Island Shoal as
to prevent the enemy from turning that end of the
line. Forty rods in the rear of this line lay ten
gunboats, kept in position by their sweeps; two
north and in rear of the Eagle, the others opposite the intervals between the larger craft.

At nine o'clock the hostile fleet came to anchor
in a line about three hundred yards from ours,
Captain Downie's flagship, the Confiance, opposed
to the Saratoga; his brig Linnet to the Eagle;
his twelve galleys to our schooner, sloop, and a division of galleys; while one of the sloops taken

from us the year before assisted the Confiance and
Linnet, the other the enemy's galleys. The British
fleet had 95 guns, and 1,050 men; the American,
86 guns, and 820 men. In such position of the
fleets the action began.

The first broadside of the Confiance killed and
disabled forty of the Saratoga's crew. The head
of one of his men, cut off by a cannon-shot, struck
Macdonough in the breast and knocked him into
the scuppers. A shot upset a coop and released a
cock, which flew into the shrouds and crowed lustily,
and the crew, cheering this augury of victory,
served the guns with increased ardor. The Eagle,
unable to bring her guns to bear, cut her cable and
took a position between the Saratoga and the Ticonderoga, where she greatly annoyed the enemy, but
left the flagship exposed to a galling fire from the
British brig. Nearly all the Saratoga's starboard
guns were dismounted, and Macdonough winded
her, bringing her port guns to bear upon the Confiance, which ship attempted the same manœuvre,
but failed. After receiving a few broadsides, her
gallant commander dead, half her men killed and
wounded, with one hundred and five shots in her
hull, her rigging in tatters on the shattered masts,
the British flagship struck her colors.

The guns of the Saratoga were now turned on
the Linnet, and in fifteen minutes she surrendered,
as the Chub, crippled by the Eagle's broadsides
and with a loss of half her men, had done some
time before.

The Finch, driven from her position by the Ticonderoga, drifted upon Crab Island Shoals, where, receiving the fire of a battery on the island manned by invalids, she struck and was taken possession of by them. The galleys remaining afloat made off. Our galleys were signaled to pursue, but were all in a sinking condition, unable to follow, and, the other vessels being crippled past making sail, the galleys escaped.

The havoc wrought in this conflict proves it to have been one of the hottest naval battles ever fought. A British sailor who was at Trafalgar declared that battle as "but a flea-bite to this." The British lost in killed and wounded one fifth of their men, the commander of the fleet, and several of his officers; the Americans, one eighth of their men. Among the killed were Lieutenant Stansbury of the Ticonderoga, and Lieutenant Gamble of the Saratoga. The Saratoga was twice set on fire by the enemy's hot shot, and received fifty-five shots in her hull. At the close of the action, not a mast was left in either squadron on which a sail could be hoisted.[1]

The result, so glorious to the Americans, was due to the superior rapidity and accuracy of their fire.

For more than two hours the unremitting thunder-peal of the battle had rolled up the Champlain valley to thousands who listened in alternating hope and fear. For a time, none but the combat-

[1] Macdonough's report, Palmer's *Lake Champlain.*

ants and immediate spectators knew how the fight had gone, till the lifting smoke revealed to the anxious watchers on the eastern shore the stars and stripes alone floating above the shattered ships; then horsemen rode in hot speed north, east, and south, bearing the glad tidings of victory.

The opening of the naval fight was the signal for the attack of the British land force. A furious fire began from all the batteries. At two bridges, and at a ford above Plattsburgh, its strength was exerted in attempts to cross the Saranac. The attacks at the bridges were repulsed by the American regulars, firing from breastworks formed of planks of the bridges. At the ford, the enemy were met by the volunteers and militia. A considerable number succeeded in crossing the river, but an officer riding up with news of the naval victory, the citizen soldiers set upon the enemy in a furious assault, and with cheers drove them back.

A fire was kept up from the English batteries until sundown, but when the evening, murky with the cloud of battle, darkened into the starless gloom of night, the British host began a precipitate retreat, abandoning vast quantities of stores and munitions, and leaving their killed and wounded to the care of the victors. They had lost in killed, wounded, prisoners, and deserters 2,500; the Americans, 119. But bitterest of all to the vanquished invaders was the thought that they who had overcome the armies of Napoleon were now beaten

back by an "insignificant rabble" of Yankee yeomen.

The retreat had been for some hours in progress
before it was discovered, and a pursuit begun,
which, after the capture of some prisoners, and
covering the escape of a number of deserters, was
stopped at Chazy by the setting in of a drenching
rainstorm.

Three days later, their present service being no
longer necessary, the Vermont volunteers were dismissed by General Macomb, with thanks of warm
commendation for their ready response to his call,
and the undaunted spirit with which they had met
the enemy.

Through General Strong they received the
thanks of Governor Chittenden, and, later, the
thanks of the general government "to the brave
and patriotic citizens of the State for their prompt
succor and gallant conduct in the late critical state
of the frontier."

Their promptness was indeed commendable, for
they had rallied to Macomb's aid, and the battle
was fought, four days before the government at
Washington had issued its tardy call for their
assistance. The State of New York presented to
General Strong an elegant sword in testimony of
"his services and those of his brave mountaineers
at the battle of Plattsburgh," and the two States
united in making a gift to Macdonough of a tract
of land on Cumberland Head lying in full view of
the scene of his brilliant victory.

The army of Sir George Prevost was beaten back to Canada, but it was still powerful, and the danger of another invasion was imminent. Governor Chittenden issued another proclamation, unequivocal in its expressions of patriotism, enjoining upon all officers of the militia to hold their men in readiness to meet any invasion, and calling on all exempts capable of bearing arms to equip themselves and unite with the enrolled militia when occasion demanded.

As there was nothing to apprehend from any naval force which could be put afloat this season by the British, Macdonough requested that he might be employed on the seaboard under Commodore Decatur. On the approach of winter, the fleet was withdrawn to Fiddler's Elbow, near Whitehall, never again to be called forth to battle. There, where the unheeding keels of commerce pass to and fro above them, the once hostile hulks of ship and brig, schooner and galley, lie beneath the pulse of waves in an unbroken quietude of peace.

There were rumors of a projected winter invasion from Canada to destroy the flotilla while powerless in the grip of the ice. It was reported that an immense artillery train of guns mounted on sledges was preparing; that a multitude of sleighs and teams for the transportation of troops, with thousands of buffalo robes for their warmth, had been engaged and bought. Vermont did not delay preparation for such an attack.

The rancor of politics among her people had given place to a nobler spirit of patriotism, and, without distinction of parties, all good men stood forth in defense of their country, and those who had opposed the war were now as zealous as its advocates in prosecuting it to an honorable close.

Major-General Strong issued a general order to the militia to be ready for duty at any moment, requested the exempts to aid them, and urged the selectmen to make into cartridges the ammunition with which the towns were supplied, and place them at convenient points for distribution. All responded promptly, and, moreover, matrons and maids diligently plied their knitting-needles in the long winter evenings to make socks and mittens for the brave men who would need them in the bitter weather of such a campaign.

But, instead of the expected invasion, came the good news of the treaty of peace, signed at Ghent on the twenty-fourth day of December.

Peace was welcome to the nation, though the treaty was silent concerning the professed causes of the declaration of war, and the only compensation for the losses and burdens entailed by the conflict, so wretchedly conducted by our government, was the glory of the victories gained by our little navy and undisciplined troops over England's invincible warships and armies of veterans.

CHAPTER XX.

OLD-TIME CUSTOMS AND INDUSTRIES.

PEACE was indeed welcome to a people so long deprived of an accessible market as had been the inhabitants of Vermont.

The potash fires were relighted; the lumberman's axe was busy again in the bloodless warfare against the giant pines; new acres of virgin soil were laid bare to the sun, and added to the broadening fields of tilth. White-winged sloops and schooners, and unwieldy rafts, flocked through the reopened gate of the country, and the clumsy Durham boat spread its square sail to the favoring north wind, and once more appeared on the broad lake where it had so long been a stranger. The shores were no longer astir with military preparations, but with the bustle of awakened traffic; soldiers had again become citizens; the ravages of war had scarcely touched the borders of the State, and in a few months there remained hardly a trace of its recent existence.

There had not been, nor was there for years after this period, a marked change in the social conditions of the people, for the old fraternal bonds of interdependence still held pioneer to pioneer almost as closely as in the days when the strong hand was more helpful than the long purse.

Class distinctions were marked vaguely, if at all, and there was no aristocracy of idleness, for it was held that idleness was disgraceful. The farmer who owned five hundred acres worked as early and as late as he who owned but fifty, and led his half-score of mowers to the onslaught of herdsgrass and redtop with a ringing challenge of whetstone on scythe, and was proud of his son if the youngster " cut him out of his swathe."

The matron taught her daughters and maids how to spin and weave flax and wool. The beat of the little wheel, the hum of the great wheel, the ponderous thud of the loom, were household voices in every Vermont homestead, whether it was the old log-house that the forest had first given place to, or its more pretentious framed and boarded successor. All the women-folk knitted stockings and mittens while they rested or visited, the click of the needles accompanied by the chirp of the cricket and the buzz of gossip.

For workday and holiday, the household was clad in homespun from head to foot, save what the hatter furnished for the first and the traveling cobbler for the last.

Once a year the latter was a welcome visitor of every homestead in his beat, bringing to it all the gossip for the women-folk, all the weighty news for the men, and all the bear stories for the children which he had gathered in a twelve months'

" whipping of the cat," as his itinerant craft was termed. These he dispensed while, by the light of the wide fireplace, he mended old foot-gear or fashioned new, that fitted and tortured alike either foot whereon it was drawn on alternate days.

The old custom of making " bees," instituted when neighborly help was a necessity, was continued when it was no longer needed, for the sake of the merry-makings which such gatherings afforded. There were yet logging-bees for the piling of logs in a clearing, and raising-bees when a new house or barn was put up ; drawing-bees when one was to be moved to a new site, with all the ox-teams of half a township; and bees when a sick or short-handed neighbor's season-belated crops needed harvesting.

When the corn was ripe came the husking-bee, in which old and young of both sexes took part, their jolly labor lighted in the open field by the hunter's moon or a great bonfire, around which the shocks were ranged like a circle of wigwams; or, if in the barn, by the rays sprinkled from lanterns of punched tin. When the work was done, the company feasted on pumpkin pie, doughnuts, and cider. Then the barn floor was cleared of the litter of husks, the fiddler mounted the scaffold, and made the gloom of the roof-peak ring with merry strains, to which twoscore solidly clad feet threshed out time in " country dance " and " French four."

The quilting party, in its first laborious stage,

A Moving Bee   Rowland E. Robinson, 1880

THE SUGAR BUSH

TAPPING THE TREES.

GATHERING THE SAP.

BOILING THE SAP.

Seasonable Scenes in The Sugar Orchard　　　Rowland E. Robinson, circa 1875

was participated in only by the womenkind; but, when that was passed, the menfolk were called in to assist in the ceremony of " shaking the quilt," and in the performance of this the fiddler was as necessary as in the closing rites of the husking-bee.

When the first touch of spring stirred the sap of the maples, sugar-making began, a labor spiced with a woodsy flavor of camp life and small adventure. The tapping was done with a gouge; the sap dripped from spouts of sumach stems into rough-hewn troughs, from which it was gathered in buckets borne on a neck-yoke, the bearer making the rounds on snowshoes, and depositing the gathered sap in a big " store trough " set close to the boiling-place. This was an open fire, generously fed with four-foot wood, and facing an open-fronted shanty that sheltered the sugar-maker from rain and " sugar snow," while he plied his daily and nightly labor, now with the returning crow and the snickering squirrel for companions, now the unseen owl and fox, making known their presence with storm-boding hoot and husky bark. The sap-boiling was done in the great potash kettle that in other seasons seethed with pungent lye, but now, swung on a huge log crane, sweetened the odors of the woods with sugar-scented vapor. Many families saw no sweetening, from one end of the year to the other, but maple sugar and syrup, the honey from their few hives, or the uncertain spoil of the bee-hunter. All the young folks of a neighborhood were invited to

the " sugaring off," and camp after camp in turn,
during the season of melting snow and the return
of bluebird and robin, rung with the chatter and
laughter of a merry party that was as boisterous
over the sugar feast as the blackbirds that swung
on the maple-tops above them rejoicing over the
return of spring.

In the long evenings of late autumn and early
winter, there were apple or paring bees, to which
young folk and frolicsome elder folk came and
lent a hand in paring, coring, and stringing to
dry, for next summer's use, the sour fruit of the
ungrafted orchards, and, when the work was done,
to lend more nimble feet to romping games and
dances, that were kept up till the tallow dips paled
with the stars in the dawn, and daylight surprised
the coatless beaux and buxom belles, all clad in
honest homespun.

Very naturally, weddings often came of these
merry-makings, and were celebrated with as little
ostentation and as much hearty good fellowship.
The welcome guests brought no costly and useless
presents for display ; there were no gifts but the
bride's outfit of home-made beds, homespun and
hand-woven sheets, table-cloths, and towels given
by parents and nearest relations. The young
couple did not parade the awkwardness of their
newly assumed relations in a wedding journey, but
began the honeymoon in their new home, and spent
it much as their lives were to be spent, taking up
at once the burden that was not likely to grow

lighter with the happiness that might increase. But if the burden became heavy, and the light of love faded, there was seldom separation or divorce. If there were more sons and daughters than could be employed at home, they hired out in families not so favored without loss of caste or sense of degradation in such honest service. They often married into the family of the employer, and their position was little changed by the new relation.

For many years the wheat crop in Vermont continued certain and abundant, and formed a part of almost every farmer's income, as well as the principal part of his breadstuff, for the pioneer's Johnny-cake had fallen into disrepute among his thrifty descendants, who held it more honorable to eat poor wheat-bread than good Johnny-cake, and despised the poor wretch who ate buckwheat. It is quite possible that the first demarcation between the aristocrats and the plebeians of Vermont was drawn along this food line.

Wool-growing was fostered in the infancy of the State by public acts, and almost every farmer was more or less a shepherd. A marked improvement in the fineness and weight of the fleeces began with the introduction of the Spanish merinos in 1809.[1] By the judicious breeding by a few intelligent Vermont farmers, the Spanish sheep were brought to

---

[1] Chancellor Livingston brought merinos to this country as early as 1802. In 1809 William Jarvis, our consul at Lisbon, brought a considerable number of merinos to Vermont, and from his famous Weathersfield flocks most of the Vermont merinos are descended.

a degree of perfection which they had never attained in their European home, and Vermont merinos gained a world-wide reputation that still endures; while the wool product of the State, once so
famous for it that Sheffield cutlers stamped their
best shears " The True Vermonter," has become
almost insignificant, compared with that of states
and countries whose flocks yearly renew their impov-
erished blood with fresh draughts from Vermont
stock. Shearing-time was the great festival of the
year. The shearers, many of whom were often the
flock-owner's well-to-do neighbors, were treated
more as guests than as laborers, and the best the
house afforded was set before them. The great
barn's empty bays and scaffolds resounded with the
busy click of incessant shears, the jokes, songs, and
laughter of the merry shearers, the bleating of the
ewes and lambs, and the twitter of disturbed swal-
lows, while the sunlight, shot through crack and
knot-hole, swung slowly around the dusty interior
in sheets and bars of gold that dialed the hours
from morning till evening.

A distinctive breed of horses originated in Vermont, and the State became almost as famous for
its Morgan horses as for its sheep. But, though
Vermont horses are still of good repute, this noted
strain, the result of a chance admixture of the blood
of the English thoroughbred and the tough little
Canadian horse, has been improved into extinction
of its most valued traits.

The laborious life of the farmer had an occasional break in days of fishing in lulls of the spring's work, and between that and haymaking; of hunting when the crops were housed, and the splendor of the autumnal woods was fading to sombre monotony of gray, or when woods and fields were white with the snows of early winter.

The clear mountain ponds and streams were populous with trout, the lakes and rivers with pike, pickerel, and the varieties of perch and bass; and in May and June the salmon, fresh run from the sea and lusty with its bounteous fare, swarmed up the Connecticut and the tributaries of Lake Champlain.

The sonorous call of the moose echoed now only in the gloom of the northeastern wilderness, but the deer still homed in the mountains, often coming down to feed with domestic cattle in the hillside pastures. The ruffed grouse strutted and drummed in every wood, copse, and cobble. Every spring, great flights of wild pigeons clouded the sky, as they flocked to their summer encampment; and in autumn, such innumerable hordes of wild fowl crowded the marshes that the roar of their startled simultaneous uprising was like dull thunder. These the farmer hunted in his stealthy Indian way, and after New England fashion, — the fox on foot, with hound and gun; and so, too, the raccoon that pillaged his cornfields when the ears were in the milk. When a wolf came down from the mountain fastnesses, or crossed the frozen lake from the Adirondack wilds, to ravage the folds, every arms-bearer

turned hunter. The marauder was surrounded in
the wood where he had made his latest lair ; the circle, bristling with guns, slowly closed in upon him ;
and as he dashed wildly around it in search of some
loophole of escape, he fell to rifle-ball or charge of
buckshot, if he did not break through the line at a
point weakly guarded by a timid or flurried hunter.
His death was celebrated at the nearest store or
tavern with a feast of crackers and cheese, — a
droughty banquet, moistened with copious draughts
of cider, beer, or more potent liquors, and the bounty
paid the reckoning. The bounty, and the value of
the skins and grease of bears were added incen-
tives to the taking off of these pests, which was frequently accomplished by trap and spring-gun.

Many farmers made a considerable addition to
their income by trapping the fur-bearers, for though
the beaver had been driven from all but the wildest
streams, and the otter was an infrequent visitor of
his old haunts, their little cousins, the muskrat and
mink, held their own in force on every stream and
marsh ; and the greater and lesser martins, known
to their trappers as fisher and sable, still found
home and range on the unshorn mountains. A few
men yet followed for their livelihood the hunter's
and trapper's life of laziness and hardship, for the
most part unthrifty, and poor in everything but
shiftless contentment and the wisdom of woodcraft.
There were exceptions in this class : at least one
mighty hunter laid the foundation of a fortune
when he set his traps. When the trapping season

was ended, he sold his peltry in Montreal, bought goods there, and peddled them through his State till the falling leaves again called him to the woods. He gained wealth and a seat in Congress, but neither is likely to be the reward of one who now follows such a vocation in Vermont.

The annual election of legislators, justices, judges, state officers, and members of Congress, which falls on the first Tuesday of September, had then other than political excitement to enliven the day in the wrestling matches and feats of strength that were interludes of the balloting. In one instance the name of a town was decided by the result of a wrestling match on election day. One figure constant at the elections of the first half of this century, and by far the most attractive one to the unfledged voters who never failed in attendance, was he who dispensed, from his booth or stand, pies, cakes, crackers, cheese, and spruce beer to the hungry and thirsty. When the result of the election was announced, the successful candidate for representative bought out the remaining stock of the victualer, and invited his friends to help themselves, which they did with little ceremony. Nothing less than a reception given at the house of the representative-elect will satisfy the mixed multitude in these progressive times. The once familiar booth and its occupant have drifted into the past with the wrestlers, the jumpers, and pullers of the stick.

Gradually the primitive ways of life, the earliest industries, and the ruder methods of labor gave way to more luxurious living, new industries, and labor-saving machinery.

The log-house, that was reared amid its brotherhood of stumps, decayed with them, and was superseded by a more pretentious frame-house, whose best apartment, known as the " square room," came to know the luxury of a rag carpet, or at least a painted floor, that heretofore had been only sanded, and a Franklin stove, a meagre apology for the generous breadth of the great fireplace whose place it took. There was yet a fireplace in the kitchen, down whose wide-throated chimney the stars might shine upon the seething samp-pot swinging on the trammel and the bake-kettle embedded and covered in embers. Great joints of meat were roasted before it on the spit, biscuits baked in a tin oven, and Johnny-cakes tilted on oaken boards. Around this glowing centre the family gathered in the evening, the always busy womenfolk sewing, knitting, and carding wool; the men fashioning axe-helves and ox-bows, the children popping corn on a hot shovel, or conning their next day's lessons; while all listened to the grandsire's stories of war and pioneer life, or to the schoolmaster's reading of some book seasoned with age, or of the latest news, fresh from the pages of a paper only a fortnight old. The fire gave better light for reading and work than the tallow dips, to whose manufacture of a year's supply one day was devoted, marked in the calendar by greasy discomfort. For the illumination of the square room on grand occasions, there were mould candles held in brass sticks, while these and the dips were attended by the now obsolete snuffers and extinguisher. Close by the kitchen fireplace, and part of the massive chimney stack, whose foundations filled many cubic yards of the cellar, the brick oven held its cavernous place, and was heated on baking days with wood specially prepared for it. Oven and fireplace gave away after a time to the sombre but more convenient cookstove, and with them many time-honored utensils and modes of cookery fell into disuse.

Wool-carding machines were erected at convenient points, and hand-carding made no longer necessary. Presently arose factories which performed all the work of cloth-making (carding, spinning, weaving, and finishing), so that housewife, daughter, and hired girl were relieved of all these labors, and the use of the spinning-wheel and hand-loom became lost arts. When it became cheaper to buy linen than to make it, the growing of flax and all the labors of its preparation were abandoned by the farmer. As wood grew scarcer and more valuable than its ashes, the once universal and important manufacture of pot and pearl ashes was gradually discontinued; and as the hemlock forests dwindled away, the frequent tannery, where the farmers' hides were tanned on shares, fell into disuse and decay.

Early in this century the dull thunder of the forge hammer resounded, and the furnace fire glared upon the environing forest, busily working up ore, brought some from the inferior mines of Vermont, but for the most part from the iron mines of the New York shore. This industry became unprofitable many years ago, and one by one the fires of forge and furnace went out. With the decline of this industry, the charcoal pit and its grimy attendants became infrequent in the new clearings, though for many years later there was a considerable demand for charcoal by blacksmiths. Of these there were many more then than now, for the scope of the smith's craft was far broader in the days when he forged many of the household utensils and farming tools that, except such as have gone out of use, are now wholly supplied by the hardware dealer. A common appurtenance of the smithy, when every farmer used oxen, was the " oxframe," wherein those animals, who in the endurance of shoeing belie their proverbial patience, were hoisted clear of the ground, and their feet made fast while the operation was performed. The blacksmith's shop was also next in importance, as a gossiping place, to the tavern bar-room and the store. At the store dry-goods, groceries, and hardware were dealt out in exchange for butter, cheese, dried apples, grain, peltry, and all such barter, and generous seating conveniences and potations free to all customers invited no end of loungers.

The merchant's goods were brought to him by teams from ports on Lake Champlain and the Connecticut, and from Troy, Albany, and Boston, whither by the same slow conveyance went the product of the farms, — the wool, grain, pork, maple sugar, cheese, butter, and all marketable products except beef, which was driven on the hoof in great droves to a market in Boston and Albany.

Daily stage - coaches traversed the main thoroughfares, carrying the mails and such travelers as went by public conveyance, to whom, journeying together day after day, were given great opportunities for gossip and acquaintance. There was much journeying on horseback. Families going on distant visits went with their own teams in the farm wagon, whose jolting over the rough roads was relieved only by the " spring of the axletree" and the splint bottoms of the double-armed wagon chairs. They often carried their own provisions for the journey, to the disgust of the innkeepers, and this was known as traveling " tuckanuck," a name and custom that savors of Indian origin.

Such were the means of interstate commerce, mail-carriage, and travel until two long-talked-of railroad lines were completed in 1849, running lengthwise of the State, east and west of the mountain range. The new and rapid means of transportation which now brought the State into direct communication with the great cities wrought great changes in trade, in modes of life, and in social traits.

There was now a demand for many perishable products which had previously found only a limited home market, and a host of middlemen arose in eager competition for the farmer's eggs, poultry, butter, veal calves, potatoes, and fruit, as well as for hay, for which until now there had been only a local demand.

The luxuries and fashions of the cities were in some degree introduced by the more rapid and easy intercourse with the outer world ; for many strove to make display beyond their means, to the loss of content and comfort. With homespun wear and simple ways of life, the old-time social equality became less general, and neighborly interdependence slackened its generous hold.

HAYING—OLD AND NEW METHODS.

WASHING.
UNDER SPOUTS, AND IN A POOL.

LAMBS AT PLAY.

THE PATRIARCH OF THE FLOCK.

CLIPPING TOES.

SHEARING.

MARKING.

SEASONABLE SCENES ON A SHEEP FARM.

CHAPTER XXI.

BEING almost wholly of New England origin, the settlers of Vermont and their descendants were in the main a religious people, and held to church-going when there was no place for public worship but the schoolhouse and the barn. In such places the members of the poorer and weaker sects held their meetings till within the memory of men now living. This was particularly the case of the Baptists and Methodists, who were viewed with slight favor by the predominant Congregational-ists. This sect organized the first religious so-ciety in Vermont at Bennington in 1762, and first erected houses of worship. These structures were unpretentious except in size, and for years were unprovided with means of warming. When the bitter chill of winter pervaded them, the congrega-tion kept itself from freezing with thick garments and little foot-stoves of sheet-iron; the minister, with the fervor of his exhortations. Folks went to church with no display of apparel or equipage. Homespun was the wear, till some ambitious wo-man aroused the envy of her kind by appearing in a gown of calico, or some gay gallant displayed his many-caped drab surtout of foreign cloth. The sled or wagon that served for week days on the farm was good enough for Sunday use, when its jolting was softened with a generous cushioning of buffalo robes for such as did not go to church on horseback, or on foot across lots.

Late in summer, after the earlier crops were gathered, the Methodists were wont to congregate in the woods at camp-meetings. These meetings were celebrated with a fervor of religious warmth, and whether by day the white tents and enthusiastic worshipers were splashed and sprinkled with sunlight shot through the canopy of leaves, or lit at night by the lateral glare of the pine-knot torches flaring from a score of scaffolds set on the tree-trunks, the scene was weird and picturesque beyond what the fancy can conjure from the modern fashionable camp-meeting, with its trim cottages and steadily burning lamps and unmoved throng, and one can but think that another fire than that of the old pine torches burned out with them.

There were few Episcopalians, though the royal charters had given them two glebe lots, and two for the Propagation of the Gospel in Foreign Parts, and there were so few Roman Catholics that no priest of that faith established himself in the State till 1833. In parts of the State there were many Friends, commonly called Quakers, who, by reason of their non-resistant principles, were exempted from military service.

The state grants gave in each town two lots of two hundred acres each to the first settled minister of the gospel, of whatever persuasion he might be. The rental of all these grants, except that of the Society for the Propagation of the Gospel, now goes to the support of public schools, with that of a similar grant originally made for that purpose.

The schoolhouse was one of the earliest recognized necessities, when the settlement of the State was fairly established. The pioneers built the schoolhouse of logs, like their dwellings, and its interior was even ruder than that of those. Rough slabs set on legs driven into augur-holes furnished the seats, and the desks, if there were any, were of like fashion. In winter, when the school was largest, if indeed it was held at all in the busier seasons, a great fireplace diffused its fervent heat through half the room, while a chill atmosphere pervaded the far corners. Among such cheerless surroundings many a Vermonter of the old time began his education, which was completed when he had learned to read and write and could cipher to the "rule o' three." Many of the scholars trudged miles through snow and storm to school, and the master, who always boarded around, had his turns of weary plodding with each distant dweller. The boy whose home was far away was in luck when he got the chance of doing chores for his board in some homestead near the schoolhouse. Increase of population and of prosperity brought better schoolhouses, set in districts of narrower bounds.

As early as 1782, nine years before the admission of the State into the Union, provision was made by legislative enactment for the division of towns into districts, and the establishment and support of schools. It directed that trustees for the general superintendence of the schools of each town should be appointed, and also a prudential committee in each district; and empowered the latter to raise half the money needed for the support of the schools on the grand list, the other half on the polls of the scholars or on the grand list, as each district should determine.

At one time the school fund, derived from the rental of lands and from the United States revenue distributed among the States in 1838, was apportioned among the heads of families according to the number of children of school age, without regard to attendance, or restriction of its use to school purposes. This singular application of the funds could not have greatly furthered the cause of education, though it may have stimulated the increase of population, for to the largest families fell the greater share in the distribution of the school money.

In 1827 the legislature provided for the examination and licensing of teachers, and for the supervision of schools by town committees; and also for a board of state commissioners, to select text-books and report upon the educational needs of the State. These provisions were repealed six years later, and there was no general supervision of schools till 1845, when an act provided for the appointment of county and town superintendents, but the first office was soon abolished. In 1856 a state board of education was created, empowered to appoint a secretary, who should devote his whole time to the promotion of education. J. S. Adams, the first secretary, served eleven years, and by his earnest efforts succeeded in awakening the people to a livelier interest in the public schools. During his service, normal schools were established, for the training of teachers; and graded schools in villages, with a high-school department, became a part of the school system.[1]

In 1874 a state superintendent was appointed in place of the board of education; while in 1888 a system of county instead of town supervision was introduced, which after an unsatisfactory trial was abolished in 1890, and the town superintendent was restored. He now has a general charge over the schools in his town, but the teachers are licensed by a county examiner appointed by the governor and state superintendent.

The common schools are now supported entirely at public expense, and are free to every child between the ages of five and twenty, and in all large villages there are free high schools, so that it is now rare to find a child of ten or twelve years who cannot read and write, and a fair education is within the reach of the poorest.

By the act of 1782, already referred to, the

---

[1] Conant, *Geography, History, and Civil Gov. of Vermont.*

judges of the county courts were authorized to appoint trustees of county schools in each county, and, with the assistance of the justices of the peace, to lay a tax for the building of a county schoolhouse in each. In most of the townships granted by Vermont, one right of land was reserved for the support of a grammar school or academy; but as less than one half of the towns were so granted, many of the schools derived little aid from this source, and in fact the establishment of county schools was not generally effected; and though there are many grammar schools and academies in the State, few of them are endowed, but depend on the tuition fees for their support. The Rutland County grammar school at Castleton was established in 1787, and is the oldest chartered educational institution in Vermont. This school, together with the Orange County and Lamoille County grammar schools, became a State Normal School in 1867. These three institutions are under the supervision of the State Superintendent of Education, and the State offers to pay the tuition of one student from each town, thus encouraging the better preparation of teachers for the common schools.[1]

The union of the sixteen New Hampshire towns with Vermont brought Dartmouth College within the limits of the latter State. After the dissolution of the union in 1785, Vermont, upon application of the president of the college, granted a town-

[1] Conant, *Geography, History, and Civil Gov. of Vermont.*

ship of land to that institution in view of "its importance to the world at large and this State in particular,"[1] and, encouraged by this success, the trustees asked for the sequestration to their use of the glebe and society lots granted in the New Hampshire charters, and of the lands granted by Vermont for educational purposes, promising, in return, to take charge of the affairs of education in the State. This gave rise to an agitation of the subject which resulted in the establishment of the University of Vermont at Burlington, for which purpose Ira Allen offered to give, himself, £4,000. A bill incorporating the university was passed in 1791. Three years later land was cleared, and a commodious house built for the president and the accommodation of a few students. Ten years later the erection of the university building was begun, and so far completed in 1804 that the first commencement was held in that year. During the War of 1812 the building was used for the storage of arms, and as quarters for the soldiery. President, professors, and students retired before this martial invasion, and collegiate exercises were suspended till the close of the war. This building was destroyed by fire in 1821 and rebuilt in 1825, the corner-stone being laid by General Lafayette. The medical department of the university was fully organized in 1822, and a course of lectures was kept up for eleven years, when they were suspended, but resumed later.

[1] Thompson's *Vermont.*

The department is now flourishing and of acknowledged importance, and occupies a fine building erected especially for its use. Large endowments and valuable gifts, made by generous and grateful sons of the university, have erected handsome new buildings, notably the fine library edifice, and improved the old to worthy occupancy of the noble site.

Upon the suggestion of Dr. Dwight, who visited Middlebury during his travels in New England, a college charter was obtained of the legislature, but all endowment by the State was refused. The institution was immediately organized with seven students, and held its first commencement in 1802. The first building, erected four years before, was of wood, but the college now occupies three substantial structures of limestone.

A military academy, under the superintendence of Captain Alden Partridge, was established in 1820 at Norwich. Some years later this was incorporated as Norwich University. It was removed to Northfield in 1866. Its distinctive feature is the course of instruction in military science and civil engineering. It contributed 273 commissioned officers to the Mexican and Civil wars,[1] and many, especially in the latter war, served their country with distinction.

The first course of medical lectures in Vermont was given in Castleton, by Doctors Gridley, Woodward, and Cazier in 1818, and laid the foundation

---

[1] Conant, *Geography, History, and Civil Gov. of Vermont.*

of a medical academy at that place, which in 1841 was incorporated as Castleton Medical College. This, and another medical college established at Woodstock some years previously, no longer exist.

The State now gives thirty scholarships to each of her three colleges, which pays the tuition and room-rent of a student. These appointments are made by the state senators, or by the trustees of the colleges. Though there is much interest in all these higher institutions of learning, as well as in the normal schools and academies, many of which are prosperous and important, yet the common schools more particularly engage the attention of the people and of the successive legislatures, resulting in a complication of school laws scarcely balanced by the improvement in the school system.

The early inhabitants of Vermont, though, for the most part, they were rough backwoodsmen, were imbued with a strong desire for useful and instructive reading, and this led to the formation of circulating libraries in several towns, almost as soon as the settlers had fairly established themselves in their new homes. This was notably the case in Montpelier, where a library was begun in 1794, only seven years after the first pioneer's axe broke the shade and solitude of the wilderness. Its two hundred volumes were well chosen, being histories, biographies, and books of travel and adventure, while all works of fiction and of a religious nature were excluded, the one class being deemed of an immoral tendency, the other apt to breed dis-

sension in the sparse and interdependent community.[1] In many other towns similar libraries were
formed; though perhaps not with like restrictions,
yet, as far as one may judge now by the scattered
volumes, they were of excellent character. A
rough corner cupboard in the log-house kitchen, or
a closet of the " square room," held the treasured
volumes of gray paper in unadorned but substantial leather binding. What a treasure they were to
those isolated settlers, to whom rarely came even a
newspaper, can scarcely be imagined by us who are
overwhelmed with the outflow of the modern press.

It is a pathetic picture to look back upon, of the
household reading of the one volume by the glare
of the open fire, spendthrift of warmth and light,
eldest and youngest member of the family listen-
ing eagerly to the slow, high-keyed words of the
reader, while between the pauses was heard the
long howl of the wolf, or the pitiless roar of the
winter wind. Yet it is questionable if they were
not richer with their enforced choice of a few good
books than we with our embarrassment of riches
and its bewildering encumberment of dross. In
1796 an act was passed incorporating the Brad-
ford Social Library Society,[2] the first corporate
body of the kind of which there is any record.

---

[1] *History of Montpelier*, by Daniel P. Thompson. D. P. Thomp-
son is best known as the author of *The Green Mountain Boys*, *The
Rangers*, and other tales that picture quite vividly early times in
Vermont.

[2] *Governor and Council*, vol. iv.

Similar associations in Fairhaven and Rockingham were incorporated soon after.

In recent years several large public libraries have been instituted, such as the libraries of St. Johnsbury, St. Albans, Rutland, and Brattleboro, the Norman Williams Library at Woodstock, the Fletcher Free Library at Burlington, and others, founded by wealthy and public-spirited Vermonters. The library of the University of Vermont includes the valuable collection of George P. Marsh, given by Hon. Frederick Billings. This now occupies one of the finest edifices of the kind in New England, the Billings Library Building. Such a wealth of literature as is now accessible to their descendants could hardly have been dreamed of by the old pioneers, even while they laid its foundation.

The first printing-office in Vermont was established at Westminster in 1778 by Judah Paddock Spooner and Timothy Green,[1] the first of whom and Alden Spooner were appointed state printers. The enactments of the two preceding legislatures had been published only in manuscript, a method of promulgation which one would think might have curbed verbosity. Judah Spooner and his first partner began the publication of the pioneer newspaper of the State, the "Vermont Gazette, or Green Mountain Post Boy," at Westminster in February, 1781. It was printed on a sheet of pot size, issued every Monday. Its motto, characteristic of its birthplace, was : —

[1] *Vermont*, by Zadock Thompson, an invaluable history.

> " Pliant as Reeds where Streams of Freedom glide,
>   Firm as the Hills to stem Oppression's tide."

Its publication was continued but two years. "The Vermont Gazette or Freeman's Depository," the second newspaper of the State, was published at Bennington in 1783, and continued for more than half a century. About this time George Hough removed the Spooner press to Windsor, and in company with Alden Spooner began the publication of a weekly newspaper entitled "The Vermont Journal and Universal Advertiser," which was continued until about 1834. The fourth paper, "The Rutland Herald or Courier," was established in 1792 by Anthony Haswell, and is still continued in weekly and daily issues, being the oldest paper in the State. William Lloyd Garrison edited "The Journal of the Times," at Bennington, not long before he became the foremost standard-bearer of the anti-slavery cause, with which his name was so intimately associated. In 1839 "The Voice of Freedom" was begun at Montpelier, as the organ of the anti-slavery society of the State, and was afterward merged in "The Green Mountain Freeman," published in the interest of the political Abolitionists or Liberty Party.. The publication of "The Vermont Precursor," the first paper established at Montpelier, was begun in 1806, and soon after changed its name to "The Vermont Watchman." For more than fifty years this paper was conducted by the Waltons, father and sons, and is still continued. In 1817 they began the publication of " Walton's Vermont Register," which is issued annually, bearing the name of its founder, and is a recognized necessity in every household and office in the State. Eliakim P. Walton, one of the sons, also rendered his State most valuable service in editing the records of the governor and council.

A majority of the newspapers have displayed with justifiable pride the name of the State in their titles. A number have had but a brief existence, scarcely remembered now but for the names of their founders or their own strange titles, such as the " Horn of the Green Mountains," " The Post Boy," " Tablet of the Times," " Northern Memento," and " The Reformed Drunkard." The Spooners seem to have been intimately connected with early newspapers and printing in the young commonwealth, for at least four of this name were engaged in such business. The famous Matthew Lyon edited for a while " The Farmer's Library," and Rufus W. Griswold the " Vergennes Vermonter ; " D. P. Thompson, the novelist, " The Green Mountain Freeman," and C. G. Eastman, the poet, " The Spirit of the Age," and " The Argus."

The dingy little papers of the olden time, with their month-old news, the brief oracular editorial comments, their advertisements of trades and industries now obsolete, their blazoning of lotteries and the sale of liquors, now alike illegal, were welcome visitors in every household ; and the weekly round of the post-rider was watched for with an eagerness that can hardly be understood by people to whom come daily and hourly, by mail and telegraph, news of recent events in all quarters of the globe. To those old-time readers of blurred type on gray paper, scanned by the ruddy glare of pine knots or the feeble light of tallow-dips, the tidings of foreign events which had happened months before came fresher than to us what but yesterday first stirred the heart of Europe.

Now, every considerable village in the State has its weekly paper, the larger towns these and daily papers. When Zadock Thompson published his " Vermont Gazetteer " in 1840, there were thirty papers published in the State, where now are, according to Walton's Register for 1891, sixty-one daily, weekly, and monthly periodicals.

For many years liquor-drinking was a universal custom, and a householder suffered greater mortification if he had no strong waters to set before his guest than if the supply of bread and meat was short. The cellar of every farmhouse in the apple-growing region had its generous store of cider, some of which went to the neighboring still to be converted into more potent apple-jack, here known as cider-brandy. This and New England rum were the ordinary tipple of the multitude, and the prolific source of hilarity, maudlin gabble, and bickerings at bees, June trainings, and town meetings. Drunkenness was disgraceful, but the limit was wide, for a man was not held to be drunk as long as he could keep upon his feet. When he fell, and clung to the grass to keep himself from rolling off the heaving earth, he became open to the charge of intoxication, and fit for the adornment of the stocks. Many a goodly farm, that had been uncovered of the forest by years of labor, floated out of its owner's hands in the continual dribble of New England rum and cider-brandy.

The signboard of the wayside inn swung at such frequent intervals along the main thoroughfares that the traveler must be slow indeed who had time to grow thirsty between these places of entertainment. The old-time landlord was a very different being from his successor, the modern hotel proprietor. Though a person of consideration, and maintaining a certain dignity, he received his guests with genial hospitality, and at once established a friendly relationship with them which he considered gave him a right to their confidence. Ensconced in his cage-like bar, paled from counter to ceiling, the landlord drew from his guests all the information they would give of their own and the world's affairs, — their whence-coming and whither-going, — while he dispensed foreign and domestic strong waters, or made sudden sallies to the fireplace where lay the ever-ready flip-iron, blushing in its bed of embers. Good old Governor Thomas Chittenden was a famous tavern-keeper, and as inquisitive concerning his guests' affairs as other publicans of those days. He used to tell with relish of a rebuff he got from a wayfarer who stopped to irrigate his dusty interior at the governor's bar. " Where might you come from, friend ? " the governor asked.

" From down below," was the curt reply.

" And where might you be going?"

" To Canada."

" To Canada? Indeed! And what might take you there?"

" To get my pension."

" A pension? And what might you get a pension for, friend?"

" For what you never can, as I judge."

" Indeed! And what is that?"

" For minding my own business."

Temperance began to have earnest advocates, men who, for the sake of their convictions, suffered unpopularity and persecution. A Quaker miller refused to grind grain for a distillery, and the owners brought a suit against him to compel him to do so. After a long and vexatious suit, the case was decided against him, but he persisted in his refusal, and the distillery was finally abandoned. Some would no longer comply with the old custom of furnishing liquor to their help in haymaking and to their neighbors who came to give a helping hand at bees, and by this infraction of ancient usage made themselves unpopular till a better sentiment prevailed.

There were zealots who cut down acres of thrifty orchard, as if there were no use for apples but cider-making. Through moral suasion and the honest example of good men, a great change was wrought in the sentiment of the people, till at last temperance became popular enough to become a matter of politics. Moral suasion was in the main abandoned, and the old workers dropped out of sight.

Vermont followed the lead of Maine in legislation for the suppression of the liquor traffic, and in 1852 passed a prohibitory law. Each succeeding assembly has legislated to increase the stringency and efficiency of the prohibitory statutes. Yet the fact remains that, after forty years' trial, prohibition does not prohibit, and presents the anomaly of an apparently popular law feebly and perfunctorily enforced.

It is a question whether the frequent and unnoticed violations of this law, and the many abortive prosecutions under it, have not made all laws less sacredly observed, and the crime of perjury appear to the ordinary mind a merely venial sin.

CHAPTER XXII.

EMIGRATION.

WHEN the tide of emigration began to flow from New England to the newly opened land of promise in the West, Vermont still offered virgin fields to be won by the enterprising and ambitious young men of the older States. Thousands of acres, capable of bounteous fruitfulness, still lay in the perpetual shadow of the woods, untouched by spade or plough; and the forest growth of centuries was itself a harvest worth the gathering, while wild cataracts still invited masterful hands to tame them to utility.

Some decades elapsed before the young State began to furnish material for the founding and growth of other new commonwealths, except such restless spirits as can never find a congenial place but in the foremost rank of pioneers. Such an one was Matthew Lyon, who, having borne his part in the establishment of the first State of his adoption, early in the century removed to Kentucky, then farther westward to Missouri, in whose territorial government he had become the most prominent figure when death set a period to his enterprise and ambition.

Though there were yet vast tracts in Vermont awaiting the axe and the plough, the fertile lands of the West began to draw from the State a steadily increasing flow of emigration. The tales of illimitable acres unencumbered by forest, and warmed by a genial climate, were attractive to men tired of warfare with the woods, and the beleaguering of bitter winters. The blood of their pioneering fathers was fresh in their veins, and impelled them to found new homes and new States.

The first migrations were made in wagons drawn by horses or oxen, and beneath whose tent-like covers were bestowed the bare necessities of household stuff and provision for the tedious journey.

After leave-takings as sad as funerals, the emigrants sorrowfully yet hopefully set forth. Slowly the beloved landmarks of the mountains sank as the miles lengthened behind them, and slowly unfolded before them level lands and sluggish streams. The earlier stages of the journey were relieved by trivial incidents, and the new experience of gypsy-like nightly encampment by the wayside; but as day after day and week after week passed, the new and unfamiliar scenes, still stranger and less home-like, grew wearisome to the tired men and jaded, homesick women and children, and incident became a monotonous round of discomfort.

In 1825 a swifter and easier path was opened to the West when, two years after the Champlain Canal had connected the waters of Lake Champlain and the Hudson, the Erie Canal was completed. The new thoroughfare was thronged with emigrants, of whom Vermont furnished her full share of families, and of enterprising young men seeking to better their fortunes in the land of plenty known there in common speech as "The 'Hio," or in that farther region of prairies whose western bound was the golden sunset, and where they whose plough had turned no virgin soil till the axe had first cleared its path should behold the miracle of fertile plains that had never been shadowed by forest. When the long journey was accomplished, a quarter of the continent lay between them and the old home; and though they lived out the allotted days of man, the separation of kindred and friends was often as final as that of death.

Mails were weeks in making the passage that is now accomplished in a few days; and the grass might be green on the graves of kindred and friends in the old or the new home before tidings of their death brought a new and sudden grief from the distant prairie, or from the New England hillside, where its pain had already grown dull with accustomed loss.

The course of emigration tended westward nearly within the parallels of latitude that bound New England, and but few pioneers of Vermont birth diverged much below the southward limit of a region whose climate, kindred, emigrants, and familiar institutions, transplanted from the East, most attracted them.

The fertile lands of Ohio were chosen by many,

while more were drawn to Michigan, Wisconsin, Indiana, Illinois, and Iowa, in all of whom Vermonters took their place as founders of homes and free commonwealths, and gave each some worthy characteristic of that from which they came. When gold was discovered in California, many Vermonters flocked thither in quest of fortune, and many remained there to become life-long citizens of the State in whose marvelous growth they were a part.

From their inauguration, the great railroad systems of the West have made another and continuous drain upon the best population of the East; and in every department of the enormous business men of Vermont birth and training are found conspicuously honored for their ability and integrity.

The rapidly growing cities, the immense sheep and cattle ranches, and all the new enterprises of the whole West, have drawn great numbers of ambitious young Vermonters to every State and Territory of the wonderful region. Indeed, there is not a State in the Union in which some Vermonters have not made their home; but however far they may have wandered from the land of their birth, they cherish the mountaineer's love of home, and a just pride in the goodly heritage of their birthright.

Wherever in their alien environment they have congregated to any considerable number, they are associated as Sons of Vermont. Chicago boasts the largest society, as its State does the greatest number of citizens, of Vermont birth.[1] St. Louis

[1] "The first president of this association was Guerdon S. Hub-

has a large association of the kind, as have other
Western cities. Even so near their old home as
Boston,[1] Worcester, Providence, and Brooklyn,
the Sons of Vermont gather annually to refresh
fond memories, and celebrate the virtues of their
beloved State.

To fill the place left by this constant drain on
its population, the State has for the most part received a foreign element, which, though it keeps her
numbers good, poorly compensates for her loss.

Invasions of Vermont from Canada did not cease
with the War of the Revolution, nor with the later
war with Great Britain. On the contrary, an insidious and continuous invasion began with the establishment of commercial and friendly relations
between the State and the Province. Early in the
century, a few French Canadians, seeking the small
fortune of better wages, came over the border, and
along the grand waterway which their noble coun-
tryman had discovered and given his name, and
over which so many armies of their people had
passed, sometimes in the stealth of maraud, sometimes in all the glorious pomp of war. At first the
few new-comers were tenants of the farmers, for
whom they worked by the day or month at fair
wages, for the men were expert axemen, familiar
with all the labors of land-clearing, and as handy as

bard, a Vermonter, who was instrumental in founding and establishing the city of Chicago, who went there in 1819, and later, ten
years afterwards, when Chicago only had a fort and one house." —
George Edmund Foss.

[1] S. E. Howard.

Yankees with scythe and sickle; while their wea-
ther-browned wives and grown-up daughters could
reap and bind as well as they, and did not hold
themselves above any outdoor work.

After a while some acquired small holdings of a
few acres, or less than one, and built thereon log-
houses, that with eaves of notched shingles and
whitewashed outer walls, with the pungent odor of
onions and pitch-pine fires, looked and smelled as
if they had been transplanted from Canada with·
their owners.

When the acreage of meadow land and grain-
field had broadened beyond ready harvesting by
the resident yeomen, swarms of Canadian laborers
came flocking over the border in gangs of two or
three, baggy-breeched and moccasined habitants,
embarked in rude carts drawn by shaggy Canadian
ponies. After a month or two of haymaking and
harvesting, they jogged homeward with their earn-
ings, whereunto were often added some small pil-
ferings, for their fingers were as light as their
hearts. This annual wave of inundation from the
north ceased to flow with the general introduction
of the mowing-machine; and the place in the
meadow once held by the rank of habitants picturesque in garb, swinging their scythes in unison to
some old song sung centuries ago in France, has
been usurped by the utilitarian device that, with
incessant chirr as of ten thousand sharded wings,
mingling with the music of the bobolinks, sweeps
down the broad acres of daisies, herdsgrass, and
clover.

Many Canadians returned with their families to live in the land which they had spied out in their summer incursions, and so in one way and another the influx continued till they have become the most numerous of Vermont's foreign population.

For years the State was infested with an inferior class of these people, who plied the vocation of professional beggars. They made regular trips through the country in bands consisting of one or more families, with horses, carts, and ricketty wagons, and a retinue of curs, soliciting alms of pork, potatoes, and breadstuffs at every farmhouse they came to, and pilfering when opportunity offered. In the large towns there were depots where the proceeds of their beggary and theft were disposed of. They were an abominable crew of vagabonds, robust, lazy men and boys, slatternly women with litters of filthy brats, and all as detestable as they were uninteresting. They worked their beats successfully, till their pitiful tales of sickness, burnings-out, and journeyings to friends in distant towns were worn threadbare, and then they gradually disappeared, no one knows whither.

Almost to a man, the Canadians who settled in Vermont were devout Catholics when they came; but after they had been scattered for a few years among such a preponderant Protestant community, most of them were held very loosely by the bonds of mother church. Except they were residents of the larger towns they seldom saw a priest, and enjoyed a comfortable immunity from fasting, penance, and all ecclesiastic exactions on stomach or purse. On New Year's Day, perhaps the members of the family confessed to the venerable grandsire, but after that suffered no religious inconvenience until the close of the year. Now and then one strayed quite out of the fold and took his place boldly among the heretics, and apparently did not thereby forfeit the fellowship of his more faithful compatriots. But when the flock had become large enough to pay for the shearing, shepherds of the true faith were not wanting. With that steadfast devotion to the interests of their church which has always characterized the Catholic priesthood, these men began their work without ostentation, and have succeeded in drawing into the domination of their church a large majority of the Canadian-born inhabitants of Vermont and of their descendants, as completely as if they were yet citizens of the province, which Parkman truly says, is "one of the most priest-ridden communities of the modern world."

What this leaven may finally work in the Protestant mass with which it has become incorporated is a question that demands more attention than it has yet received.

The character of these people is not such as to inspire the highest hope for the future of Vermont, if they should become the most numerous of its population. The affiliation with Anglo-Americans of a race so different in traits, in traditions, and in religion must necessarily be slow, and may never be complete.

No great love for their adopted country can be expected of a people that evinces so little for that of its origin as lightly to cast aside names that proudly blazon the pages of French history for poor translations or weak imitations of them in English, nor can broad enlightenment be hoped for of a race so dominated by its priesthood.

Vermont, as may be seen, has given of her best for the building of new commonwealths, to her own loss of such material as has made her all that her sons, wherever found, are so proud of, — material whose place no alien drift from northward or over seas can ever fill.

CHAPTER XXIII.

"THE STAR THAT NEVER SETS."

THERE is little to interest any but the politician in the political history of the State during the uneventful years of three decades following the War of 1812. At the next election after the close of the war the Republican party proved strong enough to elect to the governorship its candidate, Jonas Galusha, who was continued in that office for the five succeeding terms. When, in consequence of the abduction of Morgan, the opposing parties were arrayed as Masonic and anti-Masonic in the battle of ballots, the Masonic party of Vermont went to the wall.

When the two great parties of the nation rallied under their distinctive banners as Whigs and Democrats, Vermont took its place with the first, and held it steadfastly alike through defeats and infrequent triumphs of the party until its dissolution. So constantly was its vote given to the state and national candidates of the Whigs that it gained the title of "The Star that never sets."

From the adoption of its Constitution [1] in 1777,

---

[1] E. P. Walton, in *Governor and Council*, vol. i. p. 92, says, " This was the first emancipation act in America."

which prohibited slave-holding, Vermont has been the opponent of slavery. The brave partisan leader, Captain Ebenezer Allen, only expressed the freedom-loving sentiment of the Green Mountain Boys when he declared he was " conscientious that it is not right in the sight of God to keep slaves," and set free those taken prisoners with the British troops on Lake Champlain.

It was natural that among the descendants of those people, the inhabitants of a mountain land such as ever nourishes the spirit of liberty and wherein slavery has never found a congenial soil, there should be found many earnest men ready to join the crusade which, under the leadership of Garrison, began in 1833 to assail the great national sin with a storm of denunciation.

They denounced the scheme of African colonization, which had a respectable following in Vermont, as a device of the slave power to rid itself of the dangerous element of free blacks, under pretense of Christianizing Africa while here gradual emancipation should be brought about; and thus they aroused the antagonism of the body of the clergy, who had been hoodwinked by the pious plausibility of the plan.

A line of the Underground Railroad held its hidden way through Vermont, along which many a dark-skinned passenger secretly traveled, concealed during the day in the quiet stations, at night passing from one to another, helped onward by friendly hands till he reached Canada and gained the protection of that government which in later years was to become the passive champion of his rebellious master.

The star-guided fugitive might well feel an assurance of liberty when his foot touched the soil that in the old days had given freedom to Dinah Mattis and her child, and draw a freer breath in the State whose judge in later years demanded of a master, before his runaway slave would be given up to him, that he should produce a bill of sale from the Almighty.[1]

The abolitionists were no more given than other reformers to the choice of soft words in their objurgations of what they knew to be a sin against God and their fellow-men ; yet they were men of peace, almost without exception, — non-resistants, — and freedom of speech was their right. It is humiliating to remember that there was an element in this State base enough to oppose them by mob violence. An anti-slavery meeting convened at the capital in 1835 was broken up by a ruffianly rabble, who pelted the speakers with rotten eggs, and became so violent in their demonstrations that it was unsafe for the principal speaker, Rev. Samuel J. May of Boston, to leave the building, till a Quaker lady quietly stepped forward, and, taking his arm, walked out with him through the turbulent crowd, which, though noisy and threatening, had decency enough to respect a lady and her escort. There were like disturbances in some

[1] Theophilus Harrington.

other Vermont towns where the abolitionists gathered to advocate their cause, but the intensity of bitterness against them gradually wore away, and they continued to gain adherents, till the question of the extension of slave territory became the all-absorbing subject of political controversy.

In 1820 the representatives of Vermont in Congress opposed the admission of Missouri as a slave State, though her senators were divided. In 1825 the legislature passed resolutions deprecating slavery as an evil, and declaring, " This General Assembly will accord in any measures which may be adopted by the general government for its abolition in the United States that are consistent with the right of the people and the general harmony of the States." Ten years later, in the same year that the anti-slavery meeting was broken up by the rabble in the very shadow of the capitol, the legislature assembled there declared, that " neither Congress nor the state governments have any constitutional right to abridge the free expression of opinions, or the transmission of them through the public mail," and that Congress possessed the power to abolish slavery in the District of Columbia.

In 1841 the anti-slavery sentiment had so far increased in the State as to take political form, and votes enough were cast for the candidate of the Liberty party for governor to prevent an election by the people. Two years later the assembly enacted that no officer or citizen of the State should seize or assist in the seizure of " any person for the reason that he is or may be claimed as a fugitive slave," and that no officer or citizen should transport or assist in the transportation of such person to any place in or out of the State ; and that, for like reason, no person should be imprisoned " in any jail or other building belonging to the State, or to any county, town, city, or person therein." When Congress in 1850, after a fierce storm of debate, passed the odious Fugitive Slave Law, which made United States marshals, and at their behest every citizen of the republic, servants of the arrogant slave power, and withheld from whoever might be claimed as a slave the right of testifying in his own behalf, Vermont was faithful to freedom and the spirit of her Constitution. Her legislature of the same year passed an act requiring States' attorneys " diligently and faithfully to use all lawful means to protect, defend, and procure to be discharged, every such person so arrested or claimed as a fugitive slave," and judicial and executive officers in their respective counties to inform their State's attorney of the intended arrest of any person claimed as a fugitive slave.

In many of the Northern States slave-hunting waxed hot and eager under the national law, but the hunters never attempted to seize their prey in the land of the Green Mountain Boys, though there were fugitive slaves living there, and an occasional passenger still fared along the mysterious course of the Underground Railroad.

Consequent upon the annexation of Texas came

war with Mexico, — a war waged wholly in the interest of slavery extension, and forced by the great republic upon her younger sister, weak and distracted by swiftly recurring revolutions.

Having a purpose so opposite to the interest and sentiment of the people of Vermont, no possible appeal to arms could have been less popular among them. Yet upon the call of President Polk for volunteers, a company was soon recruited in the State. Under Captain Kimball of Woodstock, it formed a part of the 9th regiment, whose colonel was Truman B. Ransom, a Vermonter, who had been a military instructor in the Norwich University, and in a similar institution at the South. The 9th was attached to the brigade of General Pierce, in General Pillow's division, under General Scott. The army of Americans, always outnumbered, often three to one, by the enemy, could not have fought more bravely in a better cause; and the little band of Green Mountain Boys gave gallant proof that, in the more than thirty years which had elapsed since they were last called forth to battle, the valor of their race had not abated. Colonel Ransom fell while leading his regiment in a charge at Chepultepec; and the Vermont company was one of the foremost at the storming of the castle, it being claimed for Captain Kimball and Sergeant-Major Fairbanks that they hauled down the Mexican colors, and raised the stars and stripes above the captured fortress.[1]

[1] Dana's *History of Woodstock.*

Upon the dissolution of the Whig party, the least subservient to the slavery propagandists of the two great political parties in the North, Vermont at once took her place under the newly unfurled banner of the Republicans, — a place which she has ever since steadfastly maintained through victory and defeat. In 1856 her vote was cast for Fremont, and four years later, by an increased majority, for Lincoln. Few who cast their votes at this memorable election foresaw that its result would so soon precipitate the inevitable conflict. But five brief months passed, and all were awakened to the terrible reality of war.

CHAPTER XXIV.

THE dreariness of the long Northern winter was past. The soft air of spring again breathed through the peaceful valleys, wafting the songs of returning birds, the voice of unfettered streams, and the sound of reawakened husbandry. Though far off in the Southern horizon the cloud of rebellion lowered and threatened, men went about their ordinary affairs, still hoping for peace, till the tranquillity of those April days was broken by the bursting storm of civil war.

With the echo of its first thunder came President Lincoln's call for troops, and Vermont responded with a regiment of her sons, as brave, though their lives had been lapped in peace, as the war-nurtured Green Mountain Boys of old. The military spirit had been but feebly nursed during many tranquil years, yet, at the first breath of this storm, it blazed up in a fervor of patriotic fire such as never before had been witnessed.

At the outbreak of the Rebellion, no Northern State was less prepared for war than Vermont. Except in the feeble existence of four skeleton regiments, her militia was unorganized, the men subject

to military service not being even enrolled. Some
of the uniformed companies were without guns,
others drilled with ancient flintlocks; and the State
possessed but five hundred serviceable percussion
muskets, and no tents nor camp equipage; while
the Champlain arsenal at Vergennes, like other
United States arsenals in the North, had been
stripped by Floyd, the Secretary of War, of everything but a few superannuated muskets and useless
cannon. The continual outflow of emigration had
drawn great numbers of the stalwart young men of
the rural population to the Western States, in whose
regiments many of them were already enlisting, and
she had not the large towns nor floating population
which in most other States contributed so largely
the material for armies.

The governor, Erastus Fairbanks, immediately
issued a proclamation, announcing the outbreak of
rebellion, and the President's call for volunteers,
and summoning the legislature to assemble on the
25th of April. His proclamation bore even date
with that of the President, and is believed to have
antedated by at least a day the like proclamation
of any other governor.[1]

In the brief interval between the summoning
and the assembling of the legislature, in all parts
of the State men were drilling and volunteering.
Banks and individuals tendered their money, railroad and steamboat companies offered free transportation for troops and munitions of war, and

[1] G. G. Benedict, *Vermont in the Civil War.*

patriotic women were making uniforms of "Vermont gray" for the ten companies of militia chosen on the 19th of April to form the 1st regiment.

The train which brought the legislators to the capital was welcomed by a national salute from the two cannon captured at Bennington. Without distinction of party, senators and representatives met the imperative demands of the time with such resolute purpose that in forty-eight hours they had accomplished the business for which they were assembled, and had adjourned. A bill was unanimously passed appropriating one million dollars for war expenses. Provision was made for raising six more regiments for two years' service, for it was forecast by the legislature that the war was not likely to be confined to one campaign, nor an insignificant expenditure of money. Each private was to be paid by the State seven dollars a month in addition to the thirteen dollars offered by the United States. If his aged parents or wife and children should come to want while he was fighting his country's battles, they were not to become town paupers, but the wards of the commonwealth.

The ten companies were rapidly filled, their equipment was completed, and they assembled at Rutland on the 2d of May, with John W. Phelps as colonel, a native of Vermont, who had served with distinction in the Mexican War as lieutenant, and captain in the regular army. No fitter choice

could have been made of a commander for the
regiment than this brave and conscientious soldier,
who, though a strict disciplinarian, exercised such
fatherly care over his men that he won their love
and respect.

After some delay the regiment was mustered
into the United States service on the 8th. It was
the opinion of the Adjutant-General that there
were troops enough already at Washington for its
defense, and that the 1st Vermont might better
be held in its own State for a while. But when
General Scott learned that a regiment of Green
Mountain Boys, commanded by Phelps, was awaiting marching orders, he wished them sent on at once.
" I want your Vermont regiments, all of them. I
remember the Vermont men on the Niagara frontier," and he remembered Captain Phelps at Con-
treras and Cherubusco. A special messenger was
dispatched to Rutland with orders to march, and on
the 9th of May, the eighty-sixth anniversary of the
mustering of Allen's mountaineers for the attack
of Ticonderoga, this regiment of worthy inheritors
of their home and name set forth for Fortress
Monroe. There were heavy hearts in the cheering
throng that bade them Godspeed and farewell, —
heavier than they bore, for to them was appointed
action : to those they left behind, only waiting in
hope and fear and prayer for the return of their
beloved. On its passage through New York, the
regiment attracted much admiration for the stature and soldierly bearing of its members, each of

whom wore in his gray cap, as proudly as a knight his plume, the evergreen badge of his State.

Each succeeding regiment bore this emblem to the front, to be drenched in blood, to be scathed in the fire of war, to wither in the pestilential air of Southern prisons, but never to be dishonored.

" Who is that tall Vermont colonel ? " one spectator asked, pointing to the towering form of Colonel Phelps.

" That," answered another, " is old Ethan Allen resurrected ! "

The 1st was stationed at Fortress Monroe, and remained there and in the vicinity during its term of service. At Big Bethel, in the first engagement of the war worthy the name of a battle, it bore bravely its part, though the ill-planned attack resulted in failure. The throngs of fugitive slaves who sought refuge with Colonel Phelps were not returned to their masters, but allowed to come and go as they pleased, and thereafter were safe when they had found their way into the camps of Vermonters, though they were given up by the officers of other volunteers and of the regulars. General Butler, in command at Fortress Monroe, assuming that they were contraband of war, refused to return them to slavery, and put them to efficient service in the construction of fortifications. The regiment returned to Vermont early in August, and was mustered out, but of its members five out of every six reëntered the service in regiments subsequently raised, and two hundred and fifty held commissions.

Their colonel, now appointed brigadier-general, remaining at Fortress Monroe, greatly regretted their departure. " A regiment the like of which will not soon be seen again," he said to Colonel Washburn. Yet, before the leaves had fallen that were greening the Vermont hills when the 1st regiment left them, five other regiments in no wise inferior had gone to the front, to a more active service and bloodier fields.

The 2d Vermont, its ten companies selected from over 5,600 men who offered themselves, went to the front in time to take part in the first great battle of the war at Bull Run. Thenceforth till the close of the war this splendid regiment took part in almost every battle in which the Army of the Potomac was engaged. Its ratio of killed and mortally wounded was eight times greater than was the average in the Union army. The 3d regiment followed in July, the 4th and 5th were rapidly filled and sent forward in September, the 6th in October. These five regiments formed the First Brigade of the Sixth Corps. The heroic service [1] of this brigade is interwoven with the

---

[1] The limits of this work preclude detailed account of the noble services of Vermont troops, which are fully and graphically related in G. G. Benedict's valuable work, *Vermont in the Civil War.* Of many noble examples of heroic self-devotion where Vermonters unflinchingly endured the storm of fire, the record of the 5th regiment at Savage's Station is memorable, — in the space of twenty minutes, every other man in the line was killed or wounded. Company E went into the fight with 59 officers and privates, of whom only seven came out unhurt and 25 were killed

history of the Army of the Potomac. The estimation in which it was held is shown by the responsible and dangerous positions to which it was so often assigned, and in the praise bestowed upon it by distinguished generals under which it served. When the Sixth Corps was to be hurried with all speed to the imperiled field of Gettysburg, Sedgwick's order was, " Put the Vermonters in front, and keep the column well closed up." " No body of troops in or out of the Army of the Potomac made their record more gallantly, sustained it more heroically, or wore their honors more modestly." [1]

At the time of the draft riots in New York, in July, 1863, the First Vermont Brigade, with other most reliable troops to the number of twelve thousand, were sent thither to preserve order during the continuance of the draft. It was a strange turn of time that brought Vermont regiments to protect the city whose colonial rulers had set the ban of outlawry upon the leaders of the old Green Mountain Boys. These later bearers of the name performed their duty faithfully and without arrogance, and received warm praise of all good citizens for their orderly behavior during what was holiday service to such veterans.

or mortally wounded. Five brothers named Cummings, a cousin of the same name, and a brother-in-law, all recruited on one street of the historic town of Manchester, were members of this company. All but one were killed or mortally wounded in this action, and he received a wound so severe that he was discharged by special order of the Secretary of War.

[1] Adjutant-General McMahon of the Sixth Corps.

Vermont horses had won a national reputation as well as Vermont men, and it seemed desirable that the government should avail itself of the services of both. Accordingly, in the fall of 1861, a regiment of cavalry was recruited under direct authority of the Secretary of War; and in forty-two days after the order was issued, the men and their horses were in " Camp Ethan Allen " at Burlington. But one larger regiment, the 11th, went from the State, and none saw more constant or harder service. It brought home its flag inscribed with the names of seventy-five battles and skirmishes.

The 7th and 8th regiments of infantry and two companies of light artillery were raised early in 1862, and were assigned to service in the Gulf States, in the department commanded by General Butler. Arrived at Ship Island, much to their gratification, they were placed under the immediate command of their own general, Phelps. Faithful to the spirit of his State and his own convictions of justice, he had issued [1] a proclamation to the loyal citizens of the Southwest, declaring that slavery was incompatible with free government, and the aim of the government to be its overthrow. Fugitive slaves found a safe refuge in his camp here, as in Virginia, and in May, 1862, he began drilling and organizing three regiments of blacks. But upon his requisition for muskets to arm them, he was peremptorily ordered by General Butler to

[1] December, 1861.

desist from organizing colored troops, and he resigned his commission. "The government," says
Benedict in "Vermont in the Civil War," "which
before the war closed had 175,000 colored men under arms, thus lost the services of as brave, faithful, and patriotic an officer as it had in its army,
one whose only fault as a soldier was that he was
a little in advance of his superiors in willingness
to accept the aid of all loyal citizens, white or
black, in the overthrow of rebellion."

In July, 1862, the 9th regiment, commanded by
Colonel Stannard, went to the front, being the first
under the recent call for three hundred thousand
men. Its initial service was at Harper's Ferry,
where it presently suffered the humiliation of surrender with the rest of Miles's force. In the little
fighting that occurred, the raw regiment bore itself
bravely. Colonel Stannard begged Miles to let
him storm Loudon Heights with his command
alone, and then to cut his way out of the belea-
guered post, but both requests were refused. The
9th passed several months under parole at Chicago,
was exchanged, and at length took its place in the
Army of the Potomac. A portion of this regiment
was the first of the Union infantry to carry the
national flag into the rebel capital.

The 10th and 11th regiments were speedily forwarded in the fall of 1862. The former joined the
army in Virginia. The latter, recruited as heavy
artillery, spent two years in garrison duty in the
defenses of Washington. When Grant began the

campaign of the Wilderness, it joined the First Vermont Brigade as an infantry regiment, and its fifteen hundred men outnumbered the five other thinned regiments of the brigade that had so often been winnowed in the blasts of war, which soon swept its own ranks with deadly effect.

Before these two regiments were organized came the President's call for three hundred thousand militia to serve nine months, under which Vermont's quota was nearly five thousand. The five regiments were quickly raised and sent forward, and to three of them, just before their term of enlistment expired, fell a full share of the glories of Gettysburg, under the intrepid leader, General Stannard. The charge of his Vermont Brigade beat back Pickett's furious assault, and decided the fate of the day.[1] Once more the brave little commonwealth was called on to furnish a regiment, and the 17th was sent to the front with ranks yet unfilled. Its third battalion drill was held on the battlefield of the Wilderness. The untried troops were hurled at once into the thick of the fight and

[1] On this historic field Vermont has marked with monuments the position held by her troops. Where the war-worn First Brigade stood waiting but uncalled to stem the tide of battle, a crouching lion, alert for the onslaught, rears his majestic front, like the lion couchant of the Green Mountains. Another monument stands where the Second Brigade beat back the impetuous fury of the rebel charges ; another where the Vermont cavalry dashed like a billow of fire and steel upon the foe ; and two where, at the Hornet's Nest and the Peach Orchard, the unerring rifles of Vermont's three companies of sharpshooters rained their constant fire upon the enemy.

suffered fearful loss, and henceforth were almost continually engaged with the enemy till the fall of Richmond.

Besides these seventeen regiments of infantry and one of cavalry, the State furnished for the defense of the Union three light batteries and three companies of sharpshooters, who well sustained the ancient renown of the marksmen whom Stark and Warner led, and at the close of the war Vermont stood credited with nearly thirty-four thousand men. Thus unstintingly did she devote her strength to the preservation of the Union to which she had been so reluctantly admitted. What manner of men they were, Sheridan testified when, two years after the war, standing beneath their tattered banners in Representatives' Hall at Montpelier, he said : " I have never commanded troops in whom I had more confidence than I had in the Vermont troops, and I do not know but I can say that I never commanded troops in whom I had as much confidence as those of this gallant State," and the torn and faded battle-flags under which he stood told more eloquently than words how bravely they had been borne through the peril of many battles, and honorably returned to the State that gave them.

When, after four weary years, the war came to its successful close, the decimated regiments of Green Mountain Boys returned to their State, received a joyful but sad welcome, and then, with all the embattled host of Union volunteers, dissolved into the even, uneventful flow of ordinary life.

Notwithstanding the remoteness of the State from the arena of war, Vermont suffered a rebel raid from a quarter whence of old her enemies had often come, though of right none should come now. A majority of the people of Canada were in warm sympathy with the rebellion, their government was indifferent, and the Dominion swarmed with disloyal Americans, who were continually plotting to aid their brethren at the front by covert attacks in the rear. The federal government was on its guard, but a blow fell suddenly at an unexpected point.

On the 19th of October, 1864, while Vermont troops under Sheridan were routing the rebels at Cedar Creek, a rather unusual number of strangers appeared in the village of St. Albans, a few miles from the Canadian border. Moving about singly or in small groups, and clad in citizen's dress, they attracted no particular attention, till, at a preconcerted signal, three small parties of them entered the banks, and with cocked and leveled pistols forced the officials to deliver up all the moneys in their keeping. Other armed men in the streets at once seized and placed under guard every citizen found astir, while some attempted to fire the town by throwing vials of so-called Greek fire into some of the principal buildings. Having possessed themselves of the treasure in the banks, amounting to two hundred thousand dollars, in specie, bills, and bonds, the party took horses from the livery stables, and rode out of town, firing as they went a wanton fusilade which wounded several persons, but happily killed only a recreant New Englander who was in sympathy with their cause. They proved to be a band of rebel soldiers, commanded by a Lieutenant Young, who held a commission in the Confederate army. They beat a hurried retreat with their booty beyond the line, whither they were pursued by a hastily gathered party of mounted men under the lead of Captain Conger, who had served in the Union army. None of the raiders were taken, but later fourteen were captured in Canada, with $87,000 of the booty, by Captain Conger's men, acting under orders of General Dix, and aided by Canadian officials. During their brief imprisonment they were entertained as honored guests in the Montreal jail, and, after undergoing the farce of a trial in a Canadian court of justice, they were set at liberty amid cheers, which evinced the warm sympathy of the neutral Canadians. It appeared in the testimony of a detective that Colonel Armitinger, second in command of the Montreal militia, was aware of the contemplated raid, but took no measures to prevent it. " Let them go on," he said, " and have a fight on the frontier; it is none of our business; we can lose nothing by it."

The affair formed an important point of consideration in the Geneva arbitration, and Secretary Stanton declared it one of the important events of the war, — " not so much as transferring in part the scenes and horrors of war to a peaceful, loyal State, but as leading to serious and dangerous complications with Great Britain, through the desires and efforts of the Southern people to involve Canada, and through her Britain, in a war on behalf of their Southern friends." [1] The unfriendly attitude which the Canadians held toward our government, throughout the struggle for its maintenance, might be profitably considered whenever the frequently arising project of annexation comes to the surface.

The Fenian irruptions of 1866 and 1870, abortive except for the panic which they created in Canada, with more than the ordinary certainty of poetic justice, formed their base of operations at St. Albans, the point of rebel attack in Vermont.

Impelled by the military spirit which the war had aroused, the legislature made provision for the organization of a uniformed volunteer militia, to which every township furnished its quota. Under the instruction of veterans of the war, the militia made commendable progress in drill and discipline. But after a few years it was disbanded, and the commonwealth has drifted back into almost the condition of unpreparation which existed at the beginning of the war. For the most part, the young men who have become of military age since those troublous days are more unlearned than their mothers in the school of the soldier.

---

[1] *History of the St. Albans Raid*, p. 48, by E. A. Sowles.

CHAPTER XXV.

THE VERMONT PEOPLE.

In the years of peace that have passed since the great national conflict, many changes have taken place in the commonwealth. The speculative spirit which arose from the inflation of values during that period in some degree affected almost every one, and still survives, when all values but that of labor have sunk to nearly their former level. Too great a proportion of the people sought to gain their living by their wits as speculators, — go-betweens of the producer and consumer, agents of every real or sham business and enterprise, largely increasing the useless class who really do nothing, produce nothing, and add nothing to the wealth of a State. This class is largely drawn from the greatly predominant agricultural population.

Farmers, who in the years before the war could only bring the year around by the strictest economy, suddenly became rich men, as farmers count wealth, by the doubled or trebled value of their land, and the same increase of price of all its products, and fell into ways of extravagance that left them poorer than before, when prices went down, and withal more discontented with their lot. Men bought land at the prevailing extravagant prices, and a few years later found themselves stranded, by the subsiding tidal wave, on the barren shores of hopeless debt, and many such became ready recruits for the insane army of Greenbackers.

The extravagance of their employers infected the wage-earners, and led them to the same silly emulation of display beyond their means, rather than to the founding of comfortable homes, — the ambition for something not quite attainable, which brings inevitable unrest and discontent.

Sheep husbandry, the old and fostered industry of the State, with which it was so long identified, deserves more than a passing mention. As has been said in a former chapter, early in the century Vermont flocks were greatly improved by the introduction of the Spanish merinos. During 1809 and 1810, William Jarvis, our consul at Lisbon, obtained about 4,000 merinos from the confiscated flocks of the Spanish nobles, and imported them to this country. The flocks of pure blood bred on Mr. Jarvis's beautiful estate at Weathersfield " Bow," lying on the western bank of the Connecticut, and half inclosed by the river, were not excelled by any in this country. From the Jarvis importation, and from a small flock of the Infantado family imported about the same time by Colonel Humphreys, our minister to Spain, the most valued merinos are descended.

From various causes the value of sheep and wool has exhibited remarkable fluctuations. During the years 1809 and 1810, half-blood merino wool sold for seventy-five cents a pound, and full blood for two dollars, and during the war with England rose to the enormous price of two dollars and a half a pound ; full-blood rams sold for sums as great as the price of thoroughbred stallions, even ram lambs bringing a thousand dollars each : but such a sudden downfall followed the peace that, before the end of 1815, full-blooded sheep sold for one dollar each.

During the next ten years the price of wool continued so low that nearly all the flocks of merinos were broken up, or deteriorated through careless breeding. At that time an increase in the duties on fine wool revived the prostrate industry, but unhappily led to the general introduction of the Saxon merinos, a strain bearing finer but lighter fleeces, and far less hardy than their Spanish cousins. The cross of the puny Saxon with these worked serious injury to the flocks, but was continued for twenty years, and then abandoned so completely that all traces of the breed have disappeared. The Spanish sheep again became the favorites, or rather their American descendants, for these, through careful breeding by a few far-sighted shepherds, now surpassed in size, form, and weight of fleece their long neglected European contemporaries, if not their progenitors from whom in their best days the importations had been drawn.

Sheep-husbandry became the leading industry of Vermont, so generally entered upon that even

the dairyman's acres were shared by some number
of sheep, till every hillside pasture and broad level
of the great valleys, rank with clover and herdsgrass,
was cropped by its half hundred or hundreds of
these unconscious inheritors of mixed or unadul-
terated blue blood of the royal Spanish flocks.

Along all thoroughfares, from the Massachusetts
border to the Canadian frontier, the traveler, as he
journeyed by stage or in his own conveyance, saw
flocks dotting the close-cropped pastures with white
or umber flecks, or huddled in the comfort of the
barnyard, and the quavering bleat of the sheep was
continually in his ears; nor was the familiar sound
left quite behind as he journeyed along the lonely
woodland roads, for even there he was like to hear
it, and, chiming with the thrush's song, the inter-
mittent jangle of the tell-tale bell that marked the
whereabouts of the midwood settler's half-wild flock.

The "merino fever" again raged, and fabulous
prices were paid for full-bloods, while unscrupulous
jockeys "stubble sheared" and umbered sheep of
doubtful pedigree into a simulation of desired qual-
ities that fooled many an unsuspecting purchaser.
Breeders and growers went to the opposite extreme from that which had been reached during
the Saxon craze, and now sacrificed everything to
weight of fleece, and Vermont wool fell into ill-
repute. Prices went down again, and again the
descendants of the Paulars and Infantados went
to the shambles at prices as low as were paid for
plebeian natives.

The wool-growing industry of the East now began to find a most formidable rival in the West, the Southwest, and Australia, in whose milder climates and boundless ranges flocks can be kept at a cost far below that entailed by the long and rigorous winters of New England, and in numbers that her narrow pastures would scarcely fold. At the same time lighter duties increased the importation of foreign wools, so there was nothing apparently for Vermont shepherds to do but to give up the unequal contest, and most of them cast away their crooks and turned dairymen.

But gifted with a wise foresight, a few owners of fine flocks kept and bred them as carefully as ever, through all discouragements, and in time reaped their reward, for it presently became evident that the flocks of milder climates soon deteriorate, and frequent infusions of Eastern blood are necessary to obtain the desired weight of fleece, so that sheep-breeding is still a prosperous industry, though, as has been stated, wool-growing has become insignificant.

Dairy products have largely increased, so that now they are far more important than wool among the exports, and almost everywhere the broad foot of the Jersey, the Ayrshire, the Shorthorn, and the Holstein has usurped the place of the " golden hoof."

The butter and cheese of the State were in good repute even in the primitive days of the earthen milkpan, the slow and wearisome dash-churn, and the cheese-press that was only a rough bench and lever, as rude in construction as the plumping-mill, and when a summer store of ice was a luxury that the farmer never dreamed of possessing. The simplest utensils and means were in vogue, and modern devices and improved methods were unknown. The good, bad, and indifferent butter of a whole township went as barter to the village store, where with little assorting it was packed in large firkins, and by and by went its slow way to the city markets, in winter in sleighs, in the open seasons on lumbering wagons or creeping boats, with cargoes of cheese, pork, apples, dried and in cider sauce, maple sugar, potash, and all yields of farm and forest. Even after such long journeying, the mixed product of many dairies retained some flavor of the hills that commended it to the palates of city folk, and was in favor with them.

Cheeses were not packed, as now, each in its own neat box, but four or five together in a cask made especially for the purpose, whose manufacture kept the cooper busy many days in the year. His wayside shop, with its resonant clangor of driven hoops and heaps of fresh shavings piled about it, distilling the wholesome odor of fresh wood, was a frequent wayside landmark, now not often seen. Cheese was the chief product of the dairy, and was always home-made, while now it is almost entirely made in factories, to which the milk of neighboring dairies is brought, but by far the larger part of the milk goes to creameries for the making of butter.

As the carding, spinning, and cloth-making went from the household in the day of a former generation, and the title of " spinster " became only the designation of unmarried women, so the final labor of the dairy is being withdrawn from the farm to the creamery and cheese factory, to make an even product, better than the worst, if never so good as the best, of that of the old system, and the buxom dairymaid will exist for coming generations only in song and story.

The enormous mineral wealth of the State lay for years hidden or unheeded, copper and copperas in the hills of Vershire and Strafford, granite in the bald peaks of Barre, slate in long lines of shelving ledges here and there, and marble cropping out in blotches of dull white among the mulleins and scrubby evergreens of barren sheep pastures. Some of these resources developed slowly to their present importance, others have flourished and languished and flourished again, and others sprang from respectable existence into sudden importance.

Copper ore was discovered in Orange County about 1820,[1] and was afterwards mined and smelted in Vershire, in a small way, by a company formed of residents of the neighborhood and styled the " Farmers' Company." In 1853 the mine was purchased by residents of New York, who were granted a charter under the title of " Vermont Copper Mining Company," and they began more extensive operations under the direction of a skilled

[1] *Geology of Vermont.*

Cornish miner. In the years which have elapsed since then, the work has at times been actively carried on with excellent results, and fifty tons or more of superior copper produced each month; at times it has languished, till the populous mining village was almost deserted, and neighboring hill and vale, scathed by the sulphurous breath of roast-bed and furnace, became more desolate than when the primeval forest clothed them; again it has seasons of prosperity, when the Vershire vale is as populous with Pols, Tres, and Pens as a Cornish mining town.[1] Granite, upheaved from the core of the world, is found in immense masses in the central portions of the State. At Barre there are mountains of it; though there so overtopped by the lofty peaks of Mansfield and "Tah-be-de-wadso," they bear such humble names as Cobble Hill and Millstone Hill. The pioneer hunters who trapped beaver and otter in the wild streams,[2] and the settlers who here first brought sun and soil face to face, little dreamed that greater wealth than fertile acres bear was held in these barren hills. Yet something of it became known more than half a century ago, and the second State House was built of this Barre granite, hauled by teams nine miles over the hilly roads. For many years the working

[1] *Hearth and Home*, October, 1870.

[2] One of the first of these, named Stevens, was found in his cabin near the mouth of the stream which bears his name, dead on his piled treasure of rich peltry, with a kettle of unavailing medicinal herbs hanging over the ashes of his burned-out fire.

of the quarries increased only gradually, but within comparatively a few years it has become an immense business. The hills are noisy with the constant click of hammer and drill, the clang of machinery, and the sullen roar of blasts, and the quiet village has suddenly grown to be a busy town, with two railroads to bear away the crude or skillfully worked products of the quarries. In a single year a thousand Scotch families came to this place, bringing strong hands skilled in the working of Old World quarries to delve in those of the New, and a savor of the Scotch highlands to the highlands of the New World.

Slate of excellent quality exists in Vermont in three extensive ranges, one in the eastern part of the State, another in the central, and another in the western. Each is quarried to some extent at several points, but the last named most extensively in Rutland County. Slabs taken from the weathered surface rock were long ago used for tombstones, and may be seen among the sumacs and goldenrods of many an old graveyard, still commemorating the spiritual and physical excellences of the pioneers who sleep beneath them. No quarries were opened until 1845, nor was much progress made for five years thereafter, when an immigration of intelligent Welshmen brought skilled hands to develop the new industry, and made St. David a popular saint in the shadow of the Taconic hills.

The existence of marble in Vermont was known

long ago. On the Isle La Motte, a quarry of black marble was worked before the Revolution; and early in the present century, quarries were opened in West Rutland, and worked in rude and primitive fashion, the slabs so obtained being mostly used for headstones. A quarry was opened in Middlebury, and it is claimed that the device of sawing marble with sand and a toothless strip of iron was invented by a boy of that town, named Isaac Markham, though in fact it was known to the ancients and used by them centuries ago. But little more than fifty years ago, the site of the great quarries of West Rutland was a barren sheep-pasture, shaggy with stunted evergreens, and the wealth it roofed was undreamed of, and so cheaply valued that the whole tract was exchanged for an old horse worth less than one of the huge blocks of marble that day after day are hoisted from its depths. The working of these quarries was begun about 1836, and within ten years thereafter three companies were formed and in operation. But the growth of the business was slow, for there were no railroads, and all the marble quarried had to be hauled by teams twenty-five miles to Whitehall, the nearest shipping-point. Furthermore, its introduction to general use was difficult, for though its purity of color and firmness could not be denied, its durability was doubted. Fifty years of exposure in our variable and destructive climate have proved Vermont marble to exceed in this quality that of any foreign country. In 1852 a line of railroad running near at hand was completed, and the marble business of Rutland began to assume something of the proportions which now distinguish it as the most important of the kind on the continent.

One of the most remarkable changes in the commerce of Vermont has been in the lumber trade, which no longer flows with the current of Champlain and the Richelieu, to Canada, but from the still immense forests of the Dominion up these waterways to supply the demands of a region long since shorn of its choicest timber. Of this great trade Burlington is the centre, and one of the busiest lumber marts in New England.

The pine-tree displayed on the escutcheon of Vermont is now no more significant of the products of the commonwealth than is the wheat sheaf it bears; for almost the last of the old pines are gone with the century that nursed their growth, and the ponderous rafts of spars and square timber that once made their frequent and unreturning voyages northward have not been seen for more than half a century. The havoc of deforesting is not stayed, nor like to be while forest tracts remain. The devouring locomotive, spendthrift waste thoughtless of the future, the pulp-mill, and kindred wood-consumers gnaw with relentless persistence upon every variety of tree growth that the ooze of the swamp or the thin soil of the mountain side yet nourishes.

In 1808, only a year after Fulton's successful

experiment on the Hudson, a steamer was launched at Burlington on Lake Champlain, and astonished her spectators by her wonderful performance as she churned her way through the waters at the rate of five miles an hour. In 1815 a company was granted the exclusive right of the steam navigation of Lake Champlain, but the unjust monopoly was presently canceled. In later years the steamers of the lake were celebrated for the excellence of their appointments and superior management, a reputation which they still maintain, though the railroads that skirt their thoroughfare on either side have drawn from them the greater share of the patronage which they once enjoyed.

All the various industries have been given an impetus by the railroad system which now meshes the State, and knits it closer to the others of the Union.

With these changes in business and methods, and this constant intercourse with all inhabitants of the republic, the quaint individuality of the earlier people is fast dissolving into commonplace likeness, so that now the typical Green Mountain Boy of the olden time endures only like an ancient pine that, spared by some chance, rears its rugged crest above the second growth, still awaiting the tempest or the axe that shall lay it low; yet as the pine, changing its habit of growth with changed conditions, is still a pine, so the Vermonter of to-day, when brought to the test, proves to be of the same tough fibre as were his ancestors.

From the turbulent day of her birth through the period during which she maintained a separate and independent existence, and during the hundred years that she has borne her faithful part as a member of the great republic, the history of Vermont is one that her people may well be proud of. Such shall it continue to be, if her sons depart not from the wise and fatherly counsel of her first governor, "to be a faithful, industrious, and moral people," and in all their appointments "to have regard to none but those who maintain a good, moral character, men of integrity, and distinguished for wisdom and abilities." So may the commonwealth still rear worthy generations to uphold and increase her honorable fame, while her beautiful valleys continue, as in the long-past day of their discovery, "fertile in corn and an infinitude of other fruits."

INDEX.
